BARBED

WIRED

BARBED WIRED

A MACDUFF BROOKS FLY FISHING MYSTERY

by

award winning author

M. W. GORDON

Barbed Wired
Copyright © 2016
M.W. Gordon
All rights reserved.
Published in the United States by Swift Creeks Press,
    Sarasota, Florida
swiftcreekspress@gmail.com
www.swiftcreekspress.com

SWIFT CREEKS PRESS EDITION, APRIL 30, 2016

Library of Congress Cataloging-in-Publication Data
Gordon, M.W.
Barbed Wired/M.W. Gordon

ISBN-13 978-0-9848723-7-4
Printed in the United States of America

DEDICATION

To fly fishing guides

ACKNOWLEDGMENTS

My most humbling times are wonderful hours I spend with Iris Rose Hart, my editor, friend, and patient instructor in English grammar. At my rate of learning from Iris Rose, I have set the end of this century as my likely time for graduation from her authoritarian school of grammar.

To Christine Holmes for developing and maintaining my website and for designing advertisements.

To the graphic design staff of Renaissance Printing of Gainesville, Florida, and especially Jim O'Sullivan, for assistance with the cover, bookmarks, and posters.

To very special people who have provided quiet places for me to write, especially Julie and Jason Fleury of Bozeman, Montana.

Continued thanks to Elsbeth Waskom, Josh Dickinson, Marilyn Henderson, Roy Hunt, Paul Tarantino, and Dave Johnson.

And always thanks to my wife Buff (Elsbeth) whom I knew to be an extraordinary person the day we met. The decades have shown me wise to have proposed on our second date. Although she has assisted me in developing the characters of El and Lucinda, both fall short of my real Elsbeth.

To the Library of Congress for the cover photo, and to the photographer.

THOUGHTS ON WRITING

"That the personages in a tale should be alive, except in the case of corpses, and that always the reader shall be able to tell the corpses from the others."

Mark Twain's third rule of writing.

PROLOGUE

Elsbeth's Diary

The days dragged after Lucinda was abducted and Dad was injured by the van. Several friends had read about the St. Augustine shooting and abduction in the Bozeman News, *apparently printed because Lucinda and Dad lived as much in Montana as they did in Florida.*

I was not pleased about the newspaper article, not that it was inaccurate but that Lucinda and Dad tried to avoid any comments about either of them appearing in any paper. Especially disturbing was the News' *comment that mentioned they lived in St. Augustine in the winter and Paradise Valley in the summer.*

After two weeks Dad was released to go home to our St. Augustine cottage. He walked short distances with a cane and occasionally began an unfulfilled smile and nodded or shook his head, but he had difficulty speaking. One day at our dinner table he suddenly got up, looked around, and mumbled, 'Lucinda!' then walked into their bedroom and went through her closet, feeling her clothing.

Dad remained mostly in a living room armchair he had moved inch-by-inch to face the wall filled with countless photos of the two together, most in Montana and Florida but a few in Cuba and Spain. He often stood with his fingers touching her photo. I once saw him kiss a favorite photo of her.

His progress, nevertheless, was remarkable. Soon he was speaking slowly in full sentences that suggested the damage had not affected his memory or intellect. We were able to have increasingly in-depth conversations.

My college friend Sue and I thought it best, confirmed by his doctor, to tell Dad that Lucinda had been missing since the incident. He didn't take the news well. Those days were hard; it is difficult to write about that time. Many days passed when not one additional word appeared in this diary. But time was what was needed for Dad's recovery, and with intensive physical therapy he improved fractionally but visibly each day.

Dad improved enough as summer began to let me take him to Montana. Sue and I had summer jobs again at Chico Hot Springs Resort in Paradise Valley about five miles south of our Mill Creek log cabin. Liz Rangley, Ken's daughter—a junior at Montana State University in Bozeman—was also scheduled to work at the resort that summer. Sue and I had promised to start in late April but were delayed by Dad's occasional need for assistance getting about.

It's hardly necessary to note that Dad did not accept a single guide trip over the summer. I took Osprey on the Yellowstone or the Madison rivers several times. He had taught me to row our drift boats and encouraged me to spend time on the rivers by myself or with Sue or Liz, developing my rowing skills.

Dad exercised at the cabin, continued physical therapy, and regained nearly full use of his leg. Wuff, our decade old rescued sheltie, and he shared slight limps. Wuff had been shot on Osprey years ago.

1

AN EARLY MAY DAY IN JACKSON HOLE, WYOMING

"WHEN THIS SHREW NAMED LUCINDA HAS been eliminated by her abductor and Brooks has her declared legally dead, he'll get *all* her money," whispered Palmer Brown to himself. "I'm sure Brooks had her abducted and killed so he could inherit her assets. She was rumored to be worth something on the high side of $40 million.

"The way I would do it," Brown continued, "were I married to this Lucinda, would be to drop our car on her by collapsing the jack while she was 'helping' me fix something underneath. Accidents happen! Instantly, I'd be millions of dollars richer."

No one was nearby who might overhear his ambitious ramblings. He was sitting on the edge of a wrought iron bench in Jackson Square in Wyoming, watching two young beginner skateboarders trying to look like pros. He thought how good it was not to have kids. He spent his money on himself.

Brown looked like a cross between Johnny Cash and Jack Palance. He was tall with a craggy face and wore black jeans and a black flannel shirt. His clothes looked expensive, but were wrinkled. His hair needed trimming, and his face needed shaving. Three years ago, at fifty-four, Brown moved to Jackson Hole from Europe, claiming to be a widower.

Parked a block off the square where it wouldn't be scratched was his 621 horsepower Mercedes-Benz S65 that cost

$231,000, about the same as a bachelor's degree from an Ivy League college. It was a gift from his current wife, Brenda Lacy.

In Brown's hands was a rumpled page from the local *Jackson Hole Times* with a brief article that he read:

The abduction several weeks ago in St. Augustine, Florida, of Lucinda Brooks, wife of Emigrant, Montana, summer resident and fly fishing guide Macduff Brooks, has stymied authorities. St. Augustine police and federal agents believed to be with the FBI or the CIA have released no evidence. Many assume Mrs. Brooks is dead because no ransom demand has been received from her abductors.

I'm Macduff Brooks, the fly fishing guide mentioned in the article. A couple of years ago I guided Palmer Brown *once* on the Wyoming Snake River. My Jackson friend and guide, John Kirby, had asked me for a favor—to take Brown for the float so John could be home with a sick child. Some favor! The day was a disaster. Brown proved to be the dreaded client from hell.

"You won't need that bottle of Knob Creek," I had said to Brown, backing my drift boat down the launching ramp at Pacific Creek.

"I'll choose what I drink," Brown responded, his eyes glassy. "Like three Bloody Mary's I had with a quick breakfast."

During the first few miles, Brown sipped his way through half the bottle. It hadn't helped his casting.

"Palmer, toss your fly over to the left. It's where Buffalo Fork joins our river."

"Dammit! You jerked the boat when I cast," he complained as his fly landed only ten feet from the boat.

"You took your back cast too far, and the tip of your rod and line went into the water behind you."

"I made a *good* cast; *you* moved the boat."

Without saying why, I rowed us closer to the left bank.

"Cast to the bank. Then strip some line out as I row back toward the center."

"I don't need you to do that. I cast as good as anyone."

He threw four more casts, the longest twenty feet.

"Give me your rod a minute. I'll show you what I mean."

"I'm doin' OK," he claimed, as his fly floated along barely beyond the tip of the oar. "You don't get my rod. Cost 800 bucks. It's a hell of a lot better than that piece of crap you got."

"You could do better if you'd listen and let me help—between your sips of Knob Creek."

"You telling me *when* and *what* I can drink?"

"No, I'm trying to help you catch some trout."

"Jeeze, you jerked the boat again, and I lost my rod overboard. It sunk!"

"Your million-dollar rod didn't float, or you were using a weighted line that pulled the rod down. You should be using a floating line to fish dry flies. Take one of my rods."

"I told you I got my own gear. I got another rod in that tube next to you. Rig it!"

I removed his second rod and asked, "Got another reel?"

"Of course. Here," he said, tossing a second reel toward me. It bounced off my right oar, hit the water, and was gone."

"How the hell do I catch fish from this damn boat? You lost one of my rods and both my reels. You pay for them!"

"I don't think so," I murmured, wrongly thinking he hadn't heard.

After a half-hour of silence, I asked, "Lunch? There's a gravel bank ahead with a great view of the Grand Tetons."

"I don't give a crap about the Grand Tetons. No big deal! I didn't come for the view; I can see boring mountains from my outside bar at home. The bar cost me $30,000. . . . What's for lunch?"

"I called your wife yesterday and asked her about your food preferences. She said to buy you fried chicken."

"That bitch told you that? I hate chicken. I want *meat*."

"We're a little short of food service here. Try the chicken."

"Here's what I think of your damn chicken. Let the fish eat it," he said, and tossed it further than any of his morning casts. Then he took the last sip of Knob Creek.

The afternoon didn't go half as well as the morning. By the time we reached the takeout, I had heard multiple times every foul word berating me, the rod I loaned him, the weather, the scenery, and the fishing.

"How'd you get to be a goddamn lousy guide, Brooks?"

"It took years of learning how to cope with people like you," I answered. I'd taken enough of his nonsense to try another profession. Like becoming a serial killer!

I rowed hard the last mile to the Deadman's Bar takeout. Brown sat in the front swearing and threatening to "kick the crap" out of me when we reached shore. I let the boat hit the land hard. Brown was standing and fell into the shallow water.

"You did that on purpose! You bastard!" he screamed, getting up slowly in his soaked clothes and half-filled waders.

"Watch the boat. I'll get the trailer," I said. That was a mistake. While I was gone, Brown unclipped the anchor at the stern and shoved the boat out into the river.

"What the hell have you done you idiot?" I yelled running to the river to see my boat drifting downstream toward the next takeout at Moose, eight miles away. The current quickly carried the boat out of sight.

Out of the corner of one eye I saw Brown charge at me. I ducked, thrust forward lifting him, and tossed him back into the river. He was too drunk to respond further. Walking toward my SUV, I wondered how to retrieve my boat. Another guide suggested I float down river with him and we'd find it.

"I will kill you, Brooks," called out Brown. "I promise you that. Someday when you're on the river, you will *die!*"

His voice faded into the distance as I joined the other guide to begin my search and we floated out of sight. My last glimpse showed Brown splashing his way to the shore.

The season ended, and Palmer Brown had made no attempt to carry out his threat. He had met Brenda Lacy Hoover, a former Manhattan socialite, and disliked her from the day they were married. But he loved her money. After her husband died and left her $42 million, she moved to Jackson Hole and spent $8 million building a 12,000 square foot house between the airport and the Snake River. When they married, Brown moved into her house.

I didn't think the marriage would last. He was greedy; she had ten times his wealth. He wanted it—NOW!

As Brown finished the newspaper article, he got up and walked out of the square, remembering his float with me, and thinking about how he might carry out his death threat made that day at Deadman's Bar. But for now, he was occupied with planning the death of his wealthy, gullible wife—Brenda Lacy.

Then Brown had another idea. The article mentioned I had a daughter in college. He thought she would be easier to kill than me.

2

TWO WEEKS LATER – ON THE
GALLATIN RIVER NEAR BOZEMAN, MONTANA

// B ETH, ARE YOU OK?" SUE ASKED. SHE WAS sitting in the bow seat of our new three-person, inflatable pontoon boat, sipping from a water bottle, and drifting downstream on the Gallatin, away from the improvised Canyon Mouth launching area where the river began to smooth out after tumbling down from its origins in Yellowstone Park, passing Big Sky, and rushing into Gallatin Valley.

Every spring the winter's deep accumulation of snow on Montana mountains begins to disappear. Proceeding at its own unannounced pace—some years beginning in March, other years delaying until April—the melting ice increases the flow and raises the water level of every creek, stream, and river.

I usually tried to arrive in Montana two weeks before the onset of the snow melt to enjoy the early "ice-out" fishing until the current became too swift and the water turned "Mississippi murky." But this year our lives had been drastically conflicted.

On the eve of our annual departure to Montana from Florida my Lucinda was abducted from the grounds surrounding the Castillo de San Marcos in St. Augustine. She was grabbed and, despite her struggle, was dragged to a van and pushed inside. I tried to save her, but failed miserably and was intentionally struck by the van, suffering injuries that required two weeks of hospital time and considerable physical therapy. It nevertheless left me with a limp.

My physical therapy in Florida over, I endured an uncomfortable eight-hour three-leg flight to Bozeman and a final hour's drive to our Montana cabin forty miles north of Yellowstone Park on Mill Creek in Paradise Valley. In years past, Lucinda and I would arrive at the perfect time to fish for a week or two, but this year I headed directly to further physical therapy sessions in Livingston.

Both Elsbeth and her Wyoming friend, Sue Mills, were employed for another summer at Chico Hot Springs. Without asking me, they became my caregivers whom I referred to as Day Nurse Cruella and Night Nurse Witch Queen.

It proved far easier to manage my physical injuries—mainly nerve and muscle damage to one leg—than to assuage my mental trauma from the abduction of Lucinda. She had been missing for a month, and I was not good company for Elsbeth and Sue. I vacillated between yin—Lucinda was dead—and yang—Lucinda was alive and trying to return to me. I wanted to fish, but not as much as I wanted her back in my life.

Local fishermen who survived another Montana winter and swear it was the worst on record—perhaps the confluence of changes in both the weather and age—had taken to the streams and rivers, relieved that this early in the year few *foreigners* were present. Foreigners were defined to include without prejudice those who came from Georgia in what was part of southwestern USSR or from Georgia in what remains part of southeastern U.S. Due to the silt-hued water and its high velocity, foreigners rarely chance making reservations at this time of the year, when drift boat float days booked in advance may prove unsuitable for fishing after the intended fly fishers have traveled long distances for naught. But the greater losers are the local guides who have been off the frigid waters for four to five months dodging creditors.

One of the deservedly most popular rivers in the West is the Gallatin, which along with the Jefferson and the Madison merge near Three Forks, Montana, to form the wide Missouri. Who was Albert Gallatin—the honoree who shares the three rivers' limelight with two illustrious presidents? He was the wealthy, Geneva born, longest serving U.S. Secretary of the Treasury who also was a senator, congressman, ambassador to Britain and France, and a founder of New York University. Gallatin is largely forgotten, except by a few who fish his namesake river and don't care what he accomplished as long as the fish are biting.

I'm Elsbeth's father. Our life story is confusingly complex. Twenty-two years ago I was finishing my tenth year as Professor Maxwell W. Hunt at the law college of the University of Florida in Gainesville. I loved every day I walked into the law school. Every day of teaching, every trip abroad to lecture, every case of consulting, and every page of writing melded to create an enviable life. It was made even more so by my wife El.

El, fully named Elsbeth, and I were expecting our first child when one spring day we flew west to fish where tragedy struck and my life's foundation crumbled. We were fly fishing from a drift boat on the Snake River north of the town of Jackson, guided by an inexperienced and hungover young man. Never before having rowed the technically complex and subtly dangerous section known as Deadman's Bar to Moose, he ran us into what is called a strainer—a huge pile of tree limbs and branches deposited by the spring snow-melt runoff. The drift boat broke apart, throwing us into the fast-moving cold water. El was lost, carrying with her our unborn child.

My life turned to melancholic self-pity. I began to travel to give lectures that the U.S. State Department arranged as my cover to gain information useful to U.S. national security. Increasingly, my life was threatened. One night in Guatemala City, a former UF law student of mine and aspiring drug lord—Juan Pablo Herzog—sought to end my already desperate life. Beaten to near death, but saved by U.S. embassy personnel and evacuated to D.C., I was treated and ultimately recovered. My attacker—unscarred physically or mentally by the thrashing he gave me—went on to become the current president of his nation.

Herzog remains possessed by a desire to finish what he started: he intends to take my life. He believes—mostly incorrectly—that I was engaged in activities contrary to the interests of Guatemala.

Our State Department deceptively announced I died from a stroke in a D.C. hospital and placed me in a protection program. I adopted a new name—Macduff Brooks, chose a new identity—a fly fishing guide, and moved to a new home—Montana. None of this was accomplished with foresight.

Since then, Herzog has tried to find and kill me, aided by his closest friend, another former law student, Abdul Khaliq Isfahani, from the Sudan. They failed, and a few years later Isfahani paid the ultimate price. I assassinated him in Khartoum. Enraged and undaunted, Herzog has continued his search for me.

Happily for me in my new life as Macduff Brooks, I met a woman—Lucinda Lang—who had broken the glass ceiling at a

New York investment firm. She became a partner and soon a wealthy young woman, using some of her proceeds to buy a large ranch in Paradise Valley, Montana, that included a mile along Mill Creek upstream from where I had built my small log cabin on six acres that were also along the creek.

We met when she invited me to Thanksgiving dinner at her ranch. We were a pair like the two people John Denver must have had in mind when he wrote the song *The Cowboy and the Lady*. Months later Lucinda would claim we'd become engaged, an act I presumably conceded two years later when I allegedly participated in a ceremony that Lucinda swore was our wedding. Since we met, murder and mayhem have occurred on or close to my drift boat, *Osprey*. Lucinda usually has been with me.

Initially, a disgruntled client named Salisbury shot Lucinda and me during a float on the Snake River in Wyoming. A stray bullet struck my sheltie Wuff and produced a permanent limp. She must doubt that having been rescued by me a couple of years earlier provided her with a better life.

Lucinda and I continued to debate about who killed Salisbury and saved the three of us; both of us had fired our guns at him. Lucinda claimed he was dead before I got my gun out and that I simply added a few bullets to a corpse.

Soon after that first shooting, several local Montana women were murdered who shuttled guides' vehicles and drift boat trailers from their launching areas to their takeout sites along various sections on the Yellowstone River. Brutally murdered one by one, they were nailed to crosses on my boat trailer for me to discover when I arrived at the takeout after a day's float.

The following year witnessed murders on successive solstices and equinoxes on different rivers in Idaho, Montana, and

Wyoming. Each victim was tied to the center seat in a drift boat, covered with a wicker man basket, draped with mistletoe, and strapped with explosives set to detonate during the float.

After we shifted to our Florida cottage a series of murders of fishermen who were found dead wrapped in gill nets again involved us.

Soon thereafter, Lucinda and I visited Cuba. I went to help locate a missing U.S. representative who was fly fishing along Cuba's South Coast; Lucinda went to photograph Hemingway's favorite Havana locations for a Canadian magazine. I discovered that the representative and later his guide had been thrown into a pen of large, voraciously hungry barracudas.

Most recently, we became unjustly linked to two murders on airboats in Florida. The victims were tied to the propeller and spun to death.

Both of us joked about my reputation as a "celebrity" guide that no sensible client would book, except to insist on talking to me more about murder than mayflies.

Not all my life was spent living under a cloud of murder; I discovered that my wife, El, in her dying moments, had given birth to our daughter on the bank of Wyoming's Snake River. An elderly couple saved the baby and took her to Maine where she was raised. Just before they died, she was told she was not their birth child, but the daughter of a Professor Maxwell Hunt. The couple had named her Elsbeth after her mother, that name discovered inscribed on a small brass plaque on the handle of her fishing net that read "To Elsbeth, my best fishing buddy."

Reunited with me seventeen years after her birth, she began to live with us in Montana summers and St. Augustine winters. Currently, Elsbeth attends the University of Florida. I wonder every day why I deserve this exquisite daughter.

Elsbeth, only recently called Beth by her friends and Lucinda,—seldom by me—started college at Maine three years ago. There she met Sue Mills, who ironically was born in the hospital in Jackson, Wyoming, a week after Elsbeth was born on the bank of the Snake River fifteen miles away.

In their first-year spring-term at Maine, Elsbeth and Sue decided to transfer to the University of Florida. They are now inseparable, sharing a house in Gainesville during the academic year. Both work each summer at Chico Hot Springs in Paradise Valley, Montana.

Of necessity, over the past two years I have told Sue the truth about some of my past, and she carefully guards our secret and has become like a second daughter.

The wicker man murders that took place on different rivers in the West were mostly the work of Robert Ellsworth-Kent, Lucinda's former English husband of two months. After his earlier release from an Isle of Wight prison, he sought her return. By that time she had moved to New York to work, bought her Mill Creek ranch, and allowed me into her life. Ellsworth-Kent reappeared in St. Augustine about a month ago and abducted Lucinda. Where he has taken her remains a mystery.

Liz Rangley was the third person in the pontoon boat, sitting in the rear seat while Elsbeth rowed and Sue sat at the bow. The same age as Elsbeth, Liz is Ken Rangley's daughter. Ken heads the Park County Sheriff's Office in Livingston and has become my close fishing friend. He knows more than does Liz about my years before I moved to Montana. Liz knows only that I have a past I never mention, which her father never discusses, and which she does not ask me about.

"You don't look OK, Beth; you seem distracted," said Sue, repeating her concern. "I'd offer to row, but I've never been in one of these inflatables and never fished on the Gallatin."

"You could row it, Sue. So could Liz. It's not difficult water, but when it's shallow, it has some complex logjams and strainers we need to avoid. We're going to float about six miles and shouldn't see many other inflatables."

"I thought we weren't permitted to fish from a boat—rubber, fiberglass, or whatever—on the Gallatin," Sue stated.

"That's not exactly right. North at Gallatin Forks, some thirty-plus miles from here, we can fish from a boat. Here we're allowed only to use a boat to float, but we can stop anywhere along the way and get out and fish. *Getting out* is a must. We can't even anchor and stand in the boat and cast."

"That sounds like something a lawyer figured out," said Liz. "You're not a lawyer, Beth—yet. Who told you?"

"A guide friend of Dad. They fish together."

When they were launching the boat earlier, a man carrying a rod was walking along the edge of the river. When he came closer, they saw from his uniform he was a Montana Fish, Wildlife & Parks warden.

"Any luck?" Liz asked him, noting that strangely he was carrying a fly rod rigged with a spinning reel.

He smiled and said, "Yeah. . . . Let me help you push off on your pontoon boat."

"Did you start here early?" asked Beth

"Daybreak. I like to get out early. I'm already here when I officially go on duty. You ladies may be the first boat this morning."

"Good," Beth remarked. "The river will be ours. Are you on duty yet? If so, I assume you want to see our licenses."

"I am on duty and I do want to check your licenses."

"I got mine yesterday," said Sue. "I'm new to this."

He looked at the license and gave it back. "Enjoy fishing," he said, smiling.

Liz had her license out and handed it to the warden.

"Rangley? Ken's daughter?"

"The same. You know Dad?"

"All law enforcement people tend to know each other." He turned to Beth, who was rigging her rod.

"Can we make it three out of three valid licenses?" he said.

"Absolutely," said Beth, handing him her worn license.

"*Brooks!* That's a name I know. Your dad must be that guide over in Paradise Valley?"

"He is."

"You're all set. Have a good float. Catch lots of fish."

"He was nice to help," said Liz as the man walked on along the river.

"What was his name?" asked Beth.

"He didn't say. And come to think of it, he didn't wear a nametag."

An hour after launching, Liz looked at Beth and asked, "Why did we start calling you Beth and not Elsbeth? Was Elsbeth too formal?"

"I guess. My mom was Elsbeth, but she was called El. Her mom was the first Elsbeth but was called Betty. I didn't know about either of them when I was growing up as Elsbeth *Carson* in Maine; I learned about my blood relatives only after I joined Dad a few years ago. The Carsons were wonderful but pretty strict—an old New England family.

"I'm Beth, except to my dad. He almost *always* calls me Elsbeth. If I ever have a daughter, I think she'll be called Ellie, but her given name will be Elsbeth."

A light drizzle started when they drifted under Williams Bridge. Sue was wearing waders and a hooded waterproof jacket. Liz, who is tall like her dad, wore his waders and poncho. Beth had on hippers with a long jacket and a visor cap.

"Comfortable or getting wet?" Beth asked both friends.

"Do we have a choice?" Sue answered. "We're in the middle of nowhere. It's all prominently posted every thirty feet as private property. On *each* side of the river. We're several miles from our takeout near the old Gallatin Gateway Inn. . . . You're going to have a wet butt, Beth. Your hippers only reach a foot-and-a-half above your knees, and your jacket's not long enough to cover your rear. You're *sitting* in cold water."

"It's pretty mild this morning and going to be warmer later. I'm OK," Beth replied.

"And don't you worry about my butt."

3

" W E'RE MAKING CONVERSATION, PROBABLY to keep warm," Sue commented a few minutes later, not able to recall what they had talked about the last half-hour. It was cold and they were shivering. Talking kept them distracted from the chill. Looking at Beth, Sue asked, "You still look bewildered. . . . Share your thoughts?"

"I think of Lucinda every day and it always ends in tears."

"It seems *so* long since she was taken," Liz commented.

"Has there been *anything* that gives even a hint about what happened?" asked Sue. "Maybe from Grace in St. Augustine? Or Dan Wilson in D.C.?"

"Grace Justice," Sue explained to Liz, "is a Florida state attorney based in St. Augustine. In the past few years, she was involved investigating both one of the gill net and one of the airboat murders. She is a good friend of Lucinda. Grace fly fishes and is an exceptional caster—a Federation of Fly Fishers certified Master Casting Instructor. It doesn't get any better than that. We don't remind Macduff that Grace casts much better than he does. He knows it, but he won't admit it when Grace is present."

"Dan Wilson," explained Beth, "works in D.C. for the CIA and has been around at least since the beginning of Dad's transformation to. . . ."

Beth stopped short. She had never told Liz about Macduff's past.

"What transformation?" asked Liz. "I know only that Macduff and Dad have been friends since I was ten. I don't know what Macduff did before that. Dad said Macduff was once a law professor back East. I assumed he had good reason to come to Montana and guide."

"He did have good reason," Beth responded, staring at Liz with a look that said: Drop it!

"Beth, I wasn't prying. My lips are sealed!"

"Dan Wilson is assigned to Lucinda's case because Lucinda's abductor was thought to be foreign," said Beth, shifting her focus. "That means there's an *international* connection and brings the CIA into the investigation."

"I won't ask another question about your dad, but I will ask about Lucinda," Liz added.

"You've heard fragments about Lucinda's disappearance, Liz. I'll fill you in," Beth whispered.

"Lucinda and I were like mother and daughter. She was grabbed and taken away in broad daylight before a crowd at the christening and launching of a replica of a Spanish ship that long ago sank off St. Augustine. Lucinda hasn't been found or heard from since.

"My dad last saw her when she walked away from the crowd toward the restrooms. A man grabbed her and dragged her to the parking lot and shoved her into a van. Dad raced to her aid only to be intentionally struck by the van's driver.

"Dad survived, returned to his St. Augustine cottage after a short hospital stay, and after that we brought him here to our cabin. Sue and I again had summer jobs waiting at Chico Hot Springs. We missed taking our spring term exams at UF because we withdrew to care for Dad. That's about it, Liz. I don't want to talk about it anymore."

"Nobody but we three seems to be on the river yet," Sue noted to change the discussion.

As Beth wiped away a tear, she bounced the inflatable off an unforgiving, partially submerged boulder. "That's the first but not the last encounter today with hard places," she said with a shy, apologetic grin.

"We started early," Liz said. "We may be lucky and not see anyone all day except the guy who launched a few minutes before we did."

"The water's has been so low it discouraged floats," said Beth. "But yesterday's rain made them possible. . . . We're going to scrape bottom here and there, and we may have to get out and drag the boat through a few shallows."

"It's worth it," Sue responded. "This section of the Gallatin can't be compared to the Madison River. Once summer begins, students flock to the Madison like the Spanish Armada. Their tire tubes are filled with six-packs."

"Get used to it," Liz urged. "It won't get any better. Bozeman's growing out of control. Montana State is talking about big time additions to its more or less 14,000 students. We're lucky there are still a few places like this in America. Enjoy it while it lasts!"

Discouraged at the prospect of a Montana State University with 30,000 students, and wanting to change the subject, Liz added, "Is all the land alongside this part of the river privately owned?"

"There's public access at the bridges, but that's about it," said Beth.

"Who owns the land? I don't see many houses."

"It's mostly ranch and farm land."

"The owners don't allow access to the Gallatin?" wondered Sue.

"Many once did," Liz responded, "but they had to deal with a few imbeciles who persistently trashed the river's edge or drove their pickups across planted crops and scared grazing cattle. Some even camped out and made fires along the riverbank. The result was owners began to shut down what little was accessible."

"Think it will open up again?" asked Sue.

"Not a chance. A few homes have been built along the river in the past decade, and I don't know of one new owner who posted welcome signs to fishermen."

"That's sad. If you owned a few acres along this river, what would you do, Beth?" Sue asked.

"Open it to family and friends and friends of friends."

"But not to the general public?"

"I hate to sound indulgent or arrogant," responded Beth, "but no, it wouldn't be open to the general public. . . . Not intending to change the subject, in about twenty minutes we'll reach a productive hole next to piles of tree debris with dead branches that hang out over the edge of the river. It provides cover for trout to collect under and wait for passing food."

"And we're going to provide that passing food?" asked Liz.

"You bet."

Before they reached the hole, Beth stopped on the edge of a promising gravel bank, and they all stepped out, spread along the bank, and began casting. After fifteen minutes, nearly sixty casts by each, and zero fish, Beth said, "A dead spot today, I guess. Sorry I chose it. Let's head further downstream to the hole I mentioned. . . . Look upriver. There's the fisherman who started a little before us but who we passed near Williams

Bridge. I suggest we let him go by and get out of sight ahead of us. I don't want to show people I don't know where we stop to fish, especially if we're catching fish as they pass. . . . That boat has a single guy, and he seems to be moving faster than we are. We draw more with our weight."

As the boat passed and the person waved, Sue asked, "How can we walk on the land at the edge of the water like we've been doing—you said it's private property?"

"Montana law helps answer that," responded Beth. "It permits the public to use rivers and streams for recreational purposes up to the ordinary high-water mark."

"Can I walk across someone's land to reach a river or stream?" asked Sue. "I can't do that in Wyoming where my parents live."

"The law differs state-to-state, but the answer here in Montana is *no*. But the land owner should announce his intentions and post his land with signs. If he doesn't, you're pretty safe to cross. Some signs are torn down by people wanting to fish and, if asked, say they saw no signs and thought it was OK to fish there. Meaning every year a lot of new 'keep out' signs are put up along the rivers by the owners."

"If I'm at a bridge over the river," posed Liz, "like the Williams Bridge we passed under, how do I get to the water? Don't I have to cross some private land?"

"*That* is where it gets confusing," answered Beth, pleased she had listened when Lucinda and her father talked about these issues. "Landowners often string up barbed wire, attaching it to the bridge. They argue it's needed to keep their cattle in and that it only incidentally keeps out the public."

"So I'm out of luck, unless I want to jump off the bridge into the water."

"Don't jump. You can use the bridge right-of-way to get to the water. The county or state *usually* owns a right of way alongside the bridge that allows access to the water."

"And can we cut down any fencing that blocks access?"

"Probably, but better not to. . . . Maybe land owners should do what the English have done for centuries: put up stiles."

"I hate how you always say 'probably,' Beth. You sound like Macduff. Why go to law school? You already talk evasively. . . . And what did you mean by access up to the high-water mark? Is that where the highest water has been—*ever*?"

"I said '*ordinary* high-water mark,'" Beth repeated.

"What's 'ordinary?'" Liz asked. "There are no tides on streams and rivers. But there are significant differences between high water during spring run-off and the dry days of late summer."

"I thought we came to fish, not dredge up never resolved legal confusion," said Sue.

"Beth," interrupted Liz, "I want to be able to fish wherever there are fish. Taking an inflatable boat like ours to get to places we could easily walk to really doesn't make sense to me."

"Remember, Liz, you can't walk freely across posted land," Sue reasserted. . . . "Is Macduff the one who first said 'the law is an ass?'" she added.

"No. It was Charles. . . ," Beth said.

"Darwin?" asked Liz.

"No. Dickens. In *Oliver Twist*," Beth replied.

"How did we get *there*?" asked Sue. "We were talking about trout fishing. Please don't mention Charles Dickens. I never made it to the end of *David Copperfield*."

"Scrooge! Even in Montana we have to read *David Copper-field*," responded Liz, unaware that it had been eliminated from Bozeman High and MSU English lit courses.

"Speaking of greed, I thought you were *allowed* to be greedy about your private property," stated Sue.

"You can, and most people are," Beth responded. "That has led to arguments that the laws permitting access are an unconstitutional taking of vested property rights."

'So it's gone to the courts?" asked Liz. "My dad's never mentioned that, and sometimes he reads those kinds of cases."

"It has been in the courts," Beth began.

"Oh my God! We're about to get a lecture on law. Just like her dad does," Liz said, turning to Sue.

"I'll make it short. Be quiet and listen. The Montana Supreme Court recently held that a man who owned ten miles of land along the Ruby River couldn't install fences along miles of the river passing through his land *if* the fences prevented access from *county* roads and bridges."

"So it's settled?" asked Liz.

"Never," responded Beth. "As the famous philosopher—Yogi Berra—said, 'It ain't over 'till it's over.' And this one ain't over."

"Have there been problems here on the Gallatin like those on the Ruby River?" asked Sue.

"I don't think so. There's a lot more public access to the Gallatin. Trout fishermen are less concerned with getting *onto* the Gallatin than they are with the dissonance of yelling and drinking by tubers and rafters and kayakers on certain sections, especially upriver from here on the faster water near Big Sky."

4

"HOW ABOUT LUNCH? YOU HUNGRY?" BETH asked, adding, "I'm glad we're not counting on eating trout. We don't have any way to cook them and, in any event, we can't eat them because it's catch and release."

"Is catch and release a *law*?" asked Sue.

"In some places," responded Beth. "But more importantly, it's *my* rule when you're in *my* boat."

"Fair enough," said Sue. "I'm hungry. . . . Are there places along here you like to stop for lunch?"

"Yes. The river narrows soon. And speeds up. Then it splits into two channels and rejoins a hundred yards later, where it widens and becomes shallow. There's a nice place to have lunch along a gravel bank."

"Any good fishing before we get there?" asked Liz.

"See the bank ahead on the right, where it's maybe six to eight feet high and the river's undercut the land?"

"Are there browns under the banks?" asked Liz with expectations.

"And rainbows. And cutthroats. And cross-breed cutbows."

"What should we use for flies?" asked Sue.

"Dropper-dropper combo," Beth proclaimed, trying to be assertive like Lucinda dealing with Macduff.

"What's on top?" asked Liz.

"I have good luck here with salmon flies," said Beth. But I haven't seen any hatches, and it may be a little early."

"Through the deeper water ahead, we want the lower fly to be a small nymph," she added. "I'll try a #18 Prince Nymph; you two try the same size Pheasant Tail. It should be about five feet below an indicator."

"I don't like using an indicator. I think I'm fishing on a placid lake with a spinning rod and using a float bobber," admitted Sue.

"I still think you *need* a small yarn indicator because there will be more than three feet of water and it's moving rapidly."

"What's magic about three feet?" asked Liz.

"You may be able to see the tip of your line and some of the tippet when we fish in the shallow riffles where we're going to stop for lunch. But we'll first stop at some deep runs, and you'll lose eye contact with your two flies if you don't have an indicator."

"Beth, your dad doesn't use an indicator even on deep water," said Liz. "My dad told me that about Macduff. Why?"

"Dad's fished a long time. He watches the line tip when he can see it. And he's developed a feel for changes in the line when he can't see it. It comes with time."

"Isn't it easier to cast without an indicator? An indicator is like throwing a lure," Sue responded.

"Much easier. Anywhere the line has an interruption on it, such as an indicator, there's something foreign obstructing a smooth cast. Some guides describe the indicator as a hinge where the line bends abruptly. If you have a dropper-dropper and the upper one is large, there's a second hinge."

"What about using a single, large fly, such as a big wooly bugger or streamer?" asked Sue.

"Much the same," said Beth, "but you can make a troublesome wind knot with *only* a single fly on your tippet."

"Why not make it easier and use a single bead head nymph? No second larger upper dropper and no indicator," she added.

"That's OK, but you're eliminating half the flies in your box."

"Then use a dropper-dropper-dropper or even five or six flies tied on to cover all depths," interjected Liz.

"Some places limit you to a single fly," responded Beth, "but most have no trouble with two. I've never seen anyone fishing three or more, probably because that's an invitation to attract wind knots and it doesn't look right. It's like long-lining for swordfish."

Sue turned around and faced Beth to watch her tie on two nymphs and an indicator as the trio rounded a sharp bend twenty yards before the deep run where they wanted to stop and fish. Beth was watching Sue more than the river, which Beth had floated many times with Lucinda. Often the two went together in the inflatable boat when Macduff was guiding using one of the drift boats for the day.

"That looks good," Beth said, as she finished Sue's rig and glanced up to watch for the spot along the river's run where she planned to stop.

She couldn't believe what she saw immediately ahead.

5

"SUE! LIZ!" YELLED BETH. *"DUCK! GET DOWN NOW!"*

Sue and Liz ducked as best they could as the boat ran into something large hanging from barbed wire strung across the river. Sue reached out to push off, cut her wrist on the wire, grabbed a cold, dangling human hand, and quickly let it go.

"Beth, *what* was that?" Sue asked, low in front of her seat. Her hands were bloody and the blood wasn't all her's.

"It was *barbed* wire! We're clear of it," Beth said, rowing to the shore and anchoring.

"That's a man's body hanging from the wire," Sue exclaimed as they reached the shallows. "It's the guy who passed us. He looks awful. Worse! He looks *dead!*"

"I'm calling 911," said Beth. "Did you see the big barbs on that wire?"

"No," answered Sue. "I made it under only because you yelled. You ducked, Beth. Were you caught?"

"One tear in my jacket. I got snagged for a moment but the jacket cloth ripped, and the current carried the boat on. I never saw the wire in time to get to shore before we hit it. I was leaning down trying to find a fly I dropped."

"What's happened?" asked Liz from the stern, looking confused. She hadn't been snagged by the wire because she was on the rear seat watching a trout rise near the bank. She had dropped to the floor when Beth yelled.

"Someone strung barbed wire across the river," exclaimed Beth. "The person floating ahead of us didn't see it, and it caught him in the throat and yanked him out of his boat. We'll find the inflatable somewhere downstream."

"I see it against the shore a few yards before the next bend. What should we do?"

"First," said Beth, "We might try and take the body down and remove the wire. There may be another boat behind us, and they may not be as lucky as we were."

They walked back along the river's edge to where the wire was draped across the river, hanging about where the head would be of a person sitting in an inflatable boat. The wire had been nailed to a tree on each side. Elsbeth had brought her dad's largest Leatherman. She opened it to the pliers and used them to twist and pull the nails from the tree.

"I'm going to let the body stay caught on the wire as we pull this end loose and hope the body swings toward the other side," Beth declared. "We shouldn't *touch* the body, but we have to get the wire off the river in case another boat comes along."

Elsbeth pulled out the last nail and the weight and buoyancy of the body carried it in an arc downstream and partly across the river. In the rapid flow the head and one arm bobbed in the current.

The three young women were exhausted and returned to their boat on the riverbank. They dropped to the ground next to a large cottonwood tree, unable to say anything, staring across the water, and seeing what minutes ago was a solo fisherman who couldn't have imagined what was ahead when he rounded the last bend above the narrows.

6

THIRTY MINUTES LATER BY THE SAME TREE

THE TRIO SAT IN SILENT DISBELIEF, TRYING TO sort out what had happened. Four Gallatin County Sheriff's Office vehicles carrying six deputies soon arrived, racing across a ranch bordering the river and ignoring the fact that they drove through private pasture land and scattered dozens of bison. Two emergency rescue vans followed, adding four medics to join the discussion.

Watching the deputies and medics staring blankly across the forty feet to where the body remained caught in the wire and twisted in the swift flow, Beth turned to Liz and asked, "Your dad's a sheriff. What would he think of this?"

"I wouldn't want him to see it. No one's doing anything. They're just standing there, looking and arguing. Voices carry."

"Can you hear what they're talking about?" Sue asked.

"They don't seem to know how they're going to bring the body to this side," said Liz. "One offered to wade, but another told him he'd never make it through the current. The water's cold and swift and they don't have waders."

"They don't have a boat," Beth observed. "Maybe I should offer ours."

She got up and walked to the deputy who seemed to be in charge. At least he was dominating the conversation. Since he acquired his uniform, it had either shrunk a couple of sizes, or he had added twenty pounds. His dark blue uniform shirt had popped its lower buttons, showing a white t-shirt only partly tucked into his pants.

"How do you plan to get to the body?" Beth asked quietly and politely.

"We've called for a *real* boat, an aluminum jon boat. Not a rubber ducky like yours," said the man, who added, "I'm Deputy Jackson. With the Gallatin County Sheriff's Office. . . . We'll want to talk to you in a few minutes, little lady. Don't leave."

"My name's not 'little lady,'" said Beth, less politely. "We don't plan to leave until you've questioned us. Why don't you take our inflatable boat?" Beth offered. "If you have someone who knows how to row. . . . If you don't, I'll row you over."

"Little lady, we have the situation in hand. We can row," Johnson said. "And we can take your boat without asking for it."

"Go ahead," responded Beth. "There's line in the boat. You might need that. And, again, my name's not 'little lady.' I'm Beth Brooks. This is Sue Mills and that's Liz Rangley. We're the ones who called your office."

"You any relation to that Brooks guy who's a guide? The one who's always in trouble?"

"You mean Macduff Brooks?"

"That's him."

"He's my dad. What does that have to do with this?"

"He's always around trouble. This murder could have been his doing. He belongs in jail. We'll find out soon enough. And I mean it when I say 'don't go anywhere.' We'll bring Macduff in for questioning later. He may be involved."

"He's at home recovering from being hit and injured by a van. He isn't exactly in any shape to 'be involved' here."

"I'm the one who decides that," said Jackson.

Two younger—and fitter—deputies shoved off in Beth's inflatable and struggled to get it across to the body. The water was moving fast enough to drag them downstream until the one in the middle seat got the hang of rowing. He had more strength than experience. Twenty-five minutes passed before they reached the body, and when they did, they couldn't get it free from the barbed wire.

Beth went over to Jackson and held out her hand. "Maybe they might want this," she said, handing him a pair of wire cutters she took from the bag that one of the deputies had thrown from Beth's boat onto the bank when launching. The bag was labeled RESCUE.

"Don't need no wire cutter. They can pull the barbed wire away from the other tree," Jackson said. But they couldn't. One deputy entangled himself on the barbs, and the second man spent fifteen minutes getting him loose. Sue could not control her laughter.

"We need to cut this wire," called one of the men in the inflatable.

Again handing Jackson the wire cutter, Beth quietly said, "I suggest you get this to them. Your men couldn't row very well, and now you don't have a boat; maybe you know how to swim."

It was not the right thing to say, but it confirmed how much Beth was like Lucinda and her dad. Jackson took the wire cutters just as a Montana FWP vehicle pulled up, towing a three-person inflatable boat. It was in the water in two minutes and reached the body in two more. Two wardens cut the body free and left the barbed wire attached to the tree so it could be examined before it was removed.

The FWP wardens brought the body back across the river and laid it out on a tarp on the bank. It *was* the fisherman who started off before the three gals. If he hadn't been ahead down-stream, they would have run into the wire first.

One of the FWP wardens took out a cell phone, tapped in a number, and spoke quietly: "White male. Not in the water long. About fifty. Looks healthy. Not a lot of blood anymore. The deceased most likely drowned, but he could have been dead and then placed across the wire. He's wearing old patched Dan Bailey waders and a Patagonian jacket. No hat. It might have fallen off. Some flies are stuck on a foam pad on the front of his jacket. No sign of a fly fishing rod, he may have dropped one when he hit the wire."

While talking the warden was going through the man's pockets underneath the waders. "I have his wallet and a folded paper that's his fishing license. Name's apparently Rudolfo Martin. Address in Bozeman. Fifty-six years old. Only other things in his pocket seem to be a handkerchief, some keys, a folded twenty-dollar bill, a Leatherman, an eyeglasses case, and a packet of fly line tippets."

Deputy Jackson hadn't stirred during the FWP's exhibition of how Jackson's men might have acted if they were better pre-pared. Jackson didn't say another word to the three young women. After a brief few words with the FWP head, Jackson and his men departed. The emergency crew left at the same time with the body, headed for the county medical examiner's office.

Beth, Sue, and Liz talked to the wardens for another forty minutes, got back in the inflatable, and headed downriver to the nearest takeout. They were anxious to get home.

7

THE SAME MAY DAY AT THE PRESIDENTIAL PALACE IN GUATEMALA

LUISA SOLARES WAS ABOUT TO VISIT HER UNCLE Juan Pablo Herzog, the President of Guatemala. Luisa called him Tío Juan. She last visited Guatemala City between semesters at the University of Florida law college where she was studying for an LL.M. Tío Juan had not been pleasant to her.

Herzog had been disappointed and angry that she had not discovered anything more about Professor Hunt other than what Thomas Davis, Jr., had told her the previous fall—when Hunt adopted his new identity he planned on working with "fish." But Davis had been drunk when he told her that bit of information at a party.

Luisa was only weeks away from graduating at the end of the summer term. She excelled as a student and was a research assistant to a prominent international law professor. Her thesis was about the Guatemala-Belize territorial dispute and she knew she could not show the thesis to Tío Juan, who as president refused to proceed with a proposed settlement with Belize. Guatemala had promised to hold a public referendum that Herzog refused to schedule. He intended to use the Guatemalan military to settle the dispute. Luisa was convinced that Guatemala was wrong on both the facts and the law of the dispute.

As she went up the steps at the Casa Presidencial, for the first time she felt distant from Tío Juan. Her remarkable intelligence blossomed during her time in Florida and raised concern about Herzog's use of violent means to achieve his goals.

Several of Luisa's fellow students had formed a study group and invited her to join. She was especially fond of Stephen Watson, a tall, handsome student from Sarasota.

Luisa preferred to remain at UF another two years and obtain the JD law degree that would allow her to take the bar exam and be able to practice law in Florida. But she suspected Tío Juan would never condone those aspirations. He had spent much time raising her to achieve one goal: presenting him the head of whoever Professor Hunt had become.

She found herself shivering as she walked the hall toward the presidential living area. When her uncle opened the door, he looked at her with an expression that frightened her.

"How are you, dear niece?" Herzog said, without touching her. "Come in. We have much to talk about." When Luisa sat, she looked at Tío Juan and tried to hide her trembling.

"You have not called me in months," he began. "Why? I have been expecting information about Professor Hunt."

"I have done the best I can, Tío Juan. The law college dean is withholding the information you wish. I think she has it, but increasingly the college has become defensive."

"Why do you suppose that is?"

"One reason: Your Coronel Alarcon visited the law school two weeks ago. He was not pleasant and became belligerent when he realized Dean Nadal wasn't going to help. He raised his voice and bragged how he would exterminate anyone involved with Hunt's participation in a protection program, including Dean Nadal, who called campus security and had Alarcon physically removed.

"I have not talked to Dean Nadal since she called me after Alarcon left, explained what happened, and expressed how upset she was. I told her I didn't believe Alarcon was acting consistent with his role as an important advisor to you."

"You like the dean, don't you?"

"Yes. This has been a special year. My professors are exciting teachers, especially the one I'm working for as a research assistant. The students are so nice to me. Compared to Guatemala City, Gainesville is a safe place to live. Recently, I have read disappointing news about Guatemala in *The N.Y. Times* and *The Wall Street Journal.* The editors have not been kind to you, especially your position regarding Belize."

Herzog was visibly upset. Over and over he nervously tapped a pencil on his desk, a habit when he was about to lose his temper.

"Luisa, I didn't send you to Gainesville to read foreign newspaper trash. You are there to help me find Professor Hunt. . . . Have you been dating?"

"I see a number of law students and a few in the undergraduate program. One is here with me to see Guatemala."

"Who is he?"

"His name is Stephen Watson."

"Am I going to meet him?"

"I don't think so. He's the one who's given me the newspaper articles about Guatemala and asked questions about the country and about you. He was hesitant to come here because of the increasing crime. We're going to Antigua tomorrow, then to Lake Atitlán, and last to Chichicastenango."

Herzog had gotten up from his chair, listening and walking about his large office. He frowned, holding his chin in his left hand, staring at Luisa with an intensity that upset her.

"Would you like to meet Stephen?" she asked.

"I do *not* wish to see him. . . . When you go back to Gainesville, I want you to see the law college dean and tell her you must withdraw immediately because I need you here. You may suggest that you might return next year to finish. But I want you back in Guatemala. Is that clear?"

"Yes, Tío Juan," Luisa answered, not wishing to anger him further by telling him she would not drop out of the LL.M. program so close to receiving her degree.

Luisa got up from her chair, quietly and politely said good-bye, and without touching Herzog walked toward the door to the hall, but turned suddenly when a side door to the president's office opened. She knew it was a direct entry to Tío Juan's bedroom.

"Juanito!" called out the figure to Herzog, only then aware Luisa was in the room. A towel was wrapped around the woman's head—she wore nothing else.

"Hola Señora Alarcon," Luisa called out. "Como esta, *Dolores?*"

It was Alarcon's wife, Dolores, who quickly left and closed the door behind her. Luisa looked at her uncle.

"Give my regards to Coronel Alarcon when you see him," Luisa said curtly. "I assume *he's* out of town."

She stepped out and pulled the door closed, smiling and laughing as she left the building. She thought she had just received unspoken permission to stay at UF. She would call Tío Juan when she reached Gainesville and tell him exactly that, and she would ask him to give her regards to Dolores Alarcon.

8

THE FOLLOWING EVENING IN GAINESVILLE

LUISA FINISHED UNPACKING THE SUITCASE SHE brought with her from Guatemala and found a gift from Stephen.

After Stephen and she had visited the highlands, he went to his hotel and Luisa went home and found an anonymous note tucked in her door that said Herzog was furious, trying to contact her, and intended to prevent her leaving the country. Luisa immediately changed her reservations and booked the only seat available on a Delta flight through Atlanta that left in two hours.

When Luisa left for the airport in Guatemala City, she called Stephen and told him only that she had to return to Gainesville earlier than they had planned. Stephen decided to follow and the best he could do on short notice was a flight the next day on Avianca with a change in Miami.

Luisa had asked Stephen to call her when he arrived in Gainesville, stating she had something important to tell him about her uncle's plans that might endanger Stephen. Sleep came slowly that night as she tried to plan the next few days.

The following day Luisa anxiously awaited Stephen's return. The flight from Miami to Gainesville was due at 4:15 p.m. At 6:55 she called his cell phone number, but the call did not go through. She knew he would call and thought she might pass the next hour with the diversion of TV, turning on the

PBS NewsHour, which had just begun. Luisa listened to the reporter in disbelief, tears welling in her eyes:

The Avianca flight had departed the La Aurora airport in Guatemala City and appeared to some observers to be flying too low. It failed to gain altitude and thirty minutes later exploded and went down in the dense tropical forests of the Petén. There were no survivors. The cause of the explosion is being investigated, including the possibility of a terrorist attack. We'll have more during this program as we receive further updates.

Only two days ago they had walked hand-in-hand through the colorful market at Chichicastenango. He had bought her a jade necklace that she wore that evening to dinner at the Mayan Inn. The memories of their trip were so vivid she couldn't believe he was dead.

She had planned to tell Stephen about the meeting with her uncle. But not the part when Herzog demanded that Luisa withdraw from the law program. She decided on her own that she would not withdraw and return as he ordered. Seeing Tío Juan with the Coronel's wife gave her a playing card that was an "ace." She planned to place that card on the table if Tío Juan acted in any way hostile towards her. . . . Could it be possible that Herzog was responsible for the crash?

Luisa was terribly disappointed in the conduct of her uncle. The more she got to know him, the more she wanted to stay away from him, even if that meant staying away from Guatemala and her family.

The worst of her uncle's character had become apparent when she caught him with the wife of Coronel Alarcon, at the very time Alarcon was obtaining the information Herzog had sought for years.

Luisa also was beginning to worry seriously about her safety. She only recently began to side with those who believed that many years ago her uncle killed his cousin, the much beloved priest Padre Bueno. It was not known outside her family that Padre Bueno was Luisa's father.

The Belize issue had made Luisa interested in Guatemala's reputation abroad. She discovered it was not good. The country was so corrupt that the UN stepped in to resolve many issues and—after careful study—to issue a long list of what the Guatemalan government must do to solve its problems. Herzog continued the policy of his predecessor in rejecting every UN proposal. Luisa wondered how her country could have gotten into such trouble and why it seemingly could not get out. Her inquiries taught her that families like her own failed to demand that Guatemala make the difficult but necessary decisions to reverse years of inept and corrupt governance.

A relatively new issue was present in her country: the increasing control over drug traffic by the Mexican drug cartel known as the Zetas. Allowing control of a critical domestic issue by another nation's crime syndicates was unimaginable. She increasingly understood why so many of her friends' families had moved to the U.S. or Spain or elsewhere.

One thing Luisa had decided: she was through with her role-playing as a party seeking to find and kill Professor Maxwell Hunt.

Even if that meant never returning to her family in Guatemala.

9

A WEEK LATER IN GAINESVILLE

LUISA LEARNED THE DAY AFTER THE PLANE crash that a Stephen Watson was on the passenger manifest. A day later she received a condolence note from Dean Nadal suggesting Luisa call her office and make an appointment to talk.

Luisa was cautious but called. The dean's secretary suggested 7:30 the following morning. Luisa suspected the dean had a full schedule but was willing to arrive at her office early for the meeting.

Luisa was at the law college waiting outside the office when the dean walked in at 7:29.

"Come in with me. We'll make some coffee."

"How were you aware I knew Stephen Watson?" Luisa asked.

"Two of our students came by the day after the crash," said Dean Nadal. "They told me you had been seeing Stephen, and they were worried about you."

"I liked Stephen," Luisa said. "We had several pleasant days in Guatemala before the fatal crash. It was his first visit to Latin America."

"I wanted to tell you how saddened we were about Stephen, all the more so when we learned he was seriously dating one of our students from Guatemala."

"He would have been a fine doctor someday," Luisa said, her voice breaking. "Thank you for being concerned."

"You've been an excellent student, Luisa. Some of your fellow students have told me that when you arrived last term you were so private they couldn't tell if you were naturally inhospitable, were having some personal problems, or were hiding from something.

"I know you've made friends with two of our LL.M. students from Costa Rica and Mexico. Last week one of them told me she had thought you might drop out and return to Guatemala because you seemed lonely, but that after meeting Stephen you were a changed person. I know his loss must especially hurt. I hope you'll stay and receive your degree. It's a matter of days rather than weeks until graduation."

Twenty minutes later Luisa rose from her chair and began to move slowly toward the door.

"Please come back and sit for another moment," requested the dean. "There's something further I want to discuss."

Luisa sat again, put her backpack of law books on the floor beside her chair, and waited for the dean to speak.

"I know you inquired before the summer session about staying and applying to study in the JD program. I'm pleased. Confidentially, I'm certain you'll be admitted for the JD because of your grades."

Luisa struggled not to break down. She was not sure the moistness in her eyes was because of Stephen's death or the dean's kindness. No one she knew only briefly had ever treated her so thoughtfully. Dean Nadal obviously considered her to be a bright young lady with a promising future as a lawyer.

"Over the past month, Dean Nadal, I gave thought to finishing the LL.M. and applying to the JD program. Having the JD from here and passing the Florida bar would allow me to practice, dealing with issues involving both our countries. Guatemala is badly in need of lawyers known for their integrity and familiarity with foreign legal systems.

"Unfortunately, there's an obstacle facing me—my being President Herzog's niece. Integrity is not a characteristic he is known for or even that he considers a positive trait. I know that the real reason I am here is a part of that."

"Can you tell me more?" Dean Nadal asked.

"I came here to obtain information about Professor Hunt and help my uncle find him."

Nadal was visibly shocked. She thought being a law school dean meant mainly raising money while assistant deans ran the college. . . . But there was something that told her that this was a young woman worth saving from her uncle.

"Why are you telling me this? I could call the police and have you arrested."

"I've decided I cannot work for my uncle any more. I don't want to return to Guatemala. If Tío Juan—as he insists I call him—learns about my intentions, he will have me killed. He is ruthless."

"I want you to talk—and talk freely—with a man in Washington who was in charge of Professor Hunt when he recovered from the beating your uncle gave him. I know our official UF policy is that Hunt died in D.C. from a stroke, but I now believe he survived and is being protected by the CIA. Who he is, where he is, and what he is doing are known by a very few. I'm not one of those."

"Dean Nadal, my uncle knows *what* Hunt is doing for a living, but not where or using what name."

"What does he know and how did he learn about that?"

"He discovered that Hunt was doing something involving fish. I learned that from a young man I dated once, the son of a retired CIA agent who was living in Guatemala."

"Can you tell me who the agent was?"

"Yes. His name was Thomas Davis. His son, Thomas Davis, Jr., was a student at Vanderbilt. I met him in Guatemala before I started the program here, and Thomas came to Gainesville last fall for a football game. I got Thomas drunk and asked him what his father said about Professor Hunt. His father stated that Hunt intended to fish.

"The senior Davis passed away two weeks ago. My uncle had Davis's Alzheimer's medicine stopped when he learned that Davis might be better able to talk if he were not taking pills that made him drowsy and confused. Stopping the medicine would almost certainly kill Davis. Apparently it did. I learned of this last week while I was in Guatemala."

"What is your uncle going to do now?"

"I don't know. He has assigned a ruthless man whom you have met, Coronel Carlos Alarcon, to find out more about Hunt. Alarcon currently is in Washington."

"Luisa, I will talk to our university president about finding you grants to remain here and attend the JD program. But you may not wish to do that if you are worried that your uncle might try to harm you for disobeying him."

"He will try," she said. "But I will not live my life in fear of him. . . . I have some funds to help pay for two or three more years here."

"Please call me frequently, Luisa. I don't want us to lose you. And I don't want to lose a friend."

10

THE SAME WEEK IN WASHINGTON, D.C.

CORONEL CARLOS ALARCON SAT BACK AGAINST the wall at a table in a corner at the Starlight Restaurant within sight of the State Department in Foggy Bottom. He was not in uniform. A raincoat and umbrella lay on one chair, dripping onto the old hickory floor.

Looking at Alarcon, one would not guess he was the second most powerful man in Guatemala. And the second most corrupt. The man who held the top spot in both was Juan Pablo Herzog.

Alarcon never wore a uniform when he was abroad carrying out the wishes of President Herzog. He sipped a glass of bourbon and appeared completely at ease. But his tranquil appearance hid his anxiety about the discussion that was about to occur.

As Alarcon watched the door across the room, at almost the exact time their meeting was scheduled, a nondescript looking man in a dark suit and white shirt entered and stood by the door glancing about the room. Sufficiently experienced with espionage, Alarcon knew the man had to be Ralph Johnson; a former CIA agent based at Langley and now retired. It was the man Alarcon was waiting for.

Johnson looked Alarcon's way and nodded slightly. Alarcon responded, and Johnson, appearing nervous, looked around as he walked across the room.

"Coronel Alarcon," Johnson said, in a soft voice barely louder than a whisper.

Alarcon gestured to his right, where Johnson carefully slid onto the seat.

"How did you come to call me last week?" asked Johnson, continuing to look around the room.

"I have friends in your CIA. I head Guatemala's national security, and we have good relations with your government. I am often in contact and working with CIA people. As long as my country is ruled by a military government that prohibits communist activities, we are considered special by the U.S. We have none of the problems that face a corrupt country like Nicaragua."

Johnson wondered how Alarcon defined "corrupt," but didn't ask.

"About the money I am to receive for the information you wish; it must be in untraceable cash."

"Already the money has been transferred to an account in the Swiss Investment Bank in Zurich. I have the number of that account in a sealed envelope to give you."

Alarcon passed bank papers to Johnson that affirmed a transfer of $4 million. Johnson examined them carefully, nodding and smiling as he finished reading each page.

"They look fine. . . . What if I refused to give you the information?" he said, grinning.

"The same thing that would happen if you ever give me *incorrect* information. The same that will happen to your wife, your daughter, and your three grandchildren. Johnson is a common name. The world will not miss a few of them," he added, with his own hint of a grin.

"I asked only for the present name of Professor Hunt," Alarcon continued, "where he lives and what he does. I will not write it down; I have an excellent memory. Please give me the information. As soon as we finish, I will return to Guatemala and personally pass the information on to President Herzog."

"All right," Johnson began. "A close friend still active at the CIA who owed me a favor recently updated me on Professor Hunt. Hunt became and currently is known as Macduff Brooks. He has a daughter about nineteen named Elsbeth after her deceased mother. Brooks is married to the former Lucinda Lang, now Lucinda Brooks. They live in two locations. From April or early May through late September, sometimes extending into November, they are in a small log cabin on the Mill Creek Road in a place called Paradise Valley near Emigrant, Montana. I don't have a house number, but you may learn exactly where the house is from most anyone at one of the few stores in Emigrant. I suggest you try the fly fishing shop or the grocery. Everyone in that area knows Brooks.

"For the winters they live about 25 miles south of St. Augustine, Florida. They have a small cottage two hundred yards off route U.S. 1 a little north of the St. John's County line that joins Flagler County in Northeast Florida. Their house is on stilts and faces the salt marsh flats. There is no house number. It is on Pellicer Creek and accessed by a dirt road. There is a locked gate and a mailbox that says only M.B."

"What does Hunt, or rather Brooks, do for a living?"

"In the summer in Montana he does some fly fishing guiding in both Montana and Wyoming. Most other guides know him. He does not work in the winter; Lucinda and he go to Florida for the warmer weather. They use their Florida cottage as a base to travel, especially brief trips to an apartment they own in Manhattan."

"Is that it?" asked Alarcon.

"Yes, it is."

"I have been on my iPad while you were talking and have verified that a Macduff Brooks lives on Mill Creek in Montana. He is also listed as a fishing guide and is on several pro staffs of major fly fishing companies. I don't need more and have erased his name from my iPad. I think we are finished."

Sweating profusely, Johnson thought a little sweat and anxiety were a small price to pay for $4 million. He pushed back his chair, rose, and quickly left. A forged passport and airline tickets for the next day under a different name would take him to Lisbon, Portugal, and on to Faro on the Algarve coast where he had recently rented a condo under a different name.

Alarcon smiled and ordered another drink. He would fly home to Guatemala City the following day, and he thought of the increased likelihood that he would succeed Herzog as President of Guatemala. Then he would be able to give out *more* than $4 million to achieve his goal to become richer and more powerful than even Herzog.

As President, Alarcon would lead his country's army into Belize to regain what was rightfully Guatemala's territory, and he would go down in history as his nation's greatest president.

11

EARLY MORNING TWO DAYS LATER IN GUATEMALA

CORONEL ALARCON PARKED HIS VEHICLE AND two-at-a-time raced up the wide marble stairs at Casa Presidencial, Herzog's official residence in Guatemala City. Alarcon was excited to be meeting with the President and giving him information about Professor Hunt. He had not made an appointment and wasn't certain the President even knew he had returned to Guatemala.

When he reached the door to Herzog's office, he heard voices inside. Not wanting to disturb the President, he sat in a chair in the hall immediately outside the door.

Alarcon wondered why there was so much laughing inside and then thought he recognized a voice. It couldn't be, but it sounded like his wife, Dolores. He went to the door and listened further and then squatted and looked through the worn keyhole of the centuries old door. What he saw stunned him. Dolores and Herzog were both naked, and Herzog was chasing her around the presidential desk.

Alarcon was incensed. He didn't know whether to break down the door, knock, or leave. He decided on the first choice, stepped to the other side of the hall and threw himself against the door, which fell with a crash into the room.

"Herzog! What are you doing with my wife?" Dolores grabbed a small oriental rug and wrapped it around her shoulders. Herzog pulled a drape off a window frame and flung the fabric around his sallow body. The two looked uncomfortably absurd.

"Alarcon, it's nothing. She will return to your home with you. . . . Call it the privileges of office."

Dolores raced for the bedroom and shut the door behind her.

"Sit down, Coronel. Calm yourself," Herzog said. "What are women made for?"

Alarcon refused to sit.

"Herzog, I will see you dead!"

"That's a little overly dramatic, Coronel. Don't take this badly. Over the past few months in this beautiful antiques-filled office, I have separately entertained a dozen different government wives.

Alarcon was livid. Humiliated. Betrayed. He could accept Herzog sleeping with lower level ministers' wives, as he did himself. But not the wife of the President's most important advisor, the man who was about to turn over information otherwise unobtainable over the past dozen years.

Herzog quietly sat down at his desk, opening his drawer to make sure his pistol was there. He moved it within reach.

"How can you do this to me, Señor Presidente?" screamed Alarcon, who had become irrational. "I have served you honorably and have willingly killed for you. I owed you no less than absolute loyalty, and look how you've repaid me!"

"Don't make me angry, Coronel. It is nothing but a minor affair. I have no interest in your wife or any other wives who have shared my bed."

Alarcon was sweating profusely. His hands were shaking. He stood and yelled at Herzog.

"I will see you dead, you scum. I was the child of a prominent family who went to military school and worked my way up the ranks. Your parents were *peasants,"* he added, knowing it was untrue but would enrage Herzog. "You lied and bribed your way to the top."

Alarcon got up and took one step toward the president's desk. Herzog was frantic, reached into his drawer, lifted the pistol, and fired four shots at Alarcon's chest.

Alarcon fell bleeding, adding more red to a priceless antique oriental carpet and looking up with shock at Herzog who stood over him ready to shoot again. Dolores had opened the bedroom door barely enough to watch her husband die.

As life flowed from his body, Dolores stated calmly, "You don't know what you've done, Juan Pablo. Carlos told me yesterday on the phone from D.C. that he had learned exactly what you wanted to know—the current name of Professor Hunt, where he lives, and what he is doing. He couldn't wait to tell you. He was so proud of his efforts. Carlos said it was such valuable information that he never wrote it down. Now he has taken it with him to his grave."

Herzog was incredulous. "Who gave him the information?"

"He didn't say anything other than he had made a very private arrangement with a man named Johnson who had been at the meeting when Professor Hunt was placed in a protection program."

"How did Alarcon pay for the information?"

"With government funds you made accessible to him. He personally transferred $4 million to a foreign account in Johnson's name."

Incredulous, Herzog slumped in his chair.

12

THAT SAME EVENING AT MILL CREEK IN MONTANA

ELSBETH DROPPED OFF LIZ IN LIVINGSTON AT her house. Liz was exhausted after the Gallatin barbed wire incident. Elsbeth and Sue went on to our Mill Creek cabin.

When Elsbeth arrived home, I was sitting in a rocker on the front porch waiting, head down drowsing. At times like this, I must have looked old to her; I *felt* old and feared that she thought of me as the mere shell of the father whom she first met only a few years ago. Part of my appearance was from the physical injury the VW van had caused. But most was mental disfigurement from worrying about Lucinda.

Without doubt Elsbeth and I were certain throughout the first two weeks after the abduction that Lucinda would walk through the door at any moment. Recently, I had begun to rely on the dozens of photos of the two of us on the cottage and cabin walls to restore my vision of her soft contours.

Elsbeth sat and told me about the tragedy on the Gallatin. More would unfold in the next few days, and the three gals would be subjected to further questioning by the authorities and harassment by the media. In my mind there wasn't the slightest chance they would be suspects. It wasn't clear whether the barbed wire was placed across the river with intent to stop boaters or to keep livestock from getting out of pasture land.

The three young women had been unimpressed with the Gallatin County Sheriff's Office deputies who showed up at the scene of the murder, especially the apparent leader, Deputy Jackson. Beth worried that the police would pursue anyone found *near* the scene of a crime because of a mixture of incompetence, understaffing, and insufficient funding.

Presumably, the fisherman died after becoming entangled in the barbed wire, but he may have been dead already and his body dumped into the river or the inflatable that was found downstream. The latter seemed implausible—the women saw the man alive in his boat as he passed them less than an hour before they discovered his body hanging from the barbed wire.

"Dad," said Elsbeth, "you haven't said a word for a half-hour. Are you OK?"

"As best I can be," I murmured.

"Would you like to take me fishing?" she asked.

"Fishing? I'm not sure about that yet, but when I am, I will want to be with *you* somewhere. Maybe we could drive south and stay in Jackson for a few days and fish in Grand Teton."

"Just say the word. I'll take a few days off. We'll fish."

"Thanks."

My cell phone rang. I ignored it, continuing to rock in my chair. But the ring persisted.

"Are you going to answer that," Elsbeth asked, "or am I your personal secretary?"

"Someone *answer!*" Sue called out from the kitchen. "Am I supposed to do that as well as wash these dishes?"

"Hello," Elsbeth said, without adding more, and listened to the caller without speaking. Turning toward me, she thrust out the phone. "It's a call from the *Gallatin Magazine*."

"They must want Lucinda. Tell them she's away."

"It's for *you*. They asked for the Brooks who is the fly fishing guide who has had lots of murders take place on his boats. She wants to interview that one specific guide. *You!* Dad."

"Damn!" I said, thinking that an interview for an article was the last thing I needed. But she might write an article without me, which could be worse.

I took the phone from Elsbeth, glowered at it as though it were the caller, and said loudly, "This is Macduff Brooks. You've caught me at a bad time."

"I'm Celeste Ransome, chief editor of the *Gallatin Magazine*. I'm calling from Bozeman. We publish a lot of articles about people who live here and have been engaged in interesting activities. You qualify in spades."

"I don't do 'interesting activities' that might attract your readers. But thank you for thinking about me."

I hung up and started to hobble down the porch stairs heading for peace on my dock. I left my phone at the cabin on the arm of the rocker. When it rang again, Elsbeth answered.

"She's on the line *again*, Dad." Reluctantly, I went back up the stairs, and she handed me the phone, contorting her face as if to add that this Ransome woman doesn't understand "no."

"This is Macduff," I said again.

"Please don't hang up on me again," she pleaded in a firm but pleasant voice. "Your name was referred to me over the past decade by a dozen people. That includes Sharon Weston, the sister of Marge Atwood. You must remember Marge?"

"Yes. She was fortunate to be one of two shuttle gals who survived the murders a decade ago." I said nothing more.

"If I drove out to Paradise Valley, could I interview you?"

"I guess. . . ." I stuttered, remembering the tragedy of the three shuttle gals who didn't survive.

"I'll take that as a yes," she interrupted before I could think of a further excuse. "When would be convenient?"

"I'm booked solid for weeks for casting lessons and guide floats." I fibbed, knowing it was a flimsy excuse this determined lady would ignore.

"Name a free time. I can talk with you at night after your casting lessons and guiding trips are over. . . . I meant we could meet some *evening* in the next week or two when your *day* is over, not your *season*."

"I'd have to look at my schedule."

"I can wait."

"I could call you back."

"*I'll wait*. Get your schedule. Find a good time and date."

"You're persistent."

"You ever heard of Joyce Ransome?"

"Montana's most famous serial killer?"

"Not quite, but she was tough. She's my great grandmother. Born in Butte. One of ten siblings. Her father was a rancher, her mother a school teacher. Joyce served in the U.S. Congress—first woman to do so."

"Father served with Custer at Little Bighorn?"

"No! It's the female side that gained prominence."

"And you're determined to carry on that tradition?"

"Anyone ever tell you you're engaging but impossible?"

"Of course not. Well, maybe some. My wife. My daughter. Our housekeeper. Some fishing guides. A few others."

"I'm not surprised. . . . Date and time?"

"Next Tuesday at 8:30 a.m.," I said, expecting it to be too soon and too early in the day for her to drive to Mill Creek from Bozeman.

"Perfect. I'm staying near the entrance to Yellowstone Park in Gardiner the night before, after interviewing Herbert

Williams. He's the rancher who's been free-ranging bison around Gardiner. He's not popular with the cattle ranchers. . . . It'll be easy to be at your place early the next morning."

"What do you want to talk about?"

"*You.*"

"I'm just a guide who's had some bad luck with some bad people. . . . What's there to know?"

"Why you decided to move to Montana a dozen years ago. More specifically, thirteen years ago this coming May. You bought land along Mill Creek near Emigrant, built a cabin and drift boat, and started guiding. A few years later you married Lucinda Lang, a New York investment advisor who owned a spacious ranch upstream from you on Mill Creek."

"That's all pretty ordinary. No secrets."

She laughed. "Our readers want to know about the Macduff Brooks *before* he arrived in Montana and why there've been so many murders involving you. And why your daughter is following in your footsteps. Wasn't she rowing your inflatable boat on the Gallatin and found a body stuck on barbed wire?"

"Elsbeth and two friends found a dead body. She didn't hang it on the barbed wire. She didn't shoot him. Or drown him. She had never met him."

"I understand she had an unpleasant conversation with Deputy Jackson."

"Do you know him?"

"More than I'd like. Word is he said Beth was a suspect."

"That's true. And she let him know she disagreed. . . . Ms. Ransome, I'll talk to you about various deaths that occurred on my boats that you've mentioned. But I won't talk about my *earlier* life. It's boring and personal. Agreed?"

"I'll try not to invade your privacy."

13

THE FOLLOWING TUESDAY AT THE MILL CREEK CABIN

CELESTE RANSOME ARRIVED AT OUR MODEST Mill Creek log cabin at 8:02 a.m. She passed Elsbeth and Sue on our road near the front gate and waved. The two were leaving for their day shifts at Chico Hot Springs.

The last thing Elsbeth said to me was "Don't throw this interview lady out before you've listened to her questions."

Through the living room window, I watched as Ms. Ransome—Celease or something like that—got out of her Mercedes sedan, pulled out a large, formal, black briefcase from the passenger seat, and started toward the porch steps.

I hadn't expected her to come dressed for a day's fashion photos for Victoria's Secret. I always associated Victoria's with New York City, but Ms. Ransome's neckline plummeted all the way from Manhattan to Montana. She wore slim-leg dark-wash denims that made her seem a size smaller. A long cabernet red cable-knit car coat looked like a coat with the comfort of a sweater. It had hidden snaps the top half of which had either malfunctioned or more likely had been intentionally left open and allowed a necklace of strands with large black beads to disappear between her breasts. It was not an outfit I expected of a working journalist. I refrained from asking if she wanted me to hang up her coat.

My dress was wrinkled faded jeans and a Wrangler long sleeved shirt. It was pink and didn't have a plunging neckline.

"You can leave that briefcase in the car," I called out, stepping onto the porch. "It'll be safe."

"This is part of my research on you, Macduff. I need it."

"I doubt it. My life is not that complex."

"We'll see," she responded, reaching out to shake my hand. . . . "I'm Celeste."

"I'm Macduff, Ms. Ransome. You just missed my daughter, Elsbeth. You will meet Wuff. She's inside."

"Wuff must be your rescued sheltie. Judge Amy Becker in Bozeman told me about you two. And I know about Wuff's limp. She was shot, wasn't she?"

"Yes. Don't remind her. She'll want a treat. . . . Sit wherever you prefer," I offered.

She chose the sofa, sitting at one end, setting her opened briefcase next to her, and leaning toward me.

"Ready?" she asked.

"Before you start, Ms. Ransome. I'm from the South, and we tend to be more hospitable than folks in other parts of the country. May I get you a proper morning drink? Bloody Mary, Mimosa, Agua de Valencia?"

"Call me Celeste, please. I know the first two drinks, but what's Agua de Valencia?"

"A little like a Mimosa. It's a good early drink. Made of a Spanish *Champagne*—Cava—with a little orange juice, vodka, and gin. I keep a jug of them in the refrigerator. Because I mix in the vodka and gin, they don't freeze, but they are *very* cold."

"I'll have one if you promise not to give me a refill."

"You're old enough to make your own decisions."

I brought the jug from the kitchen, poured two glasses, handed one to Celeste, sat back at the opposite end of the sofa, and asked, "First question?"

"You arrived in Bozeman thirteen years ago from Washington, D.C., by way of Denver. The next day on your Montana driver's license application, you stated that you were forty-five. Does that sound about right?"

"About right. I haven't given those uneventful days much recent thought."

"Within a week you bought some property on Mill Creek and began to build a log cabin."

"The cabin you're now sitting in. I live here."

"All year long?"

"No."

"You live somewhere else part of the year?"

"Yes."

"Where?"

"Florida."

"Where?"

"St. Augustine."

"Where?"

"Pelicer Creek."

"Where?"

"What does it matter? I live in the woods along the salt flats a little west of the Intracoastal Waterway. . . . Are you going to ask where again?"

"That won't be necessary. Why Florida?"

"It's warmer than here. I don't favor Montana winters."

"How long are you in Florida each year?"

"It varies."

"On average."

"October to April. Sometimes we leave here in late November after Thanksgiving; sometimes we don't leave Florida until late May around Memorial Day."

"What do you do in Florida for six months?"

"Watch *The Weather Channel,* and when it snows in Montana we talk about how good it is to be in Florida."

"And."

"Buy groceries, newspapers, gas. Have our teeth cleaned. Chase rattlesnakes off our porch. The usual chores. We live uneventful lives."

"Do you socialize much?"

"Doing what?"

"Parties, events. You don't spend the winters watching *The Weather Channel* every evening."

"A very few parties. A very few events."

"Do you have a boat in Florida?"

"Yes."

"Is it like your boats here?"

"No."

"What kind?"

"A flats boat."

"What's that?"

"A Hell's Bay."

"Meaning?"

"A 16' foot shallow-draft boat made by Hell's Bay. It's made for skinny water."

"What is 'skinny' water?"

"Shallow." Like her questions, I thought.

She took some additional papers from her briefcase and was either searching for something or fidgeting because she was uncertain how to proceed. I kept looking for her black beads.

"You've been in some well-publicized incidents here in the West. Have you been in any similar situations in Florida?"

"What do you mean by *situations?*"

"In your case anything that led to a death."

"One. A man I didn't know beyond exchanging greetings was wrapped in a gill net, placed in my flats boat, doused with gas, and ignited. Needless to say, he perished. So did my boat."

"Weren't there more gill net murders?"

"Yes, one in Southwest Florida near Captiva and one in West Florida near Apalachicola. I was not involved."

"Is it true you had words with a Florida county deputy sheriff? And again here with a Gallatin County deputy?"

"Somewhat."

"Can we talk about deaths on your boat?"

"OK. Eleven years ago a former ambassador named Anders Eckstrum was killed in my boat by a sniper hidden along the bank of the Snake River in Jackson, Wyoming. A few months later on the same river, a man—apparently the killer of Eckstrum—was, in turn, killed in my boat."

"And you were shot?"

"Yes. So were Lucinda and Wuff. . . . You must read the newspapers. Those deaths were covered in repetitive detail, including in Bozeman. I have nothing to add."

"Were you the person who the killer of the former ambassador was really targeting?"

"That's an interesting thought. I don't know why I would have been the target. . . . But we'll never know, will we?"

"Was anyone chasing you?"

"Chasing me? I don't understand. We could spend hours revisiting what you've raised and where you seem to be headed. It's been covered *ad naseum* by the media."

"The deaths continued a year later in what the press called the 'shuttle gal' deaths and again later in what they called the 'wicker man and mistletoe' deaths. Any comments?"

"I can't add anything that the media didn't cover over and over. Can we move on?"

"Certainly. Let's turn to your family. Your daughter, Elsbeth, took the fall semester off to help you recover from injuries you suffered when your wife, Lucinda, was abducted."

"That's essentially correct. It also has been covered extensively in the papers. I assume you have read those."

"I have. But I like hearing it from you."

"You're not the only journalist who has asked me to repeat exactly what I stated years ago and became part of the public record—meaning records that are easily accessible."

"I've read a few news accounts about your past few years and the gill net and airboat murders in Florida and the barracuda pens murders in Cuba. Do you have any comments about how the press treated those deaths?"

"No. Other than the press rarely gets their facts right."

"I'll change the subject. Have there been any developments about who abducted your wife? Any *ransom* requests?"

"Lots of ideas, mostly from cranks. Nothing of value. No ransom requests. As you know, it's being *investigated.*"

"By?"

"FBI, I guess," I said.

"CIA?"

"Maybe, because they deal with international issues."

"According to the newspapers, the wicker man and mistletoe killings were done by a couple, and he was from Britain. If he were the one who abducted Lucinda, wouldn't the CIA be interested?"

"I don't know enough about how the FBI and CIA work in such a case. You should ask their people."

"Since you asked me not to repeat all the media information about the incidents involving you over the past dozen years, and now we're talking about the CIA, I'd like to explore the years prior to your moving here. Where were you born?"

"I believe we agreed that this interview was about my time in Montana, not my earlier years."

I couldn't let her continue this line, but had to say something. It couldn't be the true story of my life before Montana, which would place more persons than me at risk. It would include Lucinda—when she's found—and Elsbeth. And, of course, Wuff. I don't like lying, nor do I like being backed into a corner where there is no way out without either bending the truth or hurting innocent people. Maybe an outlandish fictional story of my years before Montana would be considered a "justifiable diversion from the facts," just as some killings are considered "a justifiable diversion from normally expected behavior," usually shortened to "justifiable homicide."

I decided I would tell Ms. Ransome a fable about my earlier years that would be worthy of a novelist.

"I was born some years ago in Mexico City but never obtained a copy of my birth certificate. When I was about twenty-three, the Mexican hospital and all its records were destroyed in an earthquake. But I do have a passport."

"Issued, I imagine, about the time you arrived here?"

"Yes. I was planning to guide fly fishing in Mexico. But I changed my mind and haven't needed the passport."

"May I see your passport?"

"Of course, but it's in Florida. I've planned no foreign travel. Unless the abduction requires otherwise."

"To Britain?"

63

"I have no idea."

"As to your youth, you were born in Mexico. Why?"

"My father was in the Foreign Service but actually worked for the CIA. He was stationed in Mexico as the Economic Affairs Officer. After Mexico we moved to Lisbon, Portugal, for four years. Then D.C. for eight and London for four.

"I entered university at seventeen, graduated three years later, a year after we moved to my father's last three-year foreign assignment in Madrid. My parents retired to D.C. and lived in Virginia. I returned to the states and worked for the State Department doing work I am unable to discuss."

"You joined the State Department at twenty-six. You moved to Montana at forty-five. Were you at the State Department for all those nineteen years? That's a full career?"

"It didn't seem like nineteen years. But maybe."

"Were you abroad?"

"Sometimes."

"Europe?"

"Sometimes. And sometimes in South America, sometimes in Asia, sometimes in Africa."

"Attached to the U.S. embassies?"

"Sometimes."

"Ever at risk?"

"Sometimes."

"I can't write an article based on your 'sometimes' and my 'wheres.' If you won't tell me what you did at the State Department, tell me why you left, moved to Montana, and became a fly fishing guide. That's a huge change in location and occupation. Our readers will wonder about that as much as I do."

"My parents were returning from a vacation in the Caribbean when their plane crashed, and they were killed. I was their only child and sole heir and inherited enough to live on. I liked working, but I was burned-out doing so for the government. I decided I would make a major life change and left D.C. Because I enjoyed fly fishing, I moved to Montana to try it out. But I didn't like the winters. You know the rest to date. . . . You have far more information than you need for your article about my time here."

"So what do I write that you were doing before Montana?"

"Preparing for discovering Montana."

"I don't think I can leave it there. If I had to guess what you did during those years before you moved here, I would say you were a federal agent for something like the CIA."

"I assure you that I was never *employed* by the CIA," I said. That was the truth—I was never on the payroll of the Agency. I did receive considerable expense money for travel.

"Mr. Brooks, do you shoot?"

"What do you mean?"

"Rifles, pistols, bows?"

"Yes. I've owned and fired rifles and pistols."

"Which do you prefer?"

"I guess rifles. Pistols scare me a little."

"Have you ever engaged in a rifle competition?"

"That's a strange question."

"Please let me ask it."

"Yes, I have. A few."

"Here in Montana, specifically at the state competition held in Billings two years ago?"

"Yes," I said softly, wondering where she was headed.

"You won the long distance competition?"

"I guess so."

"With a perfect score the papers said was impossible?"

"I did well that time."

"Have you ever entered a competition in Florida?"

"Yes."

"The nationals that were held in Orlando?"

"Yes."

"You won again?"

"Yes."

"With another perfect score?"

"I was lucky."

"The *Competitive Gun World* magazine said you were one of two or three persons in the world who could shoot like that."

"An exaggeration."

"When you worked for the State Department, did you ever use your shooting skills?"

"No," I said, skirting the truth.

"Does the name Abdul Khaliq Isfahani mean anything to you?"

"If I recall reading *The New York Times*, he was a terrorist."

"I've checked on where you were at two different times. First was a decade ago, after you arrived here. Isfahani was believed to have been part of an attempt to destroy the Empire State and Chrysler buildings in New York City. Do you remember?"

"I do."

"But Isfahani didn't fly one of the planes, as expected."

"I don't know about that."

"A month before that attempt in late February, you were gone from this cabin."

"I don't remember. I traveled quite often."

"The reason Isfahani was not flying one of the planes in New York City was that he had been shot in the highlands of Guatemala. He miraculously survived. Were you the shooter?"

"This sounds like science fiction."

"Did you ever meet a Roger Ransome when you worked at the State Department?"

"No, but remember that real names are often not used."

"In the State Department or in the CIA?"

"Mostly the latter."

"Roger is my brother. He works with the FBI and has friends at the CIA. I wouldn't jeopardize his job, but he gave me some of what I have used in drafting these questions."

"I don't know where you're going."

"Isfahani was shot and killed a few years after the attempt in Guatemala. He was in front of a mosque in Khartoum in the Sudan. The shot came from an extraordinary distance. . . . I've been able to access some Army medical records. About three days after the Khartoum shooting, a Macduff Brooks was treated in the military hospital near Frankfurt in Germany. . . . Macduff, did you shoot Isfahani?"

What could I say? I had to end this. "I urge you to put down your pen for a moment. And take no notes."

"All right."

"If I said I killed Isfahani and also attempted to do so earlier in Guatemala, would you write about that?"

"Of course."

"I suggest you do not."

"Why? Are you threatening me?"

"Put it anyway you like it. If you do write about Isfahani, one of two things will happen. First, when the material is published, I will be killed. That's a given fact."

"I'm sorry, but the public has the right to know."

"The hell with that. The public doesn't have the right to witness my death. And probably my daughter's. If that happens, there will be one more death."

"You're threatening me?"

"Merely telling you what *will* happen. Accidents happen. An automobile crash, a drowning, a robbery, or a shooting."

"You said two things might happen. What's the other?"

"Before the article is published, you will be informed by the U.S. government that you have violated the Espionage Act. If you go ahead with writing the article without approval, you will vanish. Take your choice."

"I don't believe you."

"Ask your brother."

"You know that you're a son-of-a-bitch."

"Perhaps figuratively, but not documented. What'll it be?"

"What *may* I publish?"

"I think you know. Anything that doesn't compromise U.S. national security. Or that might lead to my death."

Ransome was visibly shaken. I had to give her credit. She had undertaken extraordinary research.

"I think we've talked enough," I added. "I'm going to give you a name and cell phone number at the CIA. Call him if you doubt my comments. He will warn you as I have and order you not to write anything without it first being cleared with him."

"If I don't. . . ."

"You don't want to know."

"I understand."

"I thought you would."

"It's nearly noon," she said, leaning toward me and letting her car coat open further. "About that second Agua de Valencia. Forget it. Make me a double Gentleman Jack. My research told me you're likely to have some handy."

"Your research is correct."

14

THE SAME DAY IN GRAND TETON NATIONAL PARK

PALMER BROWN WAS HIGH ON INSPIRATION
Point at the edge of Jenny Lake in Grand Teton National
Park a dozen miles north of Jackson. He had hiked there alone.
It was the fourth hike he had made to the same place in the
past two weeks.

There was a reason for Brown's frequent visits to the
point. On a map of the area he had placed three "X" marks at
different locations across the edge of the point, each where a
fall should be fatal. This day he added another "X." He was
seeking the exact place most certain to rid him of his wife.

Inspiration Point rises abruptly 450 feet from the lake. At
the edge on top, one looks nearly straight down. Brown was
convinced that a person falling off would have no possibility of
survival. He knew of a case several years ago where a woman
fell from a cliff near a small town in Switzerland and, despite
allegations that her husband had pushed her off the cliff, her
death was quickly ruled an accident.

A half-dozen people were sitting on the mostly barren
rocky outcrop that ages ago formed Inspiration Point. Chip-
munks dashed across the stone from one hiding place to another, searching for tiny bits of food dropped by visitors.

The number of people on the point increased as the park
boats brought tourists across from the South Jenny Lake parking area. Brown always arrived at the parking lot early so he

would be the first person reaching the top. If a park ranger stopped him walking to the point as the first rays of dawn filtered through the trees, Brown would say he wanted to see the sunrise from Inspiration Point. He carried a camera and tripod even though he had no interest in photography.

Brown's real interest in being on the point at this hour was not to photograph or to view the spectacular scenery or to enjoy the hike. It was because Inspiration Point was the place he had chosen to push his wife—Brenda Lacy Hoover Brown—to her death. Not that he hated her—she was attractive and tolerable as a spouse. But her death would mean he would inherit her millions.

Brenda Lacy did not like heights, and Palmer wondered how he would convince her to climb to the top. She was not a hiker. But, however much Brenda Lacy might object, the lure of substantial wealth encouraged Palmer to persuade her.

On this visit Brown had brought to Inspiration Point a brief article he had cut out of the *Jackson Hole Times* and a single page downloaded from the online *Bozeman News*. Both focused on the recent death of a man found hanging from barbed wire strung across the Gallatin River in Montana.

Chewing on a protein bar, Brown reread both articles and smiled. The barbed wire seemed like much more fun than merely pushing someone off a cliff. Maybe, he thought, he should put aside the idea of pushing Brenda Lacy off Inspiration Point and instead do something more original like hanging her on barbed wire over some river.

15

A FEW DAYS LATER IN MAY

I BEGAN TO FEEL STRONG ENOUGH AND SENSED
I could row my drift boat. Elsbeth agreed.

"Dad, we're going fishing!" she declared over breakfast.
"Last night I arranged a shuttle in Jackson and got *Osprey* ready.
Get your fishing gear."

"Is this an invitation?"

"No. You're going. For three to four days. You've got two
hours to pack. Get off your butt and into the SUV. I'll drive."

She's more like Lucinda every day. . . . I selected a rod, a
reel that only yesterday I converted from right to left hand
winding, a pair of felt-soled boots, and a small bag with a big
selection of flies. Adding spare leaders, tippet material, nippers,
sunscreen, and polarized sunglasses and I was ready to go.

"Where are we headed," I asked Elsbeth.

"It's all arranged. Mavis is taking care of Wuff. We're driving through a favorite place of yours—Yellowstone Park—to
Jackson, and staying at Dornan's cabins in Moose for a couple
of nights. First thing tomorrow we meet John Kirby and fish
your favorite float—Deadman's Bar to Moose on the Snake."

"Good. With John in *Osprey*, I won't have to row."

"Wrong, *you* row. I offered him the front seat, which he
says he rarely gets because he's always rowing as a guide. . . ."

You get the middle seat. I'm in the back where you can't see me and tell me what to do. *You* are going to row *us*."

"But I'm disabled."

"Not your arms. It's your right leg. And maybe your brain. Anyway, with a cane you're walking. You don't use your feet to row. . . . Next, you'll be asking for a handicapped parking decal."

That evening we called John when we arrived at Dornan's in Moose and arranged a 7:00 a.m. meeting in front of our cabin.

I've known John for years. He guides mostly on the Snake. I learn something every time we fish. About fly selection, different special casts, identification of birds and trees, or favorite spots to toss a fly along the river. Or, too often, how his alma mater Georgia is certain to win the national football championship next season. I hope his choice of flies is better than his choice of football teams. . . . John says he likes to fish with me, but it may be Lucinda and Elsbeth that he prefers.

We launched at Deadman's Bar the next morning at 7:45.

"Beth, you take the front seat," John suggested. "I'd rather sit behind your dad where he can't criticize my casting."

"And where I can't see your fly zooming toward a hook-up with my neck or ear," I commented.

"Have I *ever* embedded a hook in you?" John asked.

"Attempts count," I responded.

John ended up in the front seat. Elsbeth's stubbornness exceeded John's, and she won a coin toss and chose the rear.

"What should I use for a fly?" she asked.

"Try a double dropper behind an indicator," I suggested.

"Don't listen to him, Beth," interrupted John. "Use a dry fly. I'll hand you one. It's a lime trude variation."

"Don't listen to *him*," I quickly pleaded. "John always uses dry flies because he can't cast using indicators and he can't see nymphs. He's given you a fly that's high on visibility and low on catching the attention of trout. It's another of his trudes with the big white tuft on the top."

"How many trout did you catch when you last fished with me?" John asked, turning his head toward me.

I remembered the day. I had caught fourteen trout, the smallest ten inches and the largest twenty-three.

"I don't remember. A few whitefish," I answered, sulking.

"If you don't remember, I'll tell you. I have it written down in my guide trips notes. Hand me my bag."

"Never mind," I said, sulking even more.

Elsbeth tied on the lime trude John handed her and cast off the drift boat's left side. It landed softly thirty feet from the boat and was immediately consumed by what, when in the net, was seventeen inches of cutthroat radiance.

"Good fly, huh Dad?" she called, grinning like Lucinda did when she one-upped me fishing. Which was often.

"*Luck*" was all I could mumble as an answer.

"Thanks for the fly, John," she said looking past me to John in the front, who was trying not to laugh.

"Luck," I repeated and said nothing more.

By lunch time Elsbeth had landed three more trout with the same fly. John had used the morning to try a broad selection of flies: from an Adams to an Elk Hair Caddis, to a Blue Winged Olive, and to a half dozen I didn't see or he didn't let me see. He had brought two fish to the net.

"John," I asked at lunch, our threesome comfortably settled on folding chairs before a collapsible table, "if a guide fishes, shouldn't he catch more fish than the client?"

"I was doing serious experimentation," he replied. "The number of fish caught was irrelevant. Isn't that true?"

"If you didn't experiment, you'd never know what fly to suggest to a client," Elsbeth said. "The two trout you caught were on an Elk Hair Caddis. Ever used it here before?"

"No, but I will from now on," John affirmed.

"Point proven, Dad," Elsbeth said, poking me in the ribs.

"It's time to get back on the river. I have more experiments to try," said John.

The afternoon was filled with negative quips from Elsbeth and John about my fly fishing skills. For a *special* trip planned for *me*, her comments sounded more like parental abuse.

After the float John announced he would follow us to Bozeman and fish for another day and maybe try the Gallatin.

The next morning we drove in tandem over Teton Pass into Victor, Idaho, where John and I each ordered a huckleberry milkshake at the Emporium. Elsbeth turned down my offer to buy her one and proceeded to drink most of mine. She must have learned that from Lucinda.

We continued north through eclectic Driggs and to West Yellowstone. After lunch we joined the Gallatin River and raced along with it downstream past Big Sky and finally onto the open expanse of greater Bozeman and the Gallatin Valley.

"Dad, we just passed the Williams Bridge road. We're close to where the Sue and Liz and I found the man hanging on barbed wire."

"Be thankful he passed you on the river. You might have been the one hung up on the barbed wire. . . . Where have you arranged for us to stay?"

"Trout Chasers—right on the Gallatin."

"John will love it there; he can walk down to the river and fish. Unseen and free from criticism."

We pulled in together and gathered our gear. Before I knew it, John was walking to the river.

Elsbeth asked me to walk out to the yard and sit and talk.

"I may be imagining things, Dad, but I thought someone followed us from Jackson. There was a Ford King Ranch F250 pickup behind John, and it stopped at the Emporium in Victor."

"Did the driver follow you in and have a milkshake?"

"No. He was behind us again when we were back on the road and he parked in view of us at West Yellowstone when we stopped for lunch. I saw him go past us as we turned in here a half-hour ago."

"Your imagination is functioning fine. Forget it."

There was barely enough water to float the Gallatin the next morning, but we were going to try to borrow an inflatable pontoon boat.

"I'll row," insisted John at breakfast.

"You're offering only because on this part of the Gallatin you can't fish when you're floating."

Soon after breakfast we were standing at the same launching spot where Elsbeth and her two friends began that fateful day that ended with a murder.

Elsbeth sat in the bow, John rowed, and I sat behind them blocked from Elsbeth's view and partly hidden behind John.

We launched and soon slipped under the Williams Bridge.

"There's a place a bit below here," I noted, "where I once walked in and fished along the shore. It was great; some good sized brown trout under the east bank. I'd like to stop."

"Anything to help you increase your catch rate," John said, applauded by Elsbeth at the bow.

Five minutes after we stopped, John hooked a beautiful brown along the bank.

"Show off," I called out.

"Dad, be nice. If you want to criticize him do it by catching more fish. . . . But of course, for you that's easier said than done."

"Siding with him are you? Maybe I can talk him into adopting you."

"You'll never get rid of me," she exclaimed. . . . "Can I say something that may appear silly?"

"Of course, you often do."

"When we passed under the Williams Bridge a half-hour ago, did you see anyone on the bridge?"

"Maybe someone walking across, but nothing that seemed unusual."

"I thought I saw a man wearing a Montana Fish, Wildlife & Parks jacket and hat. He looked like the warden we talked to at the launching site the day of the murder here. But he had on sunglasses."

"I would think you'd be happy to see a game warden out."

"I just had a bad feeling when I saw him. It made me shiver."

"This is too good a time to be worried. You did a great job planning these days. It's the first time I've really thought of how much I love fishing these rivers. Being with you and John made it all the better."

We ate on the bank of the Gallatin and enjoyed our meal so much that we didn't get back on the water until after two. A half-hour before we pulled up the anchor and started down river, another drift boat had passed by. It had a single fisherman who waved.

The afternoon started with a double by John and Elsbeth, caught while I was cleaning up after lunch. Both fish were landed, and both were about the same size and weight, although Elsbeth insisted hers was more colorful.

In mid-afternoon we reached a turn, and as we straightened and then looked ahead, we all gasped.

"There's barbed wire *across* the river," I exclaimed, "and a *body* tangled in it! It must be the person who passed us. It's like the death here on the Gallatin a few weeks ago. John, row ashore and anchor before we hit the wire. I'm calling 911."

"No," exclaimed Elsbeth. "Don't call 911. We did that with the first body on the wire. It patches you through to the Gallatin County Sheriff's Office. That means dealing with Deputy Jackson. I don't want to confront this county's deputies again. Call the Montana FWP number."

We ran the inflatable ashore not more than ten feet upstream of the wire. The body was hanging by barbed wire embedded in the person's face and neck. Fresh blood streamed down over the fishing jacket and waders and dripped into the moving water causing momentary red circles.

The arms were raised slightly above the head and were also caught in the wire, as though the person had at the last moment thrust his hands up to prevent hitting the wire full-force. It had done little good. The lower body wasn't tangled in the wire; it was hanging and swinging side-to-side.

"Should we take the body down?" asked a scared Elsbeth.

"Probably not, but we need to keep any further boats from hitting the wire," said John. "Do you have wire cutters?"

"In the guide box," I said. John took them and cut the wire attached to a cottonwood tree on our bank. With the last cut the body swung in an arc, opening a path for another boat to pass.

"John," Elsbeth asked, "would you cut off a foot of the barbed wire and give it to me?"

"Trophy?"

"No. Curious."

Five minutes later we sat on the bank staring at the body; blood was no longer draining. A siren wailed in the distance.

Elsbeth was holding the short piece of barbed wire in her hand. She got up abruptly and walked downstream nearly out of sight where she pulled something off a tree.

"What are you doing?" I asked when she returned.

She held up the two strands of wire side-by-side. "I was wondering about the wire. I went and found a piece that was attached to the tree downstream where the first death occurred. Look. They're the same."

"They are," I said. "The barbs are unusually long and sharp like razor wire. I don't think I've seen that kind of wire."

"Was the victim male or female?" asked Elsbeth.

"Can't tell from here. The clothing doesn't help. We may be lucky," John observed. "If we hadn't stayed fishing the bank for browns and talking so long, *we* would have run into the wire."

"You're probably right," said Elsbeth, "because I was looking more at places along the bank where there might be fish than downriver where the barbed wire was strung."

16

THE SAME AFTERNOON

A HALF-HOUR LATER TWO WARDENS ARRIVED from FWP. Apparently they had arranged for an emergency vehicle to meet them at the scene and for an inflatable boat to be delivered. They took photographs and some video and the body quickly was removed from the barbed wire and sent on its way to the county medical examiner's office. Warden Len Paris talked to the three of us, and copies of his notes would be sent to the Gallatin County Sheriff's Office. Deputy Jackson wouldn't be pleased with our not having called his office first, but such was the price he paid for the way he and his men had treated Elsbeth, Sue, and Liz.

Two hours after we found the body, the FWP wardens sent us on our way with thanks for helping. No accusations were made. As we drove away, we passed Deputy Jackson coming toward us with lights flashing and siren screaming.

"Our experience with the fish and game wardens is how our *county* officials should act," commented Elsbeth. "This was nothing like the first death, when Deputy Jackson immediately accused Sue, Liz, and me of being involved in the killing."

"Jackson is a special case," John reminded us. "He must know enough politicians in the county to have been reinstated. But don't blame the whole Gallatin County Sheriff's office for one man's blunders."

"John, did FWP Warden Paris tell you anything?"

"Probably nothing he didn't talk with you two about. The body was identified by a Montana fishing license found in a jacket pocket. It was a woman—Ruth Glendon. She was 33 and lived in Three Forks. She carried a card showing her to be a science teacher at Three Forks High School. Warden Paris has a friend who teaches there and called him. He said she was liked by administrators, teachers, and students. She was single but dating a Three Forks police officer. Her passion was fly fishing, and she was skilled at rowing an inflatable or drift boat."

"That leaves finding who had a motive to kill her," I said. "It sounds like there weren't many who didn't like her."

"I didn't tell Warden Paris I was one of the three who last month discovered the first body on the Gallatin," said Elsbeth. "He didn't ask. Should I have offered that information?"

"He may or may not find that out if he reviews the first case to help with this one," I answered.

"Dad, I don't want to go through what I did with Deputy Jackson. He was rude, starting every question by calling me 'little lady.' I had enough. And I didn't want *your* name dragged into this. You don't need that along with your issues with Lucinda's abduction."

"I think we're through here, as I expect you are with the first Gallatin death," I commented.

"Don't count on it," said John. "I don't think Warden Paris knows who you are, Mac. And he apparently doesn't know Beth's link to the first Gallatin barbed wire death."

"He knows where to find us," I said, wondering how far Paris might extend the investigation of Glendon's death.

17

TWO DAYS LATER ON INSPIRATION POINT

PALMER BROWN WAS BACK AGAIN SITTING ON Inspiration Point not long after his last visit. Like that last visit, he walked to the point from the south end of Jenny Lake before the first boat began to bring visitors to the area. He had his detailed trail map and carefully placed another "X" at the edge of the overlook where the drop was the furthest, then folded and put the map in his backpack.

Brown sat on a boulder and began reading yesterday's *Jackson Hole Times*, which described the second death on the Gallatin River. He smiled and chuckled as he finished the article.

"Great article!" he said, and looked around to see if anyone had heard him. But no one else was yet on the point. "I love this guy's use of barbed wire to get rid of people," he whispered. "This is the second time someone has been killed on the Gallatin in almost the same spot and by the same method. The wire caught the rower of an inflatable boat around the neck and jerked the body out to be left dangling from the wire, their neck dripping blood and legs dragging and flopping around against the current. What an incredible idea!"

"I do wish the newspaper coverage had been more descriptive," he continued. "The barbs on the wire were intended to dig into the neck, causing much bleeding and agony. The article doesn't mention that."

Brown was upset that the Wyoming newspapers didn't address whether the two different victims were the intended targets. The papers gave no indication that there was any relationship between the two victims. Were they siblings, coworkers, or perhaps friends? If either was not the intended victim, would there be another try? But the real target might not know if he or she was actually was the intended victim.

"Regardless of what happened on the Gallatin," Brown mused, "I'm committed to my idea of pushing my dear wife Brenda Lacy off this point; save the barbed wire for another day."

He had thought of another way if she absolutely refused to climb to Inspiration Point: having Brenda Lacy "help" him fix her car—put it up on the jack, slide her underneath to adjust something, and then drop the car on her. His Mercedes was heavy enough to do the job. He would keep that idea in mind for a future spouse.

Brown finished reading and making notes and began the descent to the boat. At the narrowest point on the steep trail, visions of how he would spend Brenda's money caused him to slip; if he hadn't grabbed a rock, *he* would have been the one to plummet off the point.

18

JUNE IN MONTANA

I WOKE AT FIVE IN THE MORNING, THOUGHT prematurely about tossing a few dry flies onto the tumbling surface of Mill Creek at dawn, decided otherwise, and tried but couldn't go back to sleep. Images of standing with Lucinda in Mill Creek consumed me; I lay in bed thinking the worst scenarios as the first notions of daylight came to our windows.

The recent deaths on the Gallatin were also troubling. Nothing had been discovered about the identity of the person or persons responsible for either barbed wire death.

Elsbeth arrived home from work late the previous evening, bringing Sue with her. I wanted to let them sleep in and quietly carried my coffee and cellphone to the porch, sat in my favorite rocking chair, and dialed Dan Wilson in D.C.

"You're up at sunrise, Mac. A tough day ahead fishing?"

"I thought about it but. . . ." I said quietly, as my mind wandered. "Dan, I'm sitting on my cabin porch, looking out at Mill Creek. I'm alone. . . . Anything new on Lucinda?"

"Nothing to report," Dan said. "We had help recently from the territorial police in Scotland, and it seems Lucinda and Ellsworth-Kent disappeared off the face of the earth, at least they are not thought to be in Scotland. It's likely a clever mix of multiple identities and forged passports."

"How convinced are you that the Scottish and English authorities know what they're doing? They never found Ellsworth-Kent after the wicker man and mistletoe murders."

"Maybe he never went back to the UK," suggested Dan.

"I hate to even think about this, but when is a missing person *presumed* dead? And who makes that decision?"

"It depends what department is involved. I think our Social Security system uses seven years. Some other jurisdictions reduce that to as low as four. It can cause confusion."

"Could you be legally dead in Missouri but not in Mississippi?" I wondered aloud. "Or could you be dead according to your state pension program, but not Social Security!"

"What if there's an air crash, and I'm listed as presumed dead by the carrier?" said Dan. "Why a seven-year wait? That's arbitrary."

"Can we talk about this and how it affects Lucinda?"

"Of course." Dan said. He paused and asked, "Does she have separate assets?"

"Some. The Manhattan apartment is in her name alone. The ranch, like the Montana cabin and Florida cottage, are in our joint names. We have wills designating each other as the sole heir. If something happens to *both* of us, everything goes to Elsbeth. Lucinda's will reads exactly the same as mine. . . . Would a state agency—in Montana or Florida or perhaps New York—*commence* a proceeding of its own to have her declared dead? Maybe because the state wants the estate tax revenue?"

"You need an estate lawyer. . . . Mac, do you have a reason for raising this issue? I know it's hard for you, but I don't believe it's time to consider filing a petition designating Lucinda dead. Not until we know more."

"Every day Lucinda isn't found adds to the likelihood she's dead," I said. "I won't discuss this with Elsbeth until she raises it. I try to be realistic. . . . Dan, I have some other incidents to talk about. Have you heard about the deaths on the Gallatin River?"

"No. . . . On your boat?"

"No, but close." I explained all that Elsbeth and Sue and Liz had told me about the first Gallatin death and added my observations about the second.

"Are Beth or her two friends or you suspects?"

"Not really. Elsbeth got a little testy with a county deputy who arrived at the first death. He and a couple of Montana Fish, Wildlife & Parks wardens talked to each of the gals separately after the body was brought ashore. Without telling any of them that they were *not* suspects, they were sent home. . . . When the second body was discovered, I was in an inflatable along with Elsbeth and a friend, John Kirby, who's a guide in Jackson. You've heard me speak of him.

"That stretch where both deaths occurred is one of my favorite fishing spots. I'm there often at this time of the year, and it could have been any one or more of us who ended up dead, hanging on the wire."

"Could either of the two victims have been dead *before* their boats hit the wire?" Dan asked.

"The Medical Examiner will determine that. He hasn't released a report yet."

"Who were the two who died?"

"The first was Rudolfo Martin, a 56-year-old. The second was 33-year-old Ruth Glendon. They had identification, but the authorities have to check the remains with the alleged names, given what they were carrying. It's been long enough to make a positive ID, but nothing's come from the ME's office."

"Could the ID have been made but someone is holding back its release?" Dan asked.

"Could be. I'll keep you informed. . . . One reason I called is to hear anything new you have about Guatemala and Herzog. Then I have something to share with you about an interview I did with a local magazine."

"You know I don't like you doing *any* interviews. . . . But first to Herzog. Our informant in Guatemala says Herzog is a dejected man. His leading security man—Coronel Carlos Alarcon—is dead for reasons not made public but which we know about. . . . We know his private secretary delayed leaving her job and then suddenly fled to some quiet European village."

"What's your thinking on how and why Alarcon died?"

"It involved Alarcon's wife," said Dan.

"Is she—her name is Dolores—distraught about her husband's death?"

"She can't have been too distraught," Dan responded. "She was in Herzog's office, running around nude when her husband walked in unexpectedly. She came to us because she wanted to tell all to someone she knew—Sam Bradford—in our CIA Mission in Guatemala City. Alarcon had been working with Bradford on Guatemala's drug trade issues.

"Dolores called Bradford first because she didn't know where to turn. Apparently her husband had arrived at the presidential residence to tell Herzog what he learned about Hunt. He saw his wife naked with Herzog and became angry. But before he could do anything, Herzog pulled a pistol with a silencer from his desk drawer and shot Alarcon several times. The first was enough. As Alarcon's body lay on the floor bleeding, Dolores yelled at Herzog that he had just killed the *only* person who knew *exactly* what Herzog wanted to know."

"That worries me, Dan. What had Alarcon learned?"

"Sit down if you're not already. . . . Alarcon had learned *your* name, *your* Montana address, and that *you're* a fly fishing guide. *And* he learned a lot about Lucinda and Elsbeth. But he told his wife he hadn't written the information down and he wouldn't tell anybody the specifics, except Herzog."

"Do you believe her?"

"No reason not to," Dan explained. "If *she* knew the details about you, she would have told Herzog. Probably for a price."

"Even if all that is accurate, how did Alarcon get the info? CIA agent Thomas Davis is dead. Agent Allan Whitman is dead. You told me about the other agents who were at the meeting where we decided on my name and I decided where I'd live and what I'd do. You didn't think Herzog knew *any* of their names. But Alarcon knew of at least one. Do you know who?"

"Yes. We've learned that one agent, Ralph Johnson, the guy I told you about, was a disgruntled CIA retiree living in Miami. Johnson met with Alarcon in a D.C. restaurant a week or two ago.

"Last night Johnson checked into the Connaught Hotel in Mayfair in London. He booked a room for a week. He couldn't afford the Connaught for one night without access to money well beyond his pension. He had no other source of income.

"We're trying to check his financial transactions, but we assume if he received any substantial amount from Alarcon, it went straight to a bank someplace that welcomes tarnished money."

"This is hard to believe, Dan. Herzog must be livid."

"He is, but not only for that one reason. Loyalty was never what Herzog thought he would receive without something in exchange. He believed in buying loyalty. Those he paid were *obligated* to show loyalty. Now two people have broken away from his control—I wonder how long they'll live."

"Tell me who," I asked.

"First is his former private secretary, Carlotta Boschmann, who we talked about. She's in hiding. Who knows what she could testify about, maybe Herzog's illegal activities, especially drug trade."

"So Boschmann's one. I didn't know her, and I don't envy her position now. Who's the other?"

"His niece, Luisa Solares," said Dan. "You know about her because she's at the UF law college. She's as much at risk as Boschmann. Like her, Luisa was upset with the way Herzog dealt with the dying Thomas Davis in Antigua. Luisa once dated Davis' son, who's a student at Vanderbilt.

"Herzog had two disappointments with Luisa. She couldn't get access to useful information because the UF law dean was protective of Professor Hunt and wouldn't talk about him other than to confirm the official university view that Hunt died in D.C. of a stroke. More important—Luisa recently called me to tell me about this—is that Herzog believes she's being brainwashed at UF. She's been asking Herzog questions he doesn't like, especially why he wants to kill you."

"I'm glad she's concerned. What else has she done?"

"Apparently she's dressing like a UF student. No more long silk dresses. She looks like a typical female UF undergraduate or law student. She wears sandals and shorts. She's even bought a skateboard! And worse—she reads *The New York Times!* Herzog must think she's on her way to becoming a Marxist."

"Isn't she at risk? Unlike Boschmann, Luisa's not hiding."

"She's young and seems to think Herzog won't go after her because they're related. I not sure she's right. But she may decide not to go back to Guatemala regardless. She told me Herzog expects her back as soon as classes and exams are over, if not sooner. He has instructed her *not* to stay and enroll in the JD program. Something has to give."

"Herzog must be apoplectic. With Alarcon gone, what's his next move?"

"He now knows there's a retired CIA agent who passed on to Alarcon the information Herzog wants."

"Can he get that information? You seem convinced the agent is Johnson. What can you do about him? Has he passed on other *secret* information?"

"One at a time. If *Alarcon* could get the information, there's no reason to think someone else can't. But Johnson apparently was paid at least $1 million, probably much more. If he's greedy, he'll offer to repeat the information for more money. Alarcon was going to disclose everything he knew to Herzog, but he died without giving Herzog any information about you. There's no reason to think Alarcon mentioned Johnson by name, but I suspect he did. Another possibility: if *Johnson* learns about Alarcon's death, he could initiate contact with Herzog directly."

"Dan, what would you do if you knew Johnson was planning to meet directly with Herzog in Guatemala City."

"Convince him not to deal with Herzog."

"Would Johnson listen?"

"He was one of us. He knows we can be persuasive."

"One other matter," I said. "I've been interviewed by a writer named Ransome for the *Bozeman Magazine*."

"Why did you do that?"

"She was persistent and threatened she was coming to the cabin and camp on my porch until I talked to her."

"What did she ask?"

"She's smart, Dan. Her brother works for the FBI. She began with some easy questions about my time in Montana. About the deaths related to my guiding. I may have convinced her I was not as involved as implied."

"Did she ask about Lucinda's abduction?"

"Some, but not much. She knew I wasn't prepared to talk about that. She shifted the focus from my move to Montana and becoming a guide to discussing my life *before* Montana."

"What did you tell her?"

"I had to say something beyond 'no comment.' I made up a fictional story about my early years."

"A plausible story?" Dan asked.

"I think so. I told her I was born in Mexico City and had never been able to obtain a copy of my birth certificate. That she had to accept my date of birth stated somewhere else."

"How did you do with questions about *where* you lived, *where* you were educated, and *what* you did between college and Montana?"

"I gave nothing accurate. I said my father was in the Foreign Service and that after graduation I took a job at the State Department. She pressed for what kind of work I did for the State Department, and I told her much of it was classified even though I wondered why. I told her I wasn't free to discuss that time beyond where I worked."

"Then she pressed me for why at the age of forty-five I gave up my State Department job and moved to Montana, built a log cabin and a boat, and became a fly fishing guide."

"How did you answer that?"

"I told her I was burned out at my job and was despondent when my parents were killed in a plane crash in the Caribbean. I told her they left me a substantial inheritance, and I decided to throw in the towel and do something I wanted to do, not what they might have wanted me to do. I said Dad had pressed me to go into the Foreign Service, and although I didn't follow him I did something similar by joining the State Department.

"I told her about a dozen jobs I *didn't* want after State and turned to something I had done occasionally and enjoyed: fly fishing in the Western mountains. I said I settled near Yellowstone Park because I admired the town of Jackson south and Paradise Valley north. I chose the latter on Mill Creek."

"Why being a guide?"

"I didn't plan that because I had enough money to live modestly. But when I began to float and fish the Yellowstone on my newly completed drift boat and talked to different guides who I admired, I thought it would be enjoyable taking people on floats. . . . How does that all sound to you, Dan?"

"Plausible, but maybe subject to being proved to be little more than creative fiction."

"What do you mean?"

"She might check to see if there was a Brooks in the Foreign Service about four decades ago, and if you told her where you lived when your dad was assigned abroad, it would even be easier. She could check to confirm you were a student at whatever university you said you attended. And she could learn if there were any plane crashes in the Caribbean when your folks died—determining the year would be easy because you were forty-five. Further, she could check the probate records, first for the D.C. area, since your parents apparently left a sizeable estate that would have been in probate, also about when you were forty-five."

"OK, but Dan, that was not the worst of my interview."

"Meaning?"

"She asked me about my skills with a rifle."

"Oh, no. What did she ask?"

"If I had entered the Montana State Rifle Competition and later the American Sniper Showdown."

"We paid your entry fees."

"Yes."

"You won both."

"Yes."

"With record scores."

"Yes."

"Ransome knew all that?"

"All except about *your* financial support."

"Macduff, I know where you're headed. To Guatemala and the Sudan."

"Yes."

"She asked you whether you were the shooter?"

"I said no but she didn't believe me."

"Was that how the interview ended?"

"No, I told her any reference to those shootings would violate the U.S. Espionage and Internal Security Acts."

"Did she decide not to publish an article based on your interview?"

"I told her she would have to have approval of what she wrote."

"From who?"

"Someone in our government who would contact her."

"That would be me?"

"Yes. . . . Dan, what if Herzog did the same kind of investigation?"

"For now, he's too busy. But I think Ms. Ransome has done us—and you—a favor. She showed how otherwise secret records of most any government action can be accessed; at least enough to write about it in something like the *Bozeman Maga-zine*."

"So what do we do?"

"You don't do anything more. I'll deal with Ransome."

"Thanks. Do you think publication by the magazine of *any-thing* about me would be of any use to Herzog?"

"Not necessarily. He has to learn *who* Professor Hunt became. The article doesn't tell him."

"Dan, the magazine article is likely to include the date I arrived in Bozeman. Herzog should know the approximate date I finished the conversion in D.C. and left for my new life."

"So how does he match them? Anyway, he's unlikely to come across the magazine article. How many similar local magazines are published? . . . I concede that if he read the article he might want to check you out. But I wouldn't worry. The odds are far in your favor."

"I don't like odds. Wouldn't it be better if the article was not published?"

"I'll see that what is published is not a threat. Let's drop it and worry about one real matter."

"Johnson?" I asked.

"Yes. I'll be checking on him. I may be able to get the IRS to open an investigation about how he could be living so lavishly without having stashed money abroad."

"Sorry to have kept you. I needed someone to talk to."

"I'm glad you chose me."

19

A JULY MORNING

O N A DRIZZLY FRIDAY MORNING WUFF AND I walked down the drive to the mailbox watching Paradise Valley unfold before us. I glanced with reverence at the Yellowstone River and the Gallatin mountains beyond. Wuff trotted a few yards ahead. Turning every few moments she glanced at my peeling a banana, expecting another bite. She thinks at a minimum she's entitled to both tips of every banana I eat.

Holiday catalogues were beginning to clog the mailbox and when I returned to the cabin with the mail, I threw them out without glancing at any. There were only three letters buried among the junk. One letter asked for a donation to a local group that in the winter provided blankets to the homeless—life support in this climate; another letter offered the services of a real estate agent to sell our cabin—which I was not aware was for sale; and the third letter was in a plain envelope with nothing except my address and United Nations stamps. At first I thought it must have been sent by some friend traveling abroad. But UN stamps!

The postage was in Euros, and each stated "HOFFNUNG PFLANZEN" across the bottom. *Hoffnung* I knew meant "hope," and I thought *pflanzen* dealt with "planting." Maybe the two words together meant "planting hope" for a better future. That was my situation, cultivating hope for Lucinda's return, which I needed for a better future. The design on the stamp didn't help much; it showed three people carrying branches or bundles of straw on their heads. At a lower corner of the stamp were the year issued and the letters "UN."

Where could the letter have come from? The cancel over the stamp was blurred and not readable. All I could guess was the letter had been sent from some country that was part of the Euro Zone because the value of the stamp was preceded by the Euro currency symbol: €.

When I looked at the writing on the envelope, I was stunned. It was properly addressed to me at the cabin. While it had no return address, I knew the sender. Without question it was *Lucinda's* writing!

I held the envelope with a thousand thoughts rocketing through my brain before I carefully opened it and withdrew two sheets. Unfolding the paper, the sheets bore an imprint at the top from a lodging named the Highland Park House in Kirkwall, Scotland. I knew about Kirkwall, the largest town and the capital of the Orkney Islands located off the north coast of Scotland. Kirkwall was where Lucinda's former hus-band—Robert Ellsworth-Kent—allegedly became a Druid high priest.

I walked outside and sat down on the front steps; my legs were numb, and my hands shook uncontrollably as I began to read:

MacDuff

I am sad that I couldn't write to you sooner but I know you will un-derstand when you read this letter. I pray to all the high priests that you will accept what I have to say. You ought not try to make any attempt to contact me—ever again.

Over the past several months, since the day High Priest Einar of Kirkwall, whom you know incorrectly as Robert Ellsworth-Kent, saved me from you at St. Augustine—that heathen town I so hate—we have traveled extensively. Einar has been sought by police authorities so they could perse-cute him for the legitimate religious ceremonies he performed on the solstices and equinoxes several years ago on six various rivers of the U.S. West.

He was acting under higher orders in carrying out those ceremonial sacrifices. Einar saved me from your slavery of me in Florida and granted me a new freedom. Taking me to Labrador in Canada, he cared for me for a month and administered medication to purify my body and spirit. Then to Scotland easily evading the police, and to the Orkney Islands where Einar obtained use of the same small cottage at Skara Brae where his family took him on vacation years ago. That had been where he first be-came fascinated by and dedicated to the ancient Pagan cultures.

The letter made little sense and terrified me. I turned to the second page and continued reading:

High Priest Einar and I were married on the summer solstice in a ceremony of the High Order of Druidry. The ceremony first cleansed me of any association with you, ordained me as High Priestess Onomaris, and then bound Einar and me forever.

We have left the isles to find a secluded place to live, safe from those who would take Einar and safe for me in the event you tried to find me. You ought not search for me.

I am no longer your wife. Elsbeth is not my daughter. My name is not Lucinda.

The letter was signed *High Priestess Onomaris of Kirkwall.*

Confusion and anger overwhelmed me. My first thought was that Lucinda was under the influence of mind-altering drugs administered by Ellsworth-Kent. There seemed to be no other reason to explain such aberrant behavior as she expressed in the letter. I didn't know who to share the letter with. Certainly Dan Wilson must receive a copy and I might show it to Elsbeth.

Dan must be told because Lucinda might turn against me and tell Juan Pablo Herzog in Guatemala what he wants to know. A simple letter would reveal what he has spent years, lives, and considerable money trying to discover. Even to imagine Lucinda would do this to me is beyond comprehension.

Elsbeth is sensitive. She knows the details of Lucinda's brief and terrifying marriage to Ellsworth-Kent more than a decade ago. Because of our conversations, Elsbeth also knows of the wicker man and mistletoe murders he committed, although she did not come to live with me until several months after the last of those five murders.

But Elsbeth is a bright and well-adjusted young lady and has witnessed the gill net, barracuda pens, and airboat murders and personally has suffered greatly from Lucinda's absence. Elsbeth is convinced we soon will hear that Lucinda is free and coming home. She need not be told that Lucinda has allegedly become a Druid high priestess, is again married to Ellsworth-Kent, and has rejected any hope of our ever again being together as a family.

There is no one else to turn to. I know nothing about whether Lucinda is under the influence of drugs or hypnosis or some other cause for her sudden change. Frighteningly, what she has written me could have been of her own free will.

Lucinda and Ellsworth-Kent will not face a normal life; for Ellsworth-Kent there is no statute of limitations for murder. Could he find a country that would welcome him, a country that would not care what he had done and accept both him and Lucinda, and not ask questions? I can't begin to answer that.

Perhaps I never will.

20

SUMMER TURNS TO FALL

I COULDN'T BELIEVE THAT AUGUST, SEPTEMBER, and October passed without another word about the barbed wire deaths appearing in the *Bozeman News*.

My interview with the *Gallatin Magazine* was published in September. It included nothing about marksmanship, rifles, or assassinations, and did not infer that my fictional life story before Montana wasn't accurate. The only comment received came from my friend, Park County Chief Deputy Ken Rangley, who said he "didn't believe a word in the magazine." I wondered what Dan Wilson said to Celeste Ransome but I wouldn't ask.

In no hurry to leave for Florida—the Montana weather was glorious—I spent hours alone on Mill Creek fishing in the dwindling flow of water that surged down the mountain and wasn't diverted to favor cattle that were to be exported while native trout perished. Each day there was less water, except after a heavy rain.

The Florida cottage beckoned. But it was where Lucinda and I were living when she was abducted, and I didn't welcome the prospect of facing the tedious drive across country without her. Elsbeth and Sue had left for Gainesville and the beginning of classes at UF.

Thanksgiving arrived and I hadn't given the trip to Florida further thought. I didn't want to celebrate Thanksgiving alone at the Mill Creek Montana cabin where years ago I received Lucinda's invitation to our first Thanksgiving dinner at her ranch. All that we had become started there, even if what brought us together began with me slipping on ice at the front door stoop and landing on my rear as Lucinda opened the door.

I uttered not a word of gratitude to anyone in late November on that day of thanks. I ate alone in the cabin. For weeks after the letter arrived, I stayed inside and snacked on preserved food and drank my coffee black and unsweetened.

Had Wuff's food not run out and made me leave to resupply her, I would have expired from malnourishment. The truth is, I ate nothing for several days after the cupboards were bare.

My gloom was shattered one evening by Elsbeth calling from Florida.

"Dad, *when* are you coming to Florida? I've called and called. Today, I contacted Ken Rangley and asked him to check on you. He'll drop by soon."

"OK."

"Just OK? Why haven't you left the cabin? I've been so worried. Are the injuries from the van bothering you again? Have you learned anything new about Lucinda? Do you think you might stay in Montana over the winter and maybe go and fish in Jackson with John? You hate the cold. Are you eating proper meals—the kind Lucinda forced down you? Do I have to fly out and put a bib on you and spoon feed you?"

"One question at a time," I mumbled.

"OK. Are you coming to Florida and when?"

"That's two questions."

"Are you coming?"

"I will. I promise."

"When?"

"Soon."

"'Soon' is a four letter word. Set a date! . . . I have exams beginning next week. Sue and I have decorated our house for Christmas. And we did some decorating at your cottage to welcome you home. I hope you're here soon or you're going to miss Christmas. *Please* come."

"I'll try to leave tomorrow," I said in little more than a whisper.

"Is something wrong, Dad? You don't sound like you."

"I'm just tired. Let me go, and I'll start packing."

"I'm going to call you tomorrow," she said. "And at least once every day while you're on the road to Florida. When you get here, plan some activities. Be in the annual *Nutcracker Suite* performance. Go to a movie. Or to a party. Or to a punk rock concert. Maybe even to a singles bar. Try out for the role of Scrooge in *A Christmas Carol.* Meet some people. You've got to get on with your life."

Her threats stimulated me to bathe and shave, pack Wuff's and my bags, lock the cabin, and drive to Livingston for a decent meal. I ate the meal, began to tremble, aborted the trip, and returned to the cabin. I wasn't ready for the interstates.

At least Elsbeth had dragged me from my stupor, which first was caused by an event she is yet to know about—the letter from Lucinda, or should I say High Priestess Onomaris? I haven't decided *not* to tell Elsbeth about the letter; I haven't decided *anything* the past few weeks. And I haven't called Dan Wilson.

Though my body had suffered from neglect, my mind was active thinking about every variation of facts that could have led to Lucinda's letter.

Lucinda's letter could have been entirely voluntary and not influenced by drugs. If so, I will never comprehend the transformation. Her letter might also have been forced from her hand by physical threats and her mental condition carefully controlled by Ellsworth-Kent administering mind-changing drugs. If the latter is what has happened, how long can she survive? The letter was by her hand, and from my repeated readings of the words she wrote and searching between the lines for messages she didn't write, it was hard to fully discredit her letter.

But I would read and reread the letter until I found a way.

21

FINALLY TO ST. AUGUSTINE

IF I DROVE IN MY CURRENT STATE, I WOULD threaten not only my own life but also that of everyone else who at the same time unfortunately chose to be on the roads I traveled. I delayed another day and then another. My condition can't be blamed on Gentleman Jack; that bottle had remained stoppered for weeks. The reason for my despondency was more likely exhaustion and confusion from my unresolved issues.

Ultimately, I had to share Lucinda's letter with Dan. Shortly before a late-to-bed day, I tried his number. I had talked to him the previous week, but receiving the letter demanded another call.

"Macduff," he said, cordiality missing from his tone, "do you know it's after midnight. This better be important. Another murder?"

"Worse."

"Are you all right?" Dan asked, "You sound lousy."

"As best as I can expect."

"What's happened?"

"I received a letter from. . . ." I said, my voice trailing off as I couldn't finish the sentence.

"Settle down, Mac. Letter from who?" Dan asked.

"Onomaris."

"Onomaris? Are you playing games with me?"

"No, it was signed 'High Priestess Onomaris of Kirkwall.'"

"Are you talking about the same Kirkwall on Scotland's Orkney Islands that was the setting for some of the events we called the 'wicker man and mistletoe' murders?" Dan asked.

"The very same," I affirmed.

"Who is this High Priestess Onomaris?"

"You know her, or knew her, as Lucinda."

"*Your* Lucinda?" he said, his voice cracking.

"She *was*," I murmured.

"Tell me about the letter."

"I scanned the letter and tapped the 'send' button. Look on your email," I said, and after a pause asked, "Have you got it?"

"I do, and I'm reading it. It sounds like science fiction. You're saying *Lucinda* actually sent this?"

"Yes. And I have no doubt it's her writing."

"Do you have the original and the envelope?"

"Yes."

"Send them to me. Make a copy for yourself. We have complex methods of analyzing correspondence. And send me something else in Lucinda's handwriting."

"Can you help?"

"I'll try. . . . I'll more than try. . . . Mac, are you OK?"

"I don't really know."

"Where are you? In Florida?"

"Not yet. I'm in Montana. But I promised Elsbeth I'd pack and get on the road."

"Don't wait for me to call back about the letter. Watch for a window of decent driving weather and get the hell away from Montana."

"In a day or two. It snowed last night—eight inches."

While I slept, the roads were mysteriously plowed, but a new system was heading toward us from the northwest bearing more snow. I did the best I could to again clean and close the cabin and finally was gone by noon, stopping first at our post office to send Dan by overnight mail the original letter Lucinda had written.

Without much thought, I drove west the few miles to Bozeman, south along the Gallatin River past Big Sky and into West Yellowstone. Another hour took me through Victor, Idaho, and I settled behind a welcome snowplow that was driving over Teton Pass to Jackson. A half-hour later I knocked on John Kirby's door; it was dinner time, and I was starved."

"Macduff!" John exclaimed. "Haven't heard from you for weeks!"

"Bring him in for dinner," his wife Sarah called from the kitchen. . . . Any news about Lucinda? What's going on?"

"I wish I knew."

For the next two hours I tried my best to control my emotions and tell them about Lucinda's letter. They both sat listening quietly and saying nothing until I finished.

"What can we do?" asked John.

"Hope. It all happened hundreds of miles from here. I have a friend in Washington helping to learn where Lucinda is living. He's not encouraging. There are a lot of places to hide in the U.S. and Europe."

"The Orkneys?" inquired Sarah, remembering the wicker man episode.

"I suspect all we'll learn from the UK authorities is that they have continued to 'watch' those islands for Ellsworth-Kent, mainly because of the five wicker man and mistletoe murders rather than Lucinda's abduction. The English have expressed far more concern about what happened on their decreasing amount of English soil than what happened abroad in a former colony, even if it involved an English national."

"What about searching for him in Montana or here in Wyoming?" added John.

"Probably not. The only reason he would be here would be to go after me again. I don't think he'll do that."

"Didn't he try to kill Lucinda as well as you on a summer solstice?" asked Sarah.

"Yes, and that's important. Why at first would he have loved her in England, then tried to kill her along with me on the Yellowstone in Montana, followed by forcibly abducting her in Florida and most recently watching her voluntarily write a letter as though all was forgiven and they were in love again?"

"That's what you meant when you said the most we can do is hope?" asked Sarah.

"Yes."

"Is that why she used the stamp with the words 'cultivating hope'; was she sending you a signal?"

"Of course! Sarah." I hadn't given the stamp further thought. "I'll convey your comment to my friend in Washington."

I went to bed that night with a bit of new hope, thanks to Sarah. The drive east would be easier with that thought in mind.

I drifted off more comfortably than any night since the letter arrived.

22

EAST TO FLORIDA

THE ROUTES LUCINDA AND I TOOK PREVIOUSLY to cross the expansive waistline of the U.S. had many memories to cherish. Not about traveling through spectacular landscapes or stopping to visit cultural treasures, but days of smelling her fragrance, talking for endless hours, and crawling into bed together in some strange motel room after a long day behind the wheel.

I left Jackson, aimed north for a dozen miles to Moran, curved east, crossed the Continental Divide, and followed the enticing Wind River southeast through Dubois, where Wuff and I sadly parted with the river and mountains. I drove through Lander, finally joined Interstate 80 at Rawlins, and we reached Laramie an hour-and-a-half later and decided to stay the night. Christmas lights brightened the town and reduced rough edges.

After many happy times over the years in Bozeman—home of Montana State University—and Missoula—home of the University of Montana—I often wondered why Wyoming chose Laramie to locate the state's flagship university. After seeing the city briefly, I wondered even more. It appeared never to have recovered fully from the impact of the gamblers, speculators, prostitutes, and preachers who helped make up the notorious Hell-on-Wheels population that ruled before the railroad arrived in the late 19th century. Maybe I was beginning to sense the coming drudgery of the mountain-less plains that I faced for the next couple of days and unfairly took my feelings out on Laramie. Maybe the town is better when approached from the East. Another year I'll try again.

The following two days did not prove to be any better by my ignoring maps and reminders of where I was—it seemed like ages passed driving a lot of miles east, then a lot of miles south, and then repeating that pattern until we crossed the Mississippi into Vicksburg.

In the morning, after visiting the civil war battlefields that have made the city's name synonymous with senseless tragedy, I drove to Jackson, turned southeast and crossed into Alabama at Mobile, and soon was in the part of Florida that should be a part of Georgia or Alabama. I chose the coastal route along the panhandle through what is not-too-affectionately called the "Redneck Riviera." It meant passing near Tallahassee—where the Riviera ended but the rednecks remained. Before I knew it, Wuff and I were on our cottage driveway and parking next to the home we'd left nearly eight months earlier.

The shock came when I unlocked and opened the cottage door. I froze in the doorway, looking at the dozens of photographs of Lucinda and me that crowded the walls. Holiday decorations had been hung, strung, and placed, apparently by my housekeeper Jen with some help from Elsbeth and Sue. A bottle of my favorite *Pouilly-Fuisse* sat waiting in the refrigerator. I could not overcome the sadness I instantly absorbed from the photographs.

Would another photograph of the two of us ever be taken?

23

THE NEXT DAY IN ST. AUGUSTINE

THERE WAS A SOLITARY MESSAGE ON MY CELL phone. It was from Grace Justice. The abduction happened on her turf, and she had spent countless hours on the case, frustrated by the absence of any developments in learning Lucinda's location. But I believe the truth is that Grace concluded that Lucinda is dead. I listened to the recorded message:

Macduff. We've closed the active search for Ellsworth-Kent. I'm assuming you haven't heard anything. . . . I'm sorry.

By the way, I fished in one of your kayaks three weeks ago. Followed a channel out to the Intracoastal and came back a different way. Pretty good fishing around some oyster bars—two nice seatrout, a keeper red, and a few small blues that kept biting off my fly. When I finished, I opened a bottle of wine and sat on your dock. I wish you'd been there to share it.

Back at the cottage to get my car, I found Jen cleaning your house and gave her a bottle of wine to put in your refrigerator.

Call me when you get back from Montana. I'll make you dinner; I've got a great recipe for braised chicken thighs with couscous, lemon, and Spanish olives. In case you're wondering, things haven't been encouraging with my fiancé, Valtr. It's another woman, and I don't want to say more. But it's over between us. By the way, Merry Christmas!

I like chicken, grilled, fried, or braised. I've eaten chicken breasts, wings, and legs but, acknowledging how little I go to a grocery store, I've never looked for or seen chicken *thighs* for sale. But it's what Grace said she would add to the chicken thighs that made me wonder about the dinner. Adding lemon sounded good; I like it in iced tea or with vodka in *limoncello*. The olives were OK *if* the pits were excised. Couscous must be good because whatever it's made from sometimes it's served as a dessert.

I suspect Grace is testing me. I'm sure Lucinda told her about my food fetishes. I shouldn't say a word about the meal when I called and accepted the invitation.

One decision I have to make is whether to show Grace the letter from Lucinda. I'll think about that, but I'm inclined to let her read it.

At sunrise the next morning—a far warmer event than a week ago—I poured some coffee, took my cup and phone to the porch, sat in a rocker, and called Grace. She was on the porch of her Camachee Island condo, looking over marsh to the north and watching a convention of ibis gathered on the mud flats surrounded by low spartina grass.

"Macduff! I can also see roseate spoonbills, woodstorks, ospreys, assorted herons, and a lone kingfisher. I feel like the lone kingfisher. . . . Are you at your cottage?"

"I am. Thanks for the wine. I see you've been depleting my private stock of trout and reds off my dock. Keep the blues."

"How about my offer of cooking you a dinner?"

"My date book shows nothing planned this week except an eye exam, a 35,000-mile car service, and something I scribbled and can't read."

"Meaning you'll come?"

"Tomorrow at seven?" I asked.

"That's good. You like thighs?" she asked.

"As compared to breasts?"

"Are we still talking about chicken?"

"See you at seven. Hold the olive pits but heavy on the couscous."

Since she was preparing chicken that included Spanish olives, I took a light gold sparkling Spanish *cava*.

A few socially acceptable minutes after seven the next evening, Grace answered my knock and gave me a hug and an enduring kiss, followed by a smile and face that made me wonder what would unfold over the evening.

We were both dressed casual. Causal means never having to say you're sorry to the host or hostess about being underdressed. I was wearing loafers, tan corduroy pants, and a French-blue dress shirt with no tie. Grace had on leather sandals, white canvas cropped pants, and a thin cotton shirt with a white mandarin collar and flared sleeves and showed off more than the outline of her breasts. I was sure the shirt was not meant to be worn in public. Grace handed me a glass of Gentleman Jack at the door and led me by the hand to the porch. The Kingfisher was back and no longer solo. A female was chasing it around a salt pond. Grace may have planned to do the same to me later.

"Where do we start?" she asked. "It's been months. I don't think I saw you and Lucinda much anytime during your last Florida winter stay, just before she was abducted. . . . Mac, that was a terrible thing to happen—to her and to you."

"I think more of the 'to her' consequences," I said. "I don't know whether she's been drugged or been killed."

"What makes you think drugged?"

"Her irrational behavior. The letter was hard to believe. The choices aren't comforting," I answered. "She could have been killed, but no body's been discovered. If she'd escaped, she would have contacted me."

"Letter? What letter are you talking about? . . . And what if Ellsworth-Kent is forcibly keeping her somewhere?"

"How could he do *that*," I questioned, "unless he drugged her?"

"How long can he do *that*?" She countered. "Drugs take a toll. If he left her for an hour or so, even for a simple thing like buying food, she might escape. Doesn't he have to make some decision about what to *do* with her?"

"I think he has," I answered.

"Why do you say that?"

"Assuming she's alive, she may be staying with him of her own free will."

"That's not a possibility," Grace insisted. "He treated her badly when they were married and he tried to kill her in Montana."

"Maybe he's changed."

"Maduff, I know how you feel, but be realistic. The chances of her being alive aren't good. If she is alive the chances of her wanting to stay with Ellsworth-Kent are beyond my imagination."

I reached into my shirt pocket, pulled out a folded copy of Lucinda's two-page letter, and handed it to Grace.

"What's this?" she asked.

"Read it."

She read it twice, got up, and walked to her sliding glass porch door, stepped inside, and sat on a small chair in her living room. I waited a few minutes and followed her. She was crying.

"I don't. . . . I don't believe any of this, Macduff," she said, stumbling on her words. "You know her handwriting. Is this like hers?"

"It *is* hers. So was the address on the envelope. I've looked for any indication that she didn't mean what she wrote and that she didn't write it voluntarily."

"And?"

"I don't know! I guess Lucinda wrote it. My last hope is she did it with a gun to her head. I can't believe she meant what she wrote."

"Where was it sent from?"

"Vienna."

"Austria?"

"Yes."

"How do you know that?"

"The UN has postal offices in a few locations. If the stamp denomination is in Euros, and it was, it must have come from Vienna."

"What does that tell you?"

"Nothing. I don't know if she ever visited Vienna when she worked in London. Likely, since she loves music and especially Strauss waltzes."

"What does the phrase on the stamp—HOFFNUNG PFLANZEN—mean?"

"The best translation seems to be 'cultivating hope.'"

"Does Lucinda speak German? Might she have used this stamp to send a message to you?"

"She knows a little German, probably not enough to disguise a message. She likely asked for any stamp Ellsworth-Kent gave her that would get the letter to me."

"Was Lucinda on any medication when she was abducted? Something that would have affected her if she stopped taking it abruptly?"

"She rarely took even an aspirin," I replied.

"Could Ellsworth-Kent have forced her to take drugs?" Grace asked.

"If he had access to them, yes. She wouldn't have taken anything voluntarily; if she were drugged, they had to have been forced on her. As she was forced to write the letter."

"What makes you think the letter was forced?"

"I reread it carefully last night. There's something I meant to mention but you may think me foolish and overreactive."

"Try me."

"I found three things that I had trouble with and made me think she was sending me a sign that the letter was not her own thoughts."

"Tell me about the three; I didn't notice anything when you gave it to me to read," requested Grace.

"The letter opened with my name spelled 'MacDuff' rather than what we both *always use*—'Macduff.' No capital 'D.'"

"What else?"

"She said that I 'ought not' make any attempt to contact her. She always corrected me when I used that phrase, saying it was no longer considered proper English. I always responded it was proper and she 'ought not' scold me. Lucinda would *never* use that in speech or writing. She did it twice in the letter!"

"Interesting. What's the last thing?"

"When she mentions the wicker man and mistletoe murders, she says they occurred on *six* different rivers. She knows they were on *five* and not six rivers."

"Is that enough to believe she was forced to write the letter?"

"I don't know whether it is or not. I may be grasping for straws."

"I think you are. . . . Macduff, is Ellsworth-Kent a violent man? Would he force her to do things such as write the letter?"

"Yes. He killed five people at different times and locations in one year. Earlier, he served time in an English jail for what he did to Lucinda. He hurt her badly enough so she could never have children. . . . I call that violent."

"Why does he want her so badly?"

"He's never accepted their divorce or our marriage. . . . She hates him for what he did to her. She knows he's a mental case."

"What will he do with her?"

"Beat her. Force her to have sex with him. Use her as his beautiful but silent partner. That's why she was made a high priestess and given the name Onomaris."

"What does that name mean?"

"It was the name of a female Druid who by legend was thought to have the power to control men."

"But would Ellsworth-Kent have given her that name if it meant she might have power over *him*?"

"That's a good observation. I don't know the answer. The name may be symbolic to him, serving little purpose other than to show his ability to have a partner with a name of such historic stature. Onomaris is said to have led her people in battle and founded a settlement that is now Belgrade in Serbia."

"Macduff, I hate to ask this, but would he kill her to keep her from returning to you?"

"Yes. Without hesitation."

"Would he tell you he's killed her?"

"Maybe. Likely yes. It's a choice of leaving me not knowing what happened or knowing and trying to find him."

"If you found him, would you kill him?"

"In a moment. . . . Without remorse."

We ate dinner on a small table on the porch. There was little room for our legs. Grace had removed her sandals and was rubbing my calf muscles with her feet.

When we finished, she suggested taking another bottle of wine to the condo community pool. It was late and dark, and no lights were on in any of the condo windows. We sat on a concrete bench by the pool.

"What are your plans, Macduff?" Grace asked. "At some time you have to assume Lucinda's dead or not returning. She was abducted eight months ago. The experience at our state attorney's office is that unless an abducted person returns within a matter of weeks, we assume they are dead and the body has likely been buried somewhere. Those bodies usually show up, discovered accidentally by a hiker in some woods."

"Elsbeth told me it's time for me to stop dreaming and get on with my life. If Lucinda's dead, I can't have her back; if she's decided to live with Ellsworth-Kent, I don't want her back."

I turned my head and in the dim moonlight saw that Grace's pants and shirt were on the walk beside the bench. She rose, took three steps and dove into the pool, swam the length and back, stepped out, and stood dripping in front me, her wet body glistening in the faint light.

She picked up her clothes in one hand, took mine in her other, and nudged me back to her apartment.

At seven the next morning I slipped out of bed, dressed, and drove home.

24

THE FOLLOWING EVENING

E LSBETH CALLED THE NEXT EVENING AND asked, "Where were you last night, Dad? Sue and I were at a party in Daytona and we drove by the cottage about midnight on the way back to Gainesville. There was no sign of you except a single half-filled wine glass and an empty wine bottle on the table beside your favorite chair. We looked on your dock, but you weren't there."

"I was out late."

"How late? All night?"

"You told me exactly a week ago to get out of the house. I did."

"Where?"

"It was *not* to a punk rock concert. If you must know, I was at a swimming pool."

"You don't have a swimming pool. Where were you? Did you swim?"

"I didn't make it into the water."

"Did you make it home before dawn?"

"Almost."

"Any other plans?"

"Yes." I'm thinking of going to Hope Town for a few days after Christmas."

"Why Hope Town? What's there?"

"I went once before with El. I never visited the Bahamas with Lucinda. I'll fish, walk, use a bicycle, and putter around in a small boat. I love the iridescent emerald color of the water around Abaco."

"Will you go alone?"

"Yes. Jen will keep Wuff for a week."

"What about Grace?"

"I haven't mentioned it to her."

"Will you?"

"I haven't planned to."

"Is there any chance you'll be gone for Christmas, and I'll miss seeing you?"

"Not a chance. I want to be with you." I'll leave for Hope Town a day or two after."

25

THE WEEK BEFORE CHRISTMAS

"*I* DIALED YOUR NUMBER A DOZEN TIMES OVER the past couple of days, but each time *you* answered, *I* hung up. I apologize," Grace said, when I answered her 8:00 a.m. call.

I had known some of the previous calls were from her but never tried to return them.

"There's a full moon tonight," she added. "It's at the closest point to the earth it will be for the year, and the tides will be especially high. The snook have been gathering around St. Augustine this year, even this late. They might be around docks if underwater lights are used. And there should be some big trout on your flats where they join the Intracoastal."

There was a pause. I knew she was waiting for me to invite her over to fish.

"Would you like to invite me over to fish tomorrow evening?" she asked before I could say anything.

I was slow to respond because I didn't know whether I wanted to see her. There was a long pause. . . .

"I'm driving to West Palm the day after Christmas and taking an hour flight to Marsh Harbour at Abaco, and then a ferry to Hope Town," I explained. "For New Year's week an old fishing friend from Wyoming, Chris Bennett, and I have rented a small cottage with a private dock and a 21' Boston Whaler. The cottage is on the harbor and overlooks much of the town."

"Do you plan to introduce yourself to Reginald Covington?" she asked.

Hope Town Bahamas resident Covington killed Floridian Grant Borders a year or two ago in the second airboat murder. Borders' death was not investigated in the U.S. because he was already dead when his body reached Florida and was tied to an airboat propeller and spun. According to Grace, he died either on one of the Bahama Islands or in international waters, outside U.S. jurisdiction. Weeks later Covington showed up one evening at Grace's Camachee Island condo, intimidated her, admitted to the murder, and quickly flew back to Abaco on his private plane. He has a mansion at Hope Town.

"I hadn't given Covington a thought. I've rented a bicycle. I'll probably pedal by his house—you've told me where it is—and see how the other half lives. But mainly my friend and I are going to fish two days for bones and two for whatever else swims my way."

"Fly rod?"

"Nothing else."

"I'm envious," she said.

I didn't respond. Nor did I tell her that Chris Bennett is male; she may think it's spelled "Kris" and that my friend is female.

"Let's fish here tomorrow night," I finally offered. "I can use the practice for Hope Town. Come over from work. When we finish, I'll grill bison bratwurst I had shipped from Wyoming."

26

THE NEXT MORNING

I PHONED DAN WILSON'S HOUSE LINE AFTER breakfast.

"Dan, right after Christmas I'm driving, flying, and ferrying to Hope Town for a week."

"Taking me with you?"

"You don't fish."

"But I drink piña coladas. . . . If you're not going to invite me to go along, why did you call?"

"Update me on Lucinda's abduction."

"Consider it done without me uttering a further word. We have no new information. Truthfully, we don't know any more than we did seven months ago, except for her letter to you."

"Speaking of the letter," I said, "I read it again several times, carefully looking for any signal from Lucinda. I found three."

I spent the next twenty minutes describing the three items in the letter—the use of "MacDuff" rather than "Macduff," the use of "ought not," and the reference to six rather than five rivers in the wicker man and mistletoe murders. Dan was not very impressed and asked if I had an emptied glass of Gentleman Jack in front of me.

"What's the CIA doing about Lucinda?" I asked. "It was an *international* incident. That's *your* jurisdiction."

"We believe from the postage stamp that the letter was mailed from Vienna," Dan explained. "We also know a private jet with false markings landed at the St. Augustine airport shortly before and took off shortly after the abduction. It disappeared, apparently flying low under the radar. Our best guess is it went to the nearest foreign airport—the Bahamas. It could have stopped on one of the islands or continued south at a low altitude to somewhere in the Caribbean. Haiti perhaps. Maybe the Dominican Republic.

"We don't know if it was Lucinda and Ellsworth-Kent. They could be anywhere in the world as we speak. We assume they made it to Europe and mailed the letter back. Every CIA mission in the world has been notified of the abduction. Whether or not they are actively searching is another matter."

"Is no news good news?"

"At least we don't have any specific bad news."

"What do you recommend?" I asked.

"I'm sorry, but I suggest you accept that Lucinda is dead. To make it legal, there will have to be some formal declaration by the government. . . . I agree Lucinda wrote the letter to you. After Ellsworth-Kent mailed it from Vienna, Lucinda probably served no further purpose."

"Then why did he have her named a high priestess?"

"Deception. To place the focus on the Orkney Islands. I don't believe the two were there more than a few days. The British authorities weren't enthused by Ellsworth-Kent's actions. But they've never put a lot of effort into finding him. Once he got out of jail on the Isle of Wight years ago and flew to the U.S., their interest in him ended."

"But he killed *five* people at five different locations!" I exclaimed. "And he was still a British citizen. I don't understand England's lack of interest."

"We won the war more than two hundred years ago. They still can't accept that."

"While I have you on the line, what about Johnson?"

"We believe he received several million dollars from Guatemala by way of Coronel Alarcon. Apparently Johnson insisted that it be transferred to a numbered account at a European bank before he gave Alarcon the information about you. Johnson's on the move. We're tracking him. We think he's using an assumed name and is in Portugal in the Algarve region along the south coast. We're searching the Faro area."

"Do you have agents in Faro?" I asked Dan.

"Not based there, but one from Lisbon is there."

"Is there any likelihood that Johnson has settled in Faro?"

"Good chance, but if he's smart, he's ready to move."

"Can I help?"

"Not yet. Keep out of it."

"What about Alarcon's death? Johnson doesn't have to worry about him anymore."

"But he has to worry about Herzog. Johnson was paid by a cash transfer for information Herzog never received. If Herzog finds Johnson, we worry Johnson will tell Herzog about you, and he might be foolish and try to squeeze more money out of Herzog."

"If I were him, I wouldn't even think of doing that," I said.

"I'd tell Johnson to give Herzog the information and run fast and find a new home and use new forged passports, a new name, and a new country."

"If Johnson gave Herzog the information, I'd have to run fast as well."

"Only if you wanted to live!"

27

LATER THAT DAY

IN THE AFTERNOON I MADE A RESERVATION TO fly from Abaco to Nassau to London to Lisbon and finally to Faro. I could spend only three nights in Hope Town, but the house remained mine for the full week. Chris canceled, but paid his half of the week's rent. It made dealing with Grace easier. I would suggest she take the house when I'm gone.

Grace arrived at the cottage at six directly from her office. She walked up the porch steps in her charcoal suit with the jacket open and a holster showing a gun under her left arm. She held a fly rod in one hand and an overnight bag in the other.

"Which of those things do you plan to use here, the fly rod or the gun?" I asked.

"If you behave only the fly rod."

She walked into my bedroom, left the door open, and facing the living room changed into khaki fishing clothes she had in her bag.

We went down to the pier where my flats boat and two kayaks were ready to go.

"Choose your transportation," I suggested. "Kayak or flats boat?"

"Flats boat," she said. "The tide is high, there's plenty of water, and I get to be with you and correct your casting."

"I thought the fishing might be good most anywhere between the dock and the Intracoastal Waterway," I said as I poled the boat away and east along the winding main channel. It was chilly but not cold enough to drive the fish to deeper, warmer holes.

"Mac, slow down. I see a tailing red ahead on the left side near the grass. Can you see the silver bronze shaded tail with the black spot?"

"Yes."

Redfish are largely bottom feeders. But a red's mouth is not so much on the bottom of the body as at the lower part of the snout.

"This one looks like a keeper, inside the slot. But I can't tell without seeing it closer, and if you want to keep it—*if* you land it—we'll need a quick measurement. . . . Whoops! No confirming measurement possible. It's gone!"

Grace's Clouser fly tied on a 2/0 hook was a white over red color that could attract almost any salt- or freshwater fish. Fly fishing legend Lefty Krey claims to have caught more than eighty species of fish with a Clouser, which must please the fly's designer Bob Clouser.

"Macduff, you should tie more of these. It's easy to tie, isn't it?"

"One of the least complex flies, but not as easy to tie as a San Juan Worm. The Clouser uses a bunch of colored bucktail, your's is red and white."

"Why *buck*tail? Why not just a deertail? Doesn't the female doe have a tail?"

"It does. I guess it was named bucktail to distinguish it from deer *body* hair, which is thinner and used for other things, like wrapping bodies."

"I've seen a white tail on a deer, but never a red," She said, grinning.

"I'll forget you said that, or we have to talk about green or pink or a dozen other deer tails. Dye is the essence of most modern fly colors. The newly famous Copper John nymph can be tied or bought in green, chartreuse, red, white, wine, black, blue, hot pink, and zebra. Or using any other color of wire that's available."

"Does that mean a white Clouser is a natural fly, but a red one is artificial?"

"You're getting close to a sensitive area. When does a fly become a lure? I'm not going to try to answer that. Just fish! . . . You've lost a chance at that red. You caught an oyster, broke off the fly, and scared the red. That was my only red and white Clouser. How can I afford you in my boat?"

"If you'd teach me how to tie flies, I wouldn't borrow so many from you. They don't last long around oyster banks. I assume they do better on Western rivers."

"I can't think of anything harder on salt water flies than oysters. You could use a floating line to keep your fly above the oysters, but you're likely to catch one only if your fly and leader sink close enough to the bottom where the reds prefer to feed. They aren't like Western fish rising to take a dry fly on the surface."

"I'm using a sinking line. Maybe I would do better with an intermediate line that sinks, but not as fast," she wondered.

"You might not catch more fish, but you'd catch fewer oysters and keep more flies. I use an intermediate line when I fish these marshes."

We fished for two hours until the light began to fade. Grace was more careful with her casts and didn't lose another fly. With a chartreuse and white Clouser, she landed a fine 27" sea trout. I cast mainly where small side channels joined our main channel, but I landed only a single mangrove snapper on a brown and tan Clouser.

Back at the cottage while Grace made drinks—we're both Gentleman Jack fans—I turned on the gas grill and started the bison bratwurst.

"Tell me about Hope Town," Grace asked while the fragrance of the meal drifted along the cottage porch to our rockers. I suspected she wanted to go to Hope Town with me, and I didn't know how to respond without disappointing her.

"Not much to tell I haven't mentioned. I think when you went there and met and spoke with Covington it was. . . . "

"Reginald Covington *the Third*," Grace interrupted with a laugh. "He insists everyone use his *full* name. And he interrupts you if you don't."

"Like you did to me."

"Of course. You might meet him while you're there, and I don't want you to commit an unnecessary social blunder."

"Or he might murder me, maybe on an airboat."

"Absolutely! And claim justifiable homicide."

"I was planning to stay a week in Hope Town and paid the rent for a small place with a second floor balcony off the master bedroom that overlooks the harbor. Now I'm having to cut it short to go to Europe after only three nights. . . . Why don't you fly down and use the house?"

"What about Kris? Will she mind?"

"Chris prefers not to be called a she. He spells his first name with a 'Ch' and not a 'K.' And he's not coming. The house is yours alone when I leave."

Grace smiled as she realized her initial assumption had been wrong.

"Are you talking about my being there the *first* three nights or after you're gone?"

"Well . . . after I leave. I'll be preparing for Europe instead of doing much fishing. When I'm gone, you'd have four nights to be wined and dined by Coving. . . . Reginald Covington *the Third.*"

"When I'm there, I'll use an assumed name and wear a wig," she said.

It was eleven when we finished the meal and sat on the sofa listening to an increasing breeze that caused the decorative white lights on the trees at the foot of the steps to jiggle and sparkle.

"Tomorrow is Christmas Eve," I said. "I'm sure you have things to do to get ready. Maybe we'd better call it a day."

"You throwing me out?" she exclaimed. "It's nearly midnight. I promise I'll be gone by daybreak. I don't want Elsbeth walking in on us again."

She was gone in the morning at 6:25. By the time Elsbeth drove up an hour later. I had made the bed, cleaned the kitchen, and was having coffee.

There wasn't a sign that Grace had been there with me.

28

FARO, PORTUGAL

CHRISTMAS PASSED. ELSBETH AND I STAYED close to the cottage. We did everything to keep busy and avoid maudlin talk about Lucinda's absence, partly because we both separately concluded that Lucinda couldn't have survived for so long. But perhaps truly voluntarily she decided to live with Ellsworth-Kent.

"Dad, are you leaving for Hope Town tomorrow?" Elsbeth asked Christmas Day.

"Yes," I said—and nothing more.

"Why didn't you invite me to go to the Bahamas with you? I don't go back to UF for another ten days."

"You know I'm going to Europe from the Bahamas?"

"I know you'll be in the Bahamas for three nights with Grace. What's going on with you two is happening kind of quickly, don't you think?"

"You're the one who said I should get on with my life."

"You and I know Grace loves you. She has since Lucinda left you a few years ago to live in Manhattan. I'm concerned Grace is coming on too hard, and it's unfair to you. I think you need to move on with your life, but you also need some space."

"I'm going alone to Portu. . . . to Europe."

"I know you're headed to the embassy at Lisbon and then to Faro on the Mediterranean," Elsbeth said. "I talked with

Dan Wilson. He didn't tell me directly, but I also know you're carrying a diplomatic passport under an assumed name. True?"

"No comment, and I won't ask why Dan would tell you so much about this trip. I agree with you that I need some time alone, at least away from Grace."

"Should I go to Europe with you?"

"You *can't* go. Do you expect me to get *you* a diplomatic passport under a different name?"

"Why not? Does your trip involve Herzog?"

"Why do you think that?"

"You told me a little. So did Dan. And I've filled in between the lines. You're looking for someone who knows about your past. Someone who has information that would be useful to Herzog. Am I right?"

"I don't know what you're talking about."

"You've already told me more than you should. Just tell me one thing. *Am I right?*"

"Yes," I answered quietly, looking away from her and thinking I don't want to lose her as I've lost El and Lucinda.

"Are you going to be in danger?" she asked.

"Not if it all goes well."

"If it does go well for you, must someone else come out a loser?"

"He already has. But he's alive, and if he's smart, he may remain alive."

"If he's not smart, you're going to kill him?"

"If he's not smart, he will try to kill me. I want to get to him first."

"Before he tells Herzog who you are, where you live, and what you do."

"That's about it."

29

GUATEMALA CITY

AS HERZOG SIPPED COFFEE, HE LOOKED OUT from the balcony of the Palacio Nacional at the magnificent spread of tiny lights that obscured the city's poverty. He was disturbed and at a loss about how to proceed in finding Professor Hunt. No one was nearby, but he spoke out loud.

"I've lost Luisa to the university that I offered $4 million dollars to not many years ago. "She has defied me and left a message on my phone that she will not return to Guatemala as long as I am president. Perhaps not ever. Coronel Alarcon is dead, killed by my hand in a fit of rage I regret, but was justified by his disrespect. To his grave he took the information I have sought for more than a decade.

"Alarcon's wife Dolores wasn't worth what I lost when I killed her husband. Carlos was my most loyal advisor. Dolores has left me. So has Carlotta Boschmann, my private secretary who I suspect is in Spain or Portugal. I have few choices left.

"The number of known CIA agents who were present at the meeting when Professor Hunt was placed in a protection program has dwindled to what may be no more than a half-dozen. Whitman is dead, shot before my eyes in a bar in Washington. Davis is dead from Alzheimer's.

'Before Alarcon died, he learned the names of two others who had been present, Ralph Johnson and Hugh Hernandez. Hernandez was killed in an auto accident last month. He was retired and living quietly in D.C. That left Johnson the only one of the group I knew about. He was a surprise to me; he was assumed to be loyal to the Agency, but he sold the information about Professor Hunt to Alarcon in exchange for $4 million transferred to a numbered foreign account.

"My principal security advisor, Alejandro Olviedo, who I promoted to replace Alarcon, told me Johnson is currently living in Portugal using an assumed name. Johnson erred by contacting us and offering to disclose what he told Alarcon, conditioned upon receiving an *additional* $4 million. *That's outrageous!*

"Olviedo is this moment on a flight to Lisbon to work from our embassy searching for Johnson. When he finds him, he'll offer nothing new and insist on a return of the original money. Johnson expectantly will reply that he completed his promise by turning over Professor Hunt's name and location to Alarcon. Olviedo won't accept that.

"If Johnson refuses, he will suffer and die. If he discloses the information and we finally learn about Professor Hunt, Johnson may suffer the same end, perhaps by some form of accident—automobile, bicycle, handling weapons, small plane crash, drowning, falling out of a window of a high building, or some other event. . . . *Maybe* we'll let him buy back his life."

Herzog stepped in off the balcony, nervously poured more coffee which spilled over the rim of the cup, sat behind his desk, and continued voicing his thoughts.

"Olviedio is bright. But he has no experience working with any U.S. CIA agents and thus may be of limited use. He is unlikely to learn the names of the remaining agents who were at the CIA meeting where Professor Hunt's name and location were changed. But he *is* capable of persuading Johnson to repeat the information he gave Alarcon."

30

THE NEXT DAY IN LISBON

A LEJANDRO OLVIEDO SAT IN A CORNER OF THE bar in Lisbon's Hotel Britannia, admiring the paintings depicting Portugal's vast overseas empire which endured for several centuries. Olviedo had never been to Portugal, and he admired this last surviving art deco hotel in the city's center off elegant Avenida da Liberdade. Across the table from him was Guatemala's ambassador to Portugal, Jorge Herzog, a distant cousin to the Guatemalan President. Both were drinking port from the rugged Douro Valley to the northwest of Lisbon.

"Jorge, you are related to our President?" asked Olviedo.

"Distantly, but yes. . . . Although I do not know him well."

"Are you fond of him?"

"I am loyal to him, Alejandro. I owe my appointment here to him. And you? Are you close to Juan Pablo?"

"Please don't repeat this, but no one is close to him these days. The weight of the presidency, according to those who work for him, seems increasingly burdensome. I don't envy his position. But my job is to serve him without reservation."

"I agree. And I hope you and I can take some of that weight off his shoulders. What can you tell me about your being here?"

"A man named Ralph Johnson—whom we believe resides in Faro—has information he promised to give us in exchange for a considerable amount of money. He received the money by means of a transfer to a numbered account at a European bank—I believe in Liechtenstein or Switzerland—and gave the information about Professor Hunt to the late Coronel Carlos Alarcon, the President's most trusted aide. Before conveying that information to the President, Alarcon died. He had told no one what he learned from Johnson, nor had he written it down anywhere."

"Why doesn't Johnson simply tell the President directly what he already told Alarcon?"

"Greed. Johnson has asked for the additional sum to again disclose the same information. President Herzog is unhappy with Johnson."

"And you are to. . . ?"

"Find Johnson."

"And obtain the information from him?"

"Yes."

"Without further payment?"

"Without further payment in money."

"Meaning?"

"I am not authorized to speak to that, Ambassador Herzog, but Johnson will be taken care of."

"Do you expect Johnson will be hard to find?"

"Yes. Remember that he was a CIA agent for many years. He must be presumed to be skilled in deception and disguise. I doubt he will answer the door of his house and invite me in."

"What do you expect?"

"That he will not even be in Portugal. He will have fled using an assumed name."

"Then what?'

"That will be up to me. I *will* find him."

31

THE SAME EVENING IN THE SAME CITY

NOT FAR FROM THE HOTEL BRITANIA, I HAD checked in at the Solar do Castelo, the only hotel within the walls of São Jorge Castelo at the top of the old quarter known as the Alfama.

"Good evening, Mr. Grace. Have you been with us before?"

"No." Truthfully, I *had* been at the hotel several times, but as Professor Maxwell Hunt nearly two decades ago when I served in Lisbon as a Fulbright professor at the faculty of law of the Universidade do Portuguesa in Lisbon.

This time I entered Portugal using an alias. The passport and all identification I carried stated I was Gregory Grace; it would be inappropriate for me to encounter Ralph Johnson as Macduff Brooks, the man Johnson was willing to sacrifice for several million dollars. He and I had not seen each other since our meeting in Washington when I entered as Professor Maxwell Hunt and departed as Macduff Brooks. If I confronted Ralph Johnson it would be as Gregory Grace.

"Mr. Grace," the hotel receptionist continued, regaining my attention, "Mr. Robert Silver is waiting for you in the bar. Here is your room key. I hope you will enjoy your stay. We will take your bags to your room so you may meet directly with Mr. Silver."

I walked into the bar and looked about the room for someone who might be Robert Silver. One man was sitting alone at a table in a corner, but he was facing away from me. As I walked past him, I heard him say softly, "Gregory?"

He pointed to a chair with a drink already on the table. I sat down and tasted it, knowing I had the right table because it was Gentleman Jack.

Silver was tall and slender, graying at the temples. Probably in his late fifties, although years working with the CIA tends to age agents prematurely.

"Have a good flight?" he inquired, searching the room for anyone watching their table.

"Is any flight good the way airlines are managed today?"

"I understand your point."

"What have you been told about my visit?" I asked.

"Only that you are here on a special assignment. And that you carry papers showing you're Gregory Grace, newly attached to the embassy as an Assistant Economic Affairs Officer. I need know nothing more. I am to assist you in whatever you require."

"You're with the mission here?"

"Mission? Well. . . . yes."

"I will be at your office at 9:00 a.m tomorrow, if that's convenient."

"I'll make it so. Join me for breakfast?"

"Of course."

"May I digress and ask you something?" said Silver.

"Tell me what it is."

"Were you ever in Khartoum?"

"Khartoum?"

"You know that's the capital of the Sudan. . . . We met there about six years ago."

"That's possible."

"I know what you did. The first day you were there I drove you to Omdurman, and we visited the camel market."

"The camels smelled atrociously," I remembered, laughing. "I rejected your suggestion that I buy one. Nor, I recall, did you buy one."

"If my memory is correct, you exited the Sudan in a curious way."

"I did. And I still regret not stopping to see Abu Simbal!"

"Another time. . . . I know I shouldn't ask, but are you here for similar reasons?"

"I know I shouldn't answer, but no, not as extreme. But I'm here for a matter that may determine whether I live to see my twilight years. When we met before, that was not the issue. It was whether a very evil man would live to do inconceivable harm. I can't say anything more. . . . I must ask about Ralph Johnson."

"That son-of-a-bitch!"

"So you share my view."

"I'll see you at 9:00 a.m."

"I look forward to it. Te vejo amanhã."

I waited for Silver to leave the building and walked out to the walls of the castle and looked over the river. I went to the very spot where my wife El and I had many times admired the Tagus River, where Prince Henry the Navigator and Vasco da Gama set sail on their voyages of exploration. El and I had been ecstatic about Portugal and often discussed retiring there.

It was too early to sleep if I wanted to adjust quickly to the time change from Florida. I took a cab to the Parque Eduardo

VII and began to walk down Avenida da Liberdade toward the river.

Blocks away Olviedo had said good evening to Ambassador Herzog and left his hotel. Welcoming the light breeze bringing fresh air off the river, he also walked down Avenida da Liberdade. It was late and few people were on the street. He stopped for a moment to admire the Armani suits in the window of a men's clothing store.

Standing there at first, he didn't see another man who also had stopped to view the display. I was that other man. Olviedo smiled and nodded, and I returned the gesture.

Realizing that it was quite late and not knowing whether he was safe at night on Lisbon's main downtown streets, Olviedo turned and walked away north in the direction of his hotel.

I turned and walked away south in the direction of mine.

Neither of us realized we both had come to Lisbon for much the same purpose: to find Ralph Johnson. But what we each expected from Johnson was quite different.

32

THE NEXT DAY IN LISBON

A MBASSADOR FULGENCIO DELGADO WAS THE only U.S. embassy staff member in Lisbon—other than the chief of the CIA mission, Roger Dawson—who knew that Gregory Grace was a temporary assumed name given me by the Agency in D.C.

We three were walking on the embassy grounds away from rooms that might be bugged, which included the ambassador's office.

"Macduff, or rather Gregory, a Señor Alejandro Olviedo arrived yesterday from Guatemala, where he is a security advisor to President Herzog. Here is a photo of him," the Ambassador said, handing me a small color photo. "Have you ever seen him before?"

"Yes," I answered, staring at the face in the photograph.

"You have! Where? When?"

"*Last night*. Walking on Avenida da Liberdade after dinner, I stopped to look in a store window. I noticed a man standing next to me was also looking at the window display. We each nodded, and he left. I did not know it was Olviedo."

"Roger," said the ambassador, turning to the CIA head, "Is there any reason Olviedo should know he was nodding at who Professor Maxwell Hunt has become?"

"No," said Dawson. "Logically the most Guatemala has are photos taken at least fifteen years ago of Professor Hunt. Olviedo wouldn't recognize Macduff."

"Did he act as though he knew who you were?" Dawson asked, turning toward me.

"Not that I recall. We looked at each other for only a moment, and then he turned and walked away."

"Possibly satisfied he had just seen the successor to Hunt?"

"Probably not."

"Only probably?"

"Probably."

We walked further between lush green bushes and flowers that made us realize—being in Lisbon—how far southwest we were from most of Europe.

Dawson was quiet, concerned with my use of *probably*.

"I don't like what I'm hearing," he said, abruptly stopping and turning toward me. "I don't want you and Olviedo both chasing Ralph Johnson around Faro with Olviedo more concerned about taking your head back to Herzog than taking information to him. What a coup it would be for Olviedo."

"We need to get to Johnson before Olviedo does," said Ambassador Delgado. "If Johnson refuses to give Olviedo the information, Johnson is assuredly going to be killed by him. Even if Johnson *does* give that information, he is *almost* assuredly going to be killed. The odds are not in his favor," I said.

"If, acting as Gregory Grace, I get to Johnson first, the most we can hope for is that Johnson assures me he won't give the information to Olviedo if caught. Hope is not enough. The only way I can be certain that he doesn't give the information to Olviedo is to make certain he *can't*. If the President back in

D.C. learns that we've taken out one of our own citizens who was a U.S. government employee, there'll be hell to pay."

"I think we have to be willing to pay hell," said Dawson.

I nodded in support.

"How do we know that Johnson isn't content with nothing more than staying alive?" asked the ambassador.

"Is he content? Apparently not. He's already *asked* for more," I noted.

Dawson stepped aside to take a phone call. Within minutes his face suggested he had learned something.

"Johnson may have left Faro!" Dawson called out.

"What?" I exclaimed.

"Our contact said his Faro apartment is empty," explained Dawson. "He left little behind, mostly clothing and bedding and some food in the refrigerator."

"Does your contact in Faro know where he's gone—if he has left?"

"We don't know what name he's using. If it is Johnson, he's not taken or booked any flight out of Faro or rented a car. But he could have left by train where he wasn't asked for identification."

"Where do you suppose he's gone? The worst case scenario would be he's gone to Guatemala with Olviedo, first by train and then a flight from Madrid or elsewhere in Europe. Or, more likely, by a Guatemalan government plane."

"Gone willingly to Guatemala where he might be killed?" asked Delgado.

"If he arrives in Guatemala and gives Herzog the information, without demanding more money, Herzog might let him live, and even live safely, in Guatemala," Dawson suggested.

"Let me make a suggestion," interjected Ambassador Delgado. "You go to Faro as Gregory Grace—as planned—and begin asking around about why Johnson left and where he went. We'll start analyzing Johnson's personnel records to determine where he has served and might feel comfortable returning to settle. We'll also keep investigating what transportation he may have used."

"There's a flight from Lisbon to Faro in two hours," I said. "I can make it. I'll let both of you know what I learn."

"Do you carry a gun," asked Dawson?

"I haven't been," I answered.

"You will now. Come along to my office and pick up a pistol and a silencer. The gun is plastic; it will pass airport security."

"Don't carry anything with you identifying you as Macduff Brooks," concluded Dawson.

33

FARO, PORTUGAL

MY TAP PORTUGAL AIRLINES FLIGHT WAS TEN minutes late departing Lisbon at the scheduled 8:50 a.m. and five minutes early arriving at Faro. A front was sliding south from the UK, and our pilot announced he was rushing to stay ahead of the bad weather.

Dawson had not only given me a gun and silencer, an un-named lady at the embassy cut my hair short and dyed it salt-and-pepper, cut off my moustache, and gave me aviator sun-glasses, khaki pants, a khaki shirt, and a khaki baseball cap that said "Picos de Europa" on the front. She waited until I put them all on.

If Olviedo also was on the plane, he wouldn't recognize me as the well-dressed person who stood next to him the pre-vious night, looking at the store window display. But I boarded with the first-class and looked carefully at each new passenger; no one even closely resembled Olviedo.

My assumption proved correct. Two minutes before I set my cell phone on airplane mode, Dawson called and said Olviedo had taken a 7:30 a.m. flight and was already in Faro. He had checked in at the luxury hotel Casa de Estoi. Dawson made a reservation for me at a budget hotel where he assumed I would not run into Olviedo. I would be careful where I ate so our paths didn't cross.

Our intelligence did not tell us if Olviedo knew Johnson's Faro address. We assumed Johnson didn't tell many people where he lived.

After checking in, I took a cab to within a block of Johnson's vacated temporary accommodation in the Olhão area about four miles east of Faro, close to the railway station, and started showing his photograph in restaurants within a four-five block radius.

There were numerous small restaurants near his lodging, and I started with the Santos & Machados, and then tried several others, but no one recognized him. Finally, at the fourth—the O Aquário—it was a different matter. According to the manager, Johnson ate there often. The manager said he was in at least four times a week but hadn't seen him for several days, perhaps as much as a week. He said Johnson seemed dejected recently and mentioned to his favorite waitress that he was planning to move.

In mid-afternoon I called Dawson at the embassy in Lisbon and reported my findings. One of Dawson's men had taken Johnson's photograph to the Lisbon train station ticket office. A woman at a ticket window thought Johnson might have bought a first-class ticket to Rome by way of Madrid.

With access to his foreign account from anywhere in Europe, Johnson could remain undetected for years, scheming about how to extract further money from Guatemala for the information he possessed.

Johnson's worries had to include being caught either by the CIA or by Herzog's men. Or even having one of the other CIA agents present at my conversion tell Herzog what he wanted to know, thus rendering Johnson's knowledge superfluous and without any bargaining value.

With Johnson gone from Faro and headed for Rome, we had to come up with a plan B. That evening back in Lisbon, Ambassador Delgado, Dawson, and I again met, this time at the ambassador's residence.

"What's next?" I asked to start our discussion.

"Anything is a gamble," Dawson said. "We need to try to think like Johnson. Where would he settle down next? Either somewhere in or near Rome, or, if he were only using Rome as a decoy, *anywhere* else."

"There are a thousand variations," commented Delgado.

"I have an idea," I said. "You two must have access to Johnson's official personal file. And hopefully to records of his bank and investment accounts, car rentals, trains and flights, and maybe even where he ate at restaurants when abroad. If we know that, can't we make a reasonable assumption of where he might head next? Specifically, if it appears to be to Italy."

"He probably wants to settle down," speculated Delgado. "But this time with a different name."

"Let me take this on," offered Dawson, adding, "Please help, we need to work fast. I'll get started immediately. Let's meet again early tomorrow."

34

THE SAME DAY

O N ANOTHER STREET IN LISBON, AT HIS HOME as Portugal's ambassador from Guatemala, Jorge Herzog sat in his library and called Alejandro Olviedo in Faro.

"Don't be so upset, Alejandro," said the ambassador, "Ralph Johnson has eluded us, but not for long. Come back to Lisbon."

"Why do you believe that, Ambassador Herzog? He has gone and left nothing to help us learn where he is headed."

"Alejandro, where would *you* go and live if you were being chased?"

"Somewhere I am familiar with."

"Where might that be?"

"I served at our Guatemalan embassy in London. I came to most enjoy a little town on the coast of Cornwall called Mevagissey. I have always thought I could live there the rest of my life, far from the problems one faces with crime in Guatemala or even London. . . . Assume I have decided that and I'm contented and settled in a small apartment or house using a different name. How would someone find me?"

"Have you left a trail from Guatemala to Cornwall?"

"Everyone leaves a trail. But the obstacles confronted in locating that trail vary."

"If I talked to your friends in Guatemala—neighbors and co-workers—might one or more tell me how much you admired Mevagissey?"

"Yes."

"Could I find out whether you ever revisited that town?"

"Maybe. There should be records in my personal file at the ministry in Guatemala that show I was granted leave and where I spent that time."

"Might that be at Mevagissey?"

"My records would show that, yes."

"What if my investigations disclosed that some years ago you had bought a small vacation house on the coast of Cornwall outside Mevagissey?"

"I know where you're going with this," said Olviedo.

"What do we know about where Johnson might go to live?"

"He was once assigned to Rome."

"And logically he might have gone from here in Portugal to Rome and rented a car to go to his version of Mevagissey?"

"I'll get started immediately looking at what we know about Johnson. It's quite a lot. Coronel Alarcon obtained a copy of Johnson's CIA file."

"Let's talk again early tomorrow when you've arrived back here," said the Ambassador.

35

THE FOLLOWING DAY

TWO MEETINGS OCCURRED THE FOLLOWING day. One was at the Guatemalan embassy in Lisbon. The other was a few blocks away at the U.S. embassy.

At the U.S. embassy I met with CIA mission head Dawson. Our ambassador had been called to Washington and was unable to be with us.

"Gregory," said Dawson, avoiding referring to me as Macduff, "I believe I know where Johnson has gone. I was awake most of the night. It paid off."

"Tell me where and why."

"In my view, Johnson has gone to Italy."

"Rome?"

"No."

"Where?" I asked.

"Barberino Val d'Elsa."

"Where is that?"

"In Chianti, between Florence and Sienna, on a ridge that discloses its early days where the concern of its citizens was on its defense. In a sense, the same way Johnson may intend to use it. It has few tourists and only an occasional one from the U.S. It's quite out-of-the-way."

"There must be dozens of small towns in Tuscany and other areas of Italy. Why this Barberino?"

"I looked at Johnson's CIA personal file," said Dawson. "He's served in Italy. Four subsequent letters request transfer back there from later assignments. I called the embassy and our mission in Rome. They investigated. *Johnson* is using a real estate agent and bank in Sienna, not far from Barberino. Last week he signed a contract to buy an apartment in the old walled city. He apparently used an assumed name for his travel, but not for purchasing the property.

"I did some further checking. He applied to a D.C. bank for a mortgage on the Italian property, but they referred him to the bank in Sienna. The current owner of the apartment—an Italian—also sold Johnson his old car. It's already been registered under Johnson's proper name.

"Travel records when Johnson was an agent with us show three vacation trips to Rome in his last decade of work. We don't know whether he went to Barberino. We're checking, looking at anything in his record that points to that hilltown."

"Is that enough for me to go to Barberino as soon as I can?" I asked.

"Sooner. Leave today. Keep using the Gregory Grace name. Rent a car at the Rome airport. Be careful where you stay. . . . Would Johnson recognize you?"

"Not if I look as I do right now. I'll stay in one of the surrounding villages, not in Barberino."

At the very same time, Olviedo was meeting not far away in Lisbon with the Guatemalan ambassador to Portugal.

"Did your idea about finding Johnson lead to any location?" Olviedo asked.

"Yes. We had help from one of *our* security people who works at the State Department in D.C. She went online to Johnson's records. They referenced an Italian hill town Johnson had visited several times. When he was serving with the CIA at its mission in Guatemala, he requested to be transferred to Italy.

"We also saw Johnson's most recent medical records in D.C., less than two years old. He specifically asked the doctor if he needed any shots because he was soon going to go to the southern coast of Portugal for a brief time and then to a small village in Tuscany.

"Our agents in Italy took it from there and talked to several attorneys in Tuscany, located in Florence, Luca, and Sienna. We struck gold. Johnson talked with one attorney in Sienna who is currently preparing property transfer documents for an apartment in a small town called Barberino Val de something. The purchaser is Ralph Johnson!"

"I should be in this Barberino," said Olviedo.

"Go! Immediately!" ordered the ambassador.

36

BARBERINO VAL D'ELSA

I WAS OVERWHELMED BY THE BEAUTY OF THE Tuscan hill country as I drove north from the Rome airport to Barberino Val d'Elsa. I had reserved a room in Panicale a few miles away. The attractive and talkative receptionist, with variations of black from hair to toenails, had a nametag that said: Giovanna. She told me that no one named Olviedo was staying there or had a reservation.

The Agency in D.C. had sent ahead to me a file with some useful information, especially the address of the apartment Johnson was buying in the old town. Apparently, the apartment was empty but needed work, and Johnson couldn't leave more than a few boxes for at least two weeks. He had taken a room at a nearby lodging.

My plan was unclear. If I encountered Johnson what would I do? Pretend to be Gregory Grace and not mention the name Macduff Brooks?

What if Johnson recognized me despite my disguise? Would I plead with him not to again give out the information Herzog sought? What if he said the information would go to the highest bidder? Or that he would immediately call Herzog in Guatemala, give him the information, and plead with Herzog to leave him alone?

If Johnson didn't recognize me, on the other hand, he might ask what interest Gregory Grace had asking questions about a person who the CIA sheltered with a new name and location. If he didn't care who I was, I'm sure he would insist on dealing with cash.

I could have called Dan Wilson in D.C. and told him I've learned exactly where Johnson is soon to be living. What then? Would Dan fly to Italy to negotiate? Or perhaps to end the threat by taking Johnson's life? What if Dan suggested that I eliminate Johnson? I don't have the same ill feeling towards him that I did towards Isfahani. But I should; I feel more directly threatened by Johnson than I was by Isfahani.

In the evening I walked through the old town and dined at one of the terrace restaurants. But my mind was so focused on Johnson that a half-hour after finishing I couldn't remember what I had eaten except Tiramisu for dessert.

It was a short walk from the restaurant to the apartment Johnson was buying, which covered the upper two floors and from a rooftop terrace allegedly had a panoramic view of the valley and distant hills.

I stood across from the front door to the stone building, wondering how to enter, and was about to leave when the front door to a hallway opened and a young couple stepped out. They must live in the ground floor apartment. Before the door closed and locked behind them, I slipped in and stood motionless in the dimly lighted hall.

Urged by the consequences of having finished an entire bottle of wine at dinner, I carefully proceeded up the stairs two flights to Johnson's floor, which, as I reached the top step, became suddenly flooded with light. I froze but nothing happened. My presence must have been detected by a sensor.

A nameplate had recently been removed from beside the apartment door that I assumed was Johnson's. Leaning against the door frame listening for several minutes, I could hear nothing from inside and placed my hand on the door knob. I half-hoped the door would be locked, but it was not and as I turned the knob, the door swung into the room, exposing piles of boxes with "Ralph Johnson" written on each box. One had been opened, and a pile of books was on the floor beside the box. I had come to the right apartment.

There was no reason to remain and good reasons to leave. I wasn't prepared to confront Johnson yet, and stepped back into the hall, closed the door, and carefully descended to the ground floor. As I opened the outer door, dusk was settling on the town, and the sun was merging with the horizon. Not a soul was in sight, prompting me to leave and pull the door closed tightly behind me.

Back at the restaurant I ordered another bottle of wine and another Tiramisu. An hour later I was in my room where I sent a message to Dan Wilson and went to bed. Sleep did not come quickly.

When I rose in the morning, I had not heard from Dan and had no clear idea about what to do.

37

THE NEXT MORNING

ALEJANDRO OLVIEDO ARRIVED IN BARBERINO the same time I was walking back to my hotel. He stayed at a small lodging within the walls of the old town, only three blocks from Johnson's apartment.

After breakfast the next morning, Olviedo returned to his room, checked his cell phone for messages and, finding none, decided how he would proceed.

He called a local real estate agent about the availability of apartments in the old town, and, looking at a list, calmly stated, "I have a friend who is buying an apartment here. Maybe you know him; his name is Ralph Johnson."

"I don't know him," the agent said. "But an agent friend of mine has a client from the U.S. in the process of moving into a place in the old town that I also had listed. I thought she said his name was Jensen. I'll give you his address."

"Thanks. I'll look at the listings you've given me and stop back about three this afternoon."

"I'll be here. I hope you find your friend."

Olviedo went back to his room, added a silencer to his pistol, placed it in his briefcase, and left, heading toward the apartment.

At the same time Johnson was on his way to his apartment to open more boxes. He felt comfortable in Barberino and thought, "No one will ever find me here; I will take Italian lessons and spend the remainder of my life enjoying this town.

"And I will write my memoirs and disclose the true, full story of Macduff Brooks."

38

THE FOLLOWING DAY

I SPENT THE MORNING TRYING TO DECIDE HOW to approach Johnson, finally concluding that after breakfast on the terrace I would walk to his apartment in the old town and hope he was there and would reason with me. But why would he do that? He has the prospect of doubling the millions he already received. Or die trying. My life was inconsequential to him. Foolishly, I left my gun locked in a suitcase in my room, holding false hope that reason would prevail over violence.

It was a sparkling morning of fragrant country air unblemished by pollution. Walking through the ancient, high-arched entrance to the old town, each step on the worn stones echoed throughout the street. Pilgrims and merchants in the 14th century had passed through this very same high Florentine gate.

A light drizzle coated the street's stones with a shine, but the rain ended by the time I reached the terrace for breakfast and watched the morning sun throw shadows across the spacious outside dining area.

My mind was on Johnson and not breakfast. I had no thought of what the morning would bring. The front door of the house I visited uninvited the evening before was easily opened; someone had placed a newspaper in the door to prevent it from locking. The entry hall was quiet, a note written only fifteen minutes before and taped to the ground floor door said the occupant would be back in an hour to meet a painter.

Ascending the stairs carefully to avoid making noise that Johnson might hear and bring him to the hall, I found his door ajar and chose to knock lightly rather than call out. No answer came, and I repeated my knock a bit louder. Still no response. I placed my head at the door and called, "Hello, Ralph Johnson?" The silence remained unbroken by any noise from inside the apartment, and with a slight push, the door opened a few inches.

On the floor a motionless arm extended from behind the sofa. Another louder call brought similar silence, and another push opened the door enough for me to step inside. Using the back of my hand, the door closed easily.

Two bodies lay on the floor. One was Olviedo, whom I had last seen a few nights before in Lisbon. From a single hole in his forehead blood no longer flowed. He was on his back with a hint of disbelief on his face. There was no sign of a weapon anywhere near his lifeless body.

Ralph Johnson was the other person; he lay on his side with his right hand holding a small pistol with a silencer. A slight trickle of blood flowed from a hole between his eyes and from another larger hole on the back of his head that must have been an exit wound. My first reaction would later prove to duplicate the conclusion of the local police: Johnson had shot and killed Olviedo and then taken his own life with the same pistol. As Johnson had wished, he did spend the remainder of his life in Barberino.

I avoided touching either body or leaving a footprint in the blood that hadn't soaked into the slickened tiled floor. I wanted to leave quickly but first took a towel from the tiny kitchen and wiped whatever I remembered I had touched on both my visits.

Stuffing the towel into my pocket, I noticed a paper on the table. The writing was unsteady and hurried. It was addressed "to anyone." Leaning over the table, I read it with disbelief. The note explained what had happened. A pencil lay on the single sheet that fluttered slightly in a morning breeze from an open window.

Without touching the paper, I read it once more and left it on the table, slipped out the door and down the stairs, left the building, and returned to my lodging.

The phone beside Dan Wilson's bed rang an hour later, 4:00 a.m. D.C. time.

"What on earth are you doing calling me at this hour."

"I have news. Ralph Johnson is dead; I believe he took his own life after killing Olviedo. Johnson left a suicide note. It was strange. Without touching anything, I left the note on the kitchen table where I found it. The note explained that Olviedo had been searching for Johnson with what Johnson believed was a murderous intention. It further spoke of two matters.

"One sentence contained words of apology for letting down his former colleagues and the Agency. But the more important portion identified the information Herzog had long sought. It said that Professor Maxwell Hunt had entered a protection program, assumed a new name, moved to a new location, and started a new career. Dan, you and I know that all Herzog previously learned was that former Professor Hunt was now doing something that involved 'fish.'

"I know you believe that Johnson gave the correct information about me to Coronel Carlos Alarcon in exchange for the millions of dollars paid into a foreign numbered account. But that information died with Alarcon when he was shot and killed by Herzog. Now Johnson has done something very different, apparently realizing that he would never get more money from Herzog. Even though he had killed Olviedo, his own life was as good as over. Herzog would never let him live, and he had run out of hiding places.

"Johnson's suicide note made no mention of a Macduff Brooks who moved to Mill Creek in Paradise Valley in Montana and became a fly fishing guide. What the note stated was that the CIA had changed the name Professor Maxwell Hunt to Walter Windsor and that Windsor had settled in Alaska intending to work in commercial fishing. Johnson gave no specific address in Alaska. Last, Johnson stated that Windsor had explained in Washington when he was given the name Walter Windsor that he would adopt a third, different name when he moved to Alaska.

"Johnson's intentions seem apparent," I told Dan. "He wanted his incorrect and deceptive information to find its way to President Herzog in Guatemala to correct—as best as he could—some of the damage he had caused. I intentionally left the suicide note on the table where the police would find it."

"I will see that the information reaches Herzog," said Dan.

39

TWO DAYS AFTER THE DEATHS

RALPH JOHNSON'S SUICIDE NOTE TOOK A FEW days for me to absorb. It was a gift from the gods.

For two more days I remained in Barberino to listen and learn what the police believed happened. Because Johnson was American and Olviedo was Guatemalan, the Italian authorities were principally concerned with the impact of the murder and suicide on tourism.

I admitted to a feeling of relief, but the pressures of the past months had been so great that I tried to shift my focus more to the Barberino restaurants and comforting scenery than to the murder and suicide. To be truthful, neither Olviedo's nor Johnson's death would be a loss to their country.

Olviedo was not a likeable fellow, and if the U.S. is truly going to help Guatemala develop, it would not be when an Olviedo or an Alarcon was in a leadership position. Nor because people like Herzog were elected the country's president.

Johnson was a traitor to his country. He was present at my secret meeting at Langley that determined my future. He used that information solely to enrich himself; he had no quarrel with me. When he first gave that information to Alarcon, he started down a path to hell and apparently was prepared to stay on that path when he was approached by Olviedo. What made him change his mind? I will go to my grave contemplating that.

If Dan Wilson had asked me to take out either Olviedo or Johnson, I would have agreed. I'm not a professional assassin unless it involves self-defense. I like to know a great deal about my target and when I have the slightest doubt, I decline agreeing to be involved. Olviedo and Johnson had earned the right to be targets. Both wanted me dead.

I wasn't excited about leaving this Italian paradise hilltop that was as beautiful as my Montana Paradise Valley.

Beginning to pack, I realized I owed Dan a call before I left Barberino. It was cocktail time in D.C. when I called, and I expected him to be in a good mood after a day at the office.

"Mac, please come directly to D.C. so we can discuss how to deal with Herzog in view of Johnson's suicide note."

"Let's meet five days from now."

"Five days! Why so long to get to D.C. from Italy?"

"My cheapest flight is through Glascow to D.C. in five days. It's a better deal than a direct flight from here."

"*Better deal?* The cost has never bothered you. You fly business or first class and we pay for it. Also, I'm looking at the fares; it's not cheaper from Glascow. What are you up to?"

"I have a package deal."

"Package? What the hell are you talking about?"

"My rate includes hotels."

"You don't need a hotel on a direct flight to D.C. You board the plane in Rome early in the morning and arrive here in D.C. in late afternoon."

"But my flight includes four nights at an historic hotel north of Aberdeen and three days with my own *ghillie.*"

"What are you doing, and what's a *ghillie?*"

"A *ghillie* is a fishing guide. There's a great run of trout right now on some of the Scottish highland rivers. I earned that!"

"Macduff, last night I was thinking that all I've done for you and Lucinda has been worth it. But now I have doubts again. How do I explain this here at the Agency?"

"I'll be working, keeping an eye out for Ellsworth-Kent. After all, he was a Brit who spent a lot of time in Scotland."

"He was on the *Orkney* Islands, miles north of Aberdeen. And he doesn't fish!"

"I'll check that out."

"This makes me want to get Lucinda back even more. She kept you in line in a way I can't."

"Just think how much better a guide I'll be in Montana when talking with a client I can compare fishing in Scotland with fishing in Montana."

"I wish Johnson had written down accurate information to give Olviedo. I'd be rid of you by now."

"Have an extra martini," I suggested. "I'll see you next week.

That evening Dan had three martinis.

40

A WEEK LATER IN D.C.

D AN WAS SO PLEASED BY THE DECEPTION THE suicide note produced that he met my plane at Dulles.

"Good flight?" he asked.

"The usual. Dirty nonfunctioning restrooms. Horrible air quality. OK food. . . . And that was business class."

"Good weather?"

"Beautiful every day. Unusual for Scotland."

"Good fishing in Scotland?"

"I didn't go."

"Why not?"

"Lucinda."

"Lucinda?"

"I was on the River Don starting to cast for a wild brown trout forty feet away when I realized I couldn't be there alone, enjoying what Lucinda did with me so often. I apologized to my *ghille*, paid him for the planned three days and then some, and went to the airport."

"That would have put you here three days ago."

"I flew to Kirkwall on the Orkney Islands direct from Aberdeen."

"Looking for Ellsworth-Kent?"

"I guess. Mainly I wanted to be where I knew Lucinda was after she was abducted. Kirkwall allegedly is where she was made a high priestess."

"How did you spend your time?"

"First looking at public records. Nothing of interest was there. Then I learned there was to be a Wiccan marriage ceremony."

"And you went?"

"Yes. Actually it was interesting and very spiritual. Not a ceremony that might be a shock to a Christian."

"How did it differ?"

"Worship of Pagan gods. And goddesses."

"Is Lucinda a goddess?" Dan inquired.

"No, but a Pagan authority told me that a high priestess embodies the promise or charge of the Star Goddess. The charge is an inspirational text, recited in rituals by the high priestess."

"That would be Lucinda."

"Yes, but as Onomaris."

"In a marriage ceremony, such as that between Lucinda and Ellsworth-Kent, is the bride drugged?" Dan asked.

"No. I know where you're headed."

"She could have been under some continuing influence of drugs taken over time."

"Yes."

"What was the marriage ceremony you went to like?"

"It was held outside at the Ring of Brodgar, a 5,000-year-old stone circle near Stenness not far from Kirkwall. The reception was nearby at Skara Brae, a site older than Stonehenge and the pyramids at Giza."

"Anything shock you?"

"Not really. The couple was married barefoot, an old Celtic wedding tradition to connect the parties with mother earth. They followed the tradition of handfasting—grasping each other's hands that are lightly tied together with a red cord. They also jumped the broomstick together—a leap of faith to celebrate their coming life together. There's a lot of freedom in what they do, making or not making any reference to a deity."

"Anything like exchanging rings?"

"Sometimes. That's an old Roman tradition."

"Is this all legal? Do they have to have a civil ceremony at some office?"

"Not needed. A couple of formalities are required—a declaration by each in the presence of the other that each takes the other in marriage, and a declaration by the celebrant that the couple are husband and wife."

"Sounds like a modern, typical Christian marriage."

"Yes, but remember the Bible prohibits Pagan worship, which is contrary to Christian monotheism."

"Did they serve you Gentleman Jack? It sounds as though you're still under its influence."

"No. They're not into Tennessee sipping whiskey, but the single malt flowed like an incoming North Sea tide. And the food was delicious. Marvelous seafood—clams, lobster, and smoots. Also beef, even buffalo burgers that made me feel at home, at least in Montana. And we drank from a cog and didn't forget to leave fried honeycakes in the garden for the Faeries."

"Cogs and smoots?"

"A cog is a large wooden drinking vessel filled with a heated mix of home brew, spices, and spirits. It's passed around to guests by the bride and groom. Needless to say it's strong and to be sipped. A smoot's easier to explain. It's razorfish."

"So you drank a lot of single malt and sang old Scottish songs?"

"Until I realized that I was at a ceremony that Lucinda allegedly went through with Ellsworth-Kent. Emotion or too many cogs got to me. I don't remember going back to my hotel at Kirkwall. That was only two days ago."

"I'm taking you to your hotel, and I'll be back at seven for dinner. No smoots. No cog."

Dinner was at Dan's club where we sat at a small table and looked out at Farragut Square. I had my first Gentleman Jack in two weeks.

"Macduff, you look tired. Time zone changes?"

"Some. Mostly too much stress before I was physically ready after being hit by the van."

"Are you up to talking about our expectations after Johnson's suicide note?"

"Yes. Are you pleased by what he did?" I asked.

"We have to be. We've bought what may be a lot of time. You're only going to live naturally so long. I want you to die quietly in your sleep."

"Thanks. Will Herzog accept Johnson's information?"

"He has to pay attention," Dan suggested. "Otherwise he has to start again and try to find out the names of the remaining people at your meeting."

"It's easier for him to check out Johnson's information than start again," I said.

"Yes. Do you think Herzog will conclude that Johnson was lying to throw Herzog off track?" Dan asked.

"No," I answered. "For now he'll accept that Johnson was telling the truth. Why do you think Johnson lied?"

"Maybe he didn't want to die with blood on his hands. Some of it *yours*. Maybe he was angry at how forceful Herzog was in trying to meet with him, sending first Alarcon and then Olviedo to find you. Maybe he wasn't himself. Drinking, drugs, scared. . . ."

"I don't think Herzog's gotten over comprehending what it meant when he shot and killed Alarcon and then learned Alarcon had obtained all the information Herzog asked for," I commented. "It was a steep price to pay for sleeping with Alarcon's wife, Dolores."

"Do you believe Herzog thought Olviedo would be successful?" Dan asked.

"Olviedo carried a silenced pistol; he was prepared for Johnson refusing to give him the information."

"But couldn't Johnson have told Olviedo the truth and saved his own life?" Dan asked. "He could have gone somewhere else under a new name. Our information suggests Johnson had over $3 million left from Alarcon's original transfer of funds."

"Johnson thought Olviedo had two jobs to do," I said. "One was to get the most information he could. The other was to kill Johnson, who was of no further use to Herzog. If Johnson lied to Olviedo, he would be killed as soon as Herzog realized he had lied. If Johnson didn't lie and repeated what he had told Alarcon, he was a possible witness if the matter ever ended up in the courts. I suspect Herzog would plan to have Johnson killed, if Olviedo didn't do it in Italy."

"What about the view that Johnson was trying to right his wrong?" asked Dan.

"If he did kill himself but got the false information to Herzog, he might have righted his earlier wrong telling Alarcon," I suggested. "But he would also be signing his own death warrant, even though the death part might not occur for months. Or maybe years. It could be a long time before Herzog realized he'd been duped. I'm sure that when Johnson began to write his suicide note he knew that when he finished he had to take his own life. . . . So where do we go from here?" I asked.

"You go home. I stay here in Washington. We forget Herzog for the moment."

"Easier said than done," I responded. "I know I have nightmares waiting for me to go to bed. Herzog nightmares. Ellsworth-Kent nightmares. Granted, Herzog now moves to the back burner. That leaves Ellsworth-Kent. I want him more than Herzog wants me."

"I hope you use better judgment in dealing with Ellsworth-Kent than Herzog has used with you."

"I'm tired," I admitted. "I always seem to feel that way after talking with you. Talking with you *in person* compounds my exhaustion. Don't call me for a week or two."

"Don't count on it."

41

BACK IN ST. AUGUSTINE A FEW DAYS LATER

AMONG THE JUNK THAT FILLED MY MAILBOX and awaited my return was one letter I had to open first when I walked into the cottage and dumped the pile of mail on the kitchen table. The envelope was postmarked Kirkwall, Scotland, and dated three days earlier. I thought the hotel was sending me a receipt for my stay. . . . Strangely, there was no return address on the envelope.

Inside was a single folded sheet of paper. I opened it and saw a large photo of a tattoo on skin. Whether it was a back, shoulder, cheek, or most anywhere else, the tattoo was a circle and an endless line that made a triangle and represented the journey of love, a place of no beginning and no end. I went on line and looked up Wiccan tattoos, remembering seeing the Wiccan symbol on several people at Kirkwall. The tattoo proved to be the commonly used triquetra, representing the past, present, and future. Christian use suggests it represents the Father, Son, and Holy Spirit and in Paganism it's the Mother, the Maiden, and the Crone or Hag approaching death. It is the triple goddess of Pagan ritual.

The paper was blank except for one statement: "I wear this as a symbol of my respect for all women." It was unsigned, but I knew the handwriting was Lucinda's!

The cottage door opened and in came Elsbeth with the grin that reminded me of Lucinda's.

"Dad, what's the drawing on that paper?'

"It's a photo, not a drawing. It's called a triquetra. This one is a tattoo."

"Are you getting a tattoo?"

"Look at the photo. It's a tattoo already on somebody's skin. Supposedly, that somebody is Lucinda. She sent it to me with this statement," I said, handing her the paper.

Elsbeth took the paper, read the statement, set down the paper, and sat down at the table looking very different from when she had come in moments ago.

"Where have you been, Dad?" Elsbeth said, regaining her composure. "We had Christmas together, and you went off the next day to Hope Town. You were gone for nearly two weeks. I tried to call you near the end of your week in the Bahamas and Grace answered. She said you weren't there but couldn't say where you were. I assumed you'd left for Portugal."

"That's right. But let's set one thing straight. I was *not* with Grace Justice. Even for the first three nights before I left. I didn't know until now talking to you that she used the cottage at Hope Town. When I knew I would be away for part of the week I had rented and paid for, I called her and offered her the time in Hope Town when I wouldn't be there. I'm glad she accepted; I haven't seen or talked to her since I've been back."

"When did you arrive back here?"

"Last night."

"Big deal! You've been back a few hours and you haven't talked to or seen Grace. Where else other than Portugal did you go? . . . And why Portugal?"

"After Portugal I went to Italy. And then a few days later I finished my trip in Great Britain."

"Finished! Who did you kill?"

"No one. I didn't need to."

"Were you looking for Herzog or one of his henchmen?"

"Mostly."

"Stop using fuzzy words. *Mostly* doesn't tell me anything."

"You know about Ralph Johnson?" I asked.

"Enough from you and Dan to believe Johnson was a former CIA agent who gave information about you to Carlos Alarcon, one of Herzog's advisors. I checked on Alarcon. He was shot and killed. Who did that?"

"Herzog shot him a few minutes before Alarcon was going to tell him my name, our address, and what I do. Alarcon paid Johnson $4 million for the information. But with Alarcon dead, Herzog had to try another tack. I suspect he wanted to find Johnson and get the information he'd paid for."

"And Johnson was hiding in Portugal?"

"Yes, in Faro."

"How was Herzog going to get to Johnson?"

"Using an aide named Olviedo. He arrived in Faro about when I did. He was probably sent to kill Johnson, after getting him to repeat the information."

"And to kill him if he refused to repeat it?"

"Of course."

"You found Johnson?"

"Yes, in Italy."

"Before you found Olviedo?"

"I located Johnson's apartment in a small Tuscan hilltown. Olviedo had gotten there before me."

"Had Olviedo killed Johnson?"

"No. Johnson killed Olviedo."

"And?"

"Johnson then killed himself."

"Taking the information to his grave," she asked.

"Taking the *correct* information to his grave. But leaving a suicide note with misinformation."

"Meaning what?"

"He said Professor Hunt's new name was Walter Windsor, he was living in Alaska, and he was involved in commercial fishing."

"Why did Johnson lie?"

"Dan and I talked about it. We don't know, but we think it has thrown Herzog off the real trail for some time. Johnson will never know how much he helped."

"You never used your gun?"

"That's right."

"Did you carry it to Johnson's?"

"No."

"You forgot!"

"I won't answer that."

"After Italy, you went where?"

"To Britain. I was tired. I thought I might do some trout fishing in Scotland."

"Did you catch anything?"

"No."

"That's often the case with you."

I didn't tell her about Kirkwall and the wedding ceremony I attended. She would learn about it in time.

"You said you talked to Dan yesterday. Did he have any new information about Lucinda?"

"No. We mainly talked about the tattoo."

"What did Dan think about it?"

"He didn't have any more to say than I did. I think he thought it was incidental as long as it was out of sight, like on her back or rear."

"Doesn't it tell us Lucinda is at least alive?"

"Maybe. We don't know the tattoo is actually on *Lucinda*."

"But she wrote the note. It's only a few days old."

"Yes. My only hope is that she's being forced to do what Ellsworth-Kent wants. I still believe drugs have been involved. They will kill her if she keeps using them; it's close to the first anniversary of her abduction."

"Dad, I think Lucinda's first letter last spring and this one a week ago were meant by her to show us one thing—that she's alive. What sense would it make for Ellsworth-Kent to suggest she send them? It would only make us try harder to locate the two."

"Any suggestions about *how* we try harder?"

"You take a rest and let Sue and me work on it. After all, it may be a 'girl thing.'"

"Where will you start?"

"I want to go to a place called Kirkwall. It's the main city in the Ork …"

"I was there last week."

"I thought you were fishing."

"For about five minutes; then I went to Kirkwall. If you can stay a little more, I'll tell you what I saw."

"Talk. And don't leave anything out."

I tried not to. Sometimes she scares me.

42

SPRING IN THE ORKNEY ISLANDS

ELSBETH AND SUE BEGAN THEIR TRIP TO THE Orkneys the first day of Spring Break. They didn't tell me anything about their plans except they would be staying at the Albert Hotel in downtown Kirkwall near the water. They rented a car so they could visit Maes Howe and the Standing Stones of Stenness, both about ten miles from town.

With the two was a stack of handouts that included a photo of Lucinda, a sheet of paper describing Ellsworth-Kent's history—jail time in England on the Isle of Wight and the five wicker man and mistletoe murders—and a copy of the sheet with the tattoo.

Elsbeth and Sue hadn't been gone for twenty-four hours when two matters arose for me in Florida. One was responding to social demands of Grace Justice; the other was responding to the anger of Celeste Ransome. Grace left a message that she wanted me to have dinner at her condo. Celeste Ransome left a message that she wanted to talk to me about what I had told her at our interview.

I thought about my time before I arrived in Montana. I could answer Celeste easier than I could answer Grace and called the *Bozeman Magazine* number and asked for Celeste.

"Macduff, did you read the article?"

"No. I don't like reading about myself."

"You lied to me when you answered my questions," she said. "I didn't appreciate that."

The article had been published several months ago, and I assumed that was the end of that. Apparently, I was wrong.

"My article was ten percent about your time since you arrived in Montana and ninety percent about your forty-some years before that arrival. I have no quarrel with the ten percent, but I'm livid about the rest. Your answers were mostly lies."

"Such as?" I asked quietly.

"There was *no one* named William Brooks who worked with the Foreign Service or CIA. I don't know what your dad did, but he didn't work with either."

"He used different names—that's common at the CIA."

"There was *no crash* of a plane in the Caribbean that allegedly killed your parents."

"They were probably flying when Dad used one of his aliases. Did you check everyone who was lost?"

"*No one* was lost. There were no reported crashes during that time."

"It was a private flight; I recall about twelve people were on the plane."

"You're *not listed* as working for the State Department for twenty years. Not for even one year. In fact, *no one* with your name *ever* worked for State."

"That's good to know. I did some things that made some powerful people in several countries declare they were coming after me. I guess they couldn't get past the State Department's records and gave up. You should also."

"I checked with every law school in D.C. *Not one* had a Macduff Brooks as a student."

"They couldn't tell you if they did. It's protected information, like students' grades and discipline issues. I suspect they told you what they did to get rid of you."

Most of my responses to her accusations were true, but a few bent the truth more than at the original interview. She wasn't in a very good position to be critical. Writing another article about her opinions regarding my answers would show she didn't check facts *before* publishing the first article, and many of her readers might side with me—pleased to see a journalist taken down a notch. Also, some would suggest the role of the *Bozeman Magazine* was not to undertake investigative reporting.

"Are you satisfied now, Celeste? I'm sorry you feel this way."

"When are you going to be out here in Montana?"

"In a couple of weeks, three at the most."

"You owe me. You're taking me to dinner."

"I'd be delighted," I answered, recalling how attractive she looked with a neckline that deepened with each half-hour of our interview.

"I'll call you when I arrive," I promised. "You have my number and you should call me if you think I'm putting you off. You can be certain I'll call if you promise to wear the outfit you wore for the interview when we meet again."

"I. . . . I'll wear it," she stuttered, and hung up.

I poured a Gentleman Jack—it was a few minutes after five—walked down to the pier, sat in a chair on the dock, and called Grace Justice.

"Elsbeth told me you made it to Hope Town and stayed three nights," Grace said without even saying hello. "I missed you," she added. "It would have been better with you. But thanks for letting me have it for the three days."

"You had your friend Reginald Covington *the Third* to take care of you," I reminded her.

"I saw him once. I don't think he saw me. He was in a bar lounge with a distinguished looking English guy, at least that's what it sounded like when the guy spoke.

"While we were there, a photographer came by and took pictures of people at each table. My picture shows I was alone. I'll show it to you so you'll know I behaved. The photographer also took one of Covington and his friend together talking, but the English guy went ballistic when he saw the photographer and quickly left. Covington looked dismayed but remained and finished his dinner, had coffee, and walked out as though nothing had happened. . . . I took a bunch of pictures with my cell phone. I'll bring them when you come to dinner."

"Dinner?"

"Tonight. I'll be by to get you at seven. You have two hours to finish your drink and get dressed. Be casual. I'm driving you back here to the Kingfish Grill near my condo. You can bring your car if you wish. We can sit outside overlooking the yacht harbor."

She arrived ten minutes early wearing designer jeans that emphasized her trim body, and a conservative pale-blue man's shirt buttoned up to the neck with the cuffs rolled up. She obviously wasn't intending to excite me. But she did.

"You look great. Classic. Enticing," I remarked. "I'm wearing jeans and a man's shirt and no one's staring at *me*."

"Do you want men to stare at you?"

"That wasn't what I meant."

"What do you want to eat?" she asked when we sat down at a table by the windows in a corner of the restaurant.

"Have we been here before?" I asked.

"I have many times. But never with you. I'll have the mixed seafood grill," Grace said to the waiter as she pulled out a group of photographs from Hope Town.

"Here are my photographs," she said, placing them in front of me.

"The first photos are around the harbor and town. The next one is me sitting alone at the bar lounge table. The waiter took it for me."

"While your companion was in the men's room?"

"I had no companion! After that is Covington. Then his English companion, who had a moustache and carefully maintained full beard."

"He looks a little familiar. OK, let's eat. I don't want to look at Covington and his friends."

Grace put away the photos. The meal was delicious and the view of the harbor entry relaxing as sailboats slowly entered after a day or evening sail.

"I have a surprise for you. I'm taking you for a ride after dinner," Grace announced.

"You drive faster than anyone I know. I'll pass on the ride. Besides, you've had two drinks."

"But I promise not to go faster than ten miles per hour."

"You'll be unable to hold it to that. You only function at full speed or full stop."

"We'll be at full speed."

"I assume you haven't bought an airplane. Even a small, two-seat Cessna flies faster."

"It's not an airplane," she assured me.

After dinner she grabbed my hand and led me along a dock to a section of the yacht harbor where there were mostly sailboats. We stopped in front of one.

"I was on one of these years ago," I commented. "They tip a lot."

"That's called listing, not tipping. . . . This one is quite stable."

"What is it, a frigate?"

"Macduff, I know you served in the Navy and were on destroyers. *They* are called frigates. *This* is a sloop. You've sailed. I'm certain of that."

"OK. I have. But not for two decades. Is this a friend's boat? Is he coming to take us out? It *is* night. I've never sailed in the dark when I can't see. We could hit a buoy. Or go aground."

"There's a full moon. I can see fine. . . . And this is not a *friend's* boat. It's mine. And I know how to sail."

"When did you buy this?"

"A month ago. It was seized in a drug bust we made in Palatka. One of the drug dealers kept it on the St. John's River. He lost it because it was being used to transport drugs from the Bahamas. It was sold at an auction of seized items. Not many buyers showed up, and I was lucky and bought this for a tenth of its value. . . . Get on board."

"Aye, aye, Madame Skipper."

"I like that. Keep saying it."

Grace started the engine. I untied the dock lines, and before I knew it, we were out in St. Augustine Harbor. We sailed around admiring the lighted city at night and then slowly powered into Salt Run near the lighthouse and far enough past the

Conch House docks to avoid the noise from the usual rowdy drinkers staggering along the piers.

"Yell when you want to turn around and go back. I'm ready," I said, trying to remember the special language used by sailors.

"It's called 'coming about.' We are *not* turning around. And we're dropping the anchor. Get up on the foredeck. Unsecure the chain and yell when the anchor hits the bottom. It's not deep here."

"You like giving orders."

"That's right, bosun. I have a lot more to give."

In a matter of minutes, the anchor was set, the sails were stowed, and the skipper gave the next order.

"We need some grog."

"I had one Gentleman Jack at my cottage, two beers at the Kingfish Grill, and you're saying we *need* grog?"

"When you've been out for a hard sail and get back to port, it's traditional to have grog."

"What's in it?"

"Most anything. Usually rum."

"What do you have on board?"

"*Only* rum."

"I'll have rum."

"Go below and pour two glasses," she ordered.

"Okeydoke," I said, avoiding her look as I climbed down the stepladder into a cozy, attractive cabin lined with varnished teak and mahogany. I came back up with the two glasses, and we sat across from each other in the cockpit.

"You like it?" she asked.

"Yeah. Good rum."

"I meant the boat."

"Yeah. Good boat."

"You're so articulate."

"Yeah. Sorry, I meant aye, aye, Madame Skipper."

"That's better."

We sat in the moonlight, slowly sipping our grog. I had no idea what was next.

"How did I get here?" I asked.

"You were shanghaied."

"I was tricked and intimidated."

"That's how it's done."

"Am I also to be keel hauled?" I said, remembering the practice I had read about during my years in the Navy.

"I haven't decided."

"Are we going to be here all night?" I asked as the last of the rum was consumed.

"That's what happens when you're shanghaied."

"I saw only one bed below."

"There's another forward. But it's stuffed with sails."

"More tricks and intimidations?"

"Let's go below and see."

43

THE FOLLOWING DAY

WE MADE IT BACK TO THE DOCK THE NEXT morning in time for Grace to dress more appropriately and be in court when it convened at nine. She left me on board to sleep in, which I did until noon.

Coffee, about the most I could make on the boat, tasted especially good as I sat alone in the cockpit, musing over the events of last evening. When I went below to clean up, I noticed that on the small cabin table Grace had left the photos she showed me at dinner. I looked through them again, paused at the one of her at the lounge, and then turned to the one of Covington and his English companion.

Looking more carefully at the companion, I imagined him without the beard and moustache. I froze. The bitter taste of the coffee I'd consumed surged up to my mouth. Next to Covington was the man who had abducted and allegedly again married Lucinda—Robert Ellsworth-Kent! I looked through all the photos, but there was no sign of Lucinda.

Hundreds of miles from Hope Town I knew no one at Abaco I might call about Covington's British friend. Certainly not Covington himself. The best choice was always Dan Wilson in D.C. Using a special number I got through to him and followed up by sending a poor copy of the photo I took with my phone's camera.

"Dan, do you see the photo? It may not be a good copy."

"It's not clear enough for me to identify people," Dan replied. "I don't know about the guy being Ellsworth-Kent. Try scanning it and sending it again."

"I can't. I'm on a boat."

"You? On a boat? Are you drinking this early?"

"Not a drop. I stayed on a friend's boat last night. She—I mean the owner—has left for the day. I'm going to leave here when we finish. I'll send you the photo in a half-hour."

"Let's assume that it is who you think it is—Ellsworth-Kent. I'll forward the photo to our man in Nassau and send him on a charter plane to Hope Town. Call me when you forward the photo from the cottage, and we'll talk. . . . And give my regards to Grace. I didn't know she had a boat."

I closed the hatch to the cabin, drove off in my car, and reached the cottage in twenty-three minutes, where I scanned the photo, sent it to Dan, and called him again.

"It's another piece of the puzzle," Dan agreed, looking at the better copy. "But it doesn't tell us anything about *Lucinda*. She could have been at Covington's and drugged, or off shopping and content. I need photos of her we can distribute around Hope Town."

"You'll have a two-year-old photo of Lucinda in fifteen minutes," I promised. "By the way, Elsbeth and Sue should have arrived in Kirkwall in the Orkney Islands a few hours ago and already started distributing Lucinda's photo in various places. I'll call Elsbeth and let her know what's happened here."

"Mac, I'm going to assume it *was* Ellsworth-Kent and that he's a friend of Covington. Remember that Covington flew to St. Augustine and back during the airboat murder investigation.

He went to Grace's condo, admitted he had been involved, and taunted her about attempting to arrest him.

"Last spring," Dan continued, "when we were trying to learn where Ellsworth-Kent might have taken Lucinda after the abduction, we discovered that a small, unmarked jet had taken off from a potato farm in Hastings west of St. Augustine and headed southeast toward the Bahamas.

"I don't know what link there might have been between Covington and Ellsworth-Kent, but they're two bad apples, and I'd like to take them both down at the same time," said Dan.

"All that sounds good," I said, "but it doesn't tell us much about Lucinda. Not even whether she's alive. Have you thought about arresting Covington?"

"In the Bahamas? You know better than to ask that."

"I didn't say *in* the Bahamas. Covington could be *brought* to the U.S., the same way Lucinda was taken. I hate to think Lucinda may have been in Hope Town when I was there before leaving for Europe. Say the word—I'll bring you Covington."

"We'll investigate. The photo could be important, Mac. "

"What about the Bahamian government cooperating with you? Covington's a crook and murderer."

"But he's politically powerful, if not untouchable. It's a crap shoot. The only gambling in the Bahamas isn't at Nassau. Let *us* deal with Covington. You keep your focus on Ellsworth-Kent and Lucinda."

"Do you mind if I tell Grace about this conversation?" I asked. "She's repeatedly had trouble with Covington. I think she's at risk dealing with him."

"Tell her. Use your discretion. I'll talk to you soon."

I called Grace. "How was work?"

"A struggle," she said. "It was worth it. I loved last night. Let's go sailing again soon. You're a pretty good crew."

"Yeah, yeah, boss. . . . I liked last night, even though this time *I* was abducted."

"It seemed to me you went without a struggle."

"The struggling came later, down in the cabin. . . . Let's be more serious. Grace, I've spent my day having evil thoughts about Covington and. . . . "

"Covington?" she interrupted. "What's he done?"

"Let me finish my sentence—Covington *and* his English friend Ellsworth-Kent."

"They're close friends?" she asked. "Tell me what's up."

I told her about the photo and my conversation with Dan.

"Have you ever seen a photo of Ellsworth-Kent before?" Grace asked.

"At the time of the wicker man and mistletoe murders, I've never seen Ellsworth-Kent close up, but I have seen enough photos to recognize him," I said. "Covington's companion in the photo is likely Ellsworth-Kent."

"That's incredible. Is Dan helping?" she asked.

"Yes. And he's after Covington," I responded. "Putting pressure on him may lead us to Ellsworth-Kent."

"Mac, it sounds as though Covington would sell his mother. . . . I'd love to see him arrested. But my first priority is Lucinda. . . . I need some private time to think. What do you think about Covington and Ellsworth-Kent being friends, maybe even business associates?"

"That's scary," I said. "I don't know. I was getting adjusted to Lucinda being dead. Maybe I was too premature."

"And I'm getting adjusted to you," she said.

"Last night was an adventure," I said. "I like adventures."

44

GUATEMALA

J UAN PABLO HERZOG CONSIDERED THAT THE
death in Italy of Alejandro Olviedo was a justified sacrifice
for finding Professor Hunt. Herzog was elated when he first
learned about Johnson's suicide note, which Herzog knew
would advance the search for Professor Hunt. . . . But Alaska!
It was, he knew, where many people from the Lower 48 moved
to get away from something—a bad marriage, a job firing, or
even criminal charges.

Herzog's initial elation moderated when he went on line
and learned the size and challenges presented searching for a
person living in Alaska. Where would Walter Windsor choose
to settle? Even though he did not have a specific address in a
specific city for Windsor, Herzog assumed it would be Anchorage even though there were more likely locations in the state
concentrating on commercial fishing.

There shouldn't be many people named Windsor in Anchorage or even all of Alaska, Herzog thought. A quick online
check showed there were twenty-eight residents in the Anchorage area with the surname Windsor. Running down the list he
crossed off fourteen females, and three males either younger
than 45 or older than 65. The remaining eleven included some
listings with first names using only single letters, such as B.
Windsor. Herzog estimated that perhaps seven or eight of the
eleven were males between 45 and 65. How many were in-

volved in commercial fishing and how many other Windsors were in Alaska living outside Anchorage should not be impossible to determine.

Herzog poured a glass of his favorite *Ron Zacapa Centenario* and took it to the balcony of the Casa Presidencial. A wisp of smoke arose from the volcano Fuego, only twenty-five miles distant, which a few years earlier had showered the capital with ash. He doubted that such an event would occur again before he had found and turned Professor Maxwell Hunt to ash.

Tomorrow, Herzog would present the wife of Alejandro Olviedo with Guatemala's highest honor, the Order of the Quetzal, given posthumously. The award didn't get off to a good start. It was first presented to Benito Mussolini. Herzog already had showed the medal to Cristina Olviedo, who, since Alejandro departed for Portugal and Italy, had spent every night in Herzog's bed.

Also tomorrow, Herzog would meet with General Hector Ramirez who next week would assume control of and commence the search for Walter Windsor.

45

KIRKWALL, SCOTLAND

THE WEATHER IN NORTHERN SCOTLAND WAS much at odds with the sunshine and warmth Elsbeth and Sue left behind in Gainesville. Kirkwall was persistently gloomy as cold rain blew in from the rough Atlantic and North Sea. The dullness was enhanced by the short days of winter.

Elsbeth and Sue were told that there was no such thing as bad weather in Scotland, only the wrong clothes. They had brought the wrong clothes. But unwelcoming weather did not discourage the two from their goal to uncover any information that might lead to finding Lucinda.

On their first day in the Orkney capital, Kirkwall, they went directly to the National Registry where marriage records were maintained. A pleasant young man, Douglas Macpherson, was thrilled to be on duty when the two lovely young women came into the building seeking information and advice.

"We have nae record of a marriage between a Lucinda Brooks and Robert Ellsworth-Kent," Macpherson said. "Are ye sure they had a civil or Pagan marriage *registered?*"

"Would they have to register a marriage that took place outside a traditional church like St. Magnus here in Kirkwall?"

Macpherson laughed. "Nae, whaur the service is performed is nae regulated. Many are celebrated out-of-doors and barefoot. The important question for us is who is to be the *cele-*

brant that performs the ceremony. The parties being married are allowed to organize the ceremony."

"I guess you're more liberal than we. Do you recognize same sex marriages?"

"Aye, certainly. Two male witches were married in Edinburgh recently. Unquestionably, it was legal. Scotland is the only place in the UK that allows Pagans to solemnize legal weddings. The Pagan Federation of Scotland conducts hundreds of weddings each year. A *lady* who headed the Federation performed the wedding between the gay male witches. Scotland is far more advanced than some of your states and for that matter far more advanced than most of the UK. . . . Have ye looked at the Federation's marriage records?" Macpherson asked. "The wedding you're askin' about may nae have been registered here."

Sue turned to Elsbeth. "When your dad was here recently, did he go and look at the *Federation's* records?"

"I don't remember him saying anything about doing that. He did come to *this* office and found the same information we have learned: there is no record of a marriage between Lucinda and Ellsworth-Kent. I don't think he went further. We need to go to the Federation. . . . Thank you for helping."

"Come back anytime. It was guid ta meet ye two lasses."

They located the Pagan Federation offices and found the staff to be equally understanding and helpful. An attractive young woman named Rosamund Gordon helped them.

"Nae problem," Rosamund began. "The 1977 Marriage Act of Scotland accepted this Federation as the regulator of authorized *celebrants* for conducting a legal Pagan marriage ceremony. The ceremony dinnae have to be registered at the National Registrar's General Office ye visited for the marriage to be recognized as lawful."

"You use the word 'celebrant' for the one who performs the ceremony," said Sue. "Who are the celebrants?"

"We regulate them; they are from many backgrounds."

"They are religious ministers or priests?" Sue asked.

"Aye, but we dinnae call them ministers."

"Are they educated in the Pagan practices?"

"Of course. They may be trained specifically in Druidry or Wicca or other forms of Witchcraft or Shamanism or Heathenry. I suspect that sounds barmy to you."

"It sounds exciting," exclaimed Sue. "How would I become a member of the group?"

"Join the Scottish Pagan Foundation."

"Is that hard?" Elsbeth asked.

"Nae if you use Pay Pal," Rosamund said, laughing. "We also take American Express, VISA, and Mastercard!"

"How do I become a *celebrant*?" Elsbeth asked.

"That's nae as easy. Celebrants are all volunteers. And almost all are women because of our Goddess-worship and partly to make up for the lack of sexual equality in the world."

"Were your parents Pagans?" Sue asked.

"Nae, my father is a Presbyterian minister. He studied at Oxford. I'm from a very traditional family. *Pagan* parents tend not to impose their beliefs on their children. To answer your question, to be a celebrant ye must be licensed. Ye must establish your knowledge of and commitment and devotion to Paganism.

"Our registered celebrants include one who lived with your Lakota Indians for two years performing sacred ceremonies. Others have included one who could perform on the Celtic harp during the service, one who worked as a nurse in terminal care, a member of the Interfaith Ministers Association, a Druid graduate, and one who held a diploma in funeral celebrancy."

"Can one study Paganism?"

"Aye. There are many books to help. Even *Harry Potter!* Institutions of varying quality offer courses. There is much help available online, or ye might find a Pagan teacher or attend Pagan ceremonies and events."

"Rosamund, we know of a couple who claim to be a high priest and high priestess of Wiccan. How would they have become what you call 'clergy'?"

"It's a long commitment of work based on substantial knowledge and service. Usually the title is bestowed by another, nae a self-serving declaration. Ye need a mentor."

"No special schooling?"

"Some Pagan traditions have a degree system for training priests. It includes helping current high priests and priestesses in performing rituals, teaching classes, and mentoring initiates."

"Could a high priest designate a *spouse* as a high priestess?"

"Only if the spouse over time separately met all the demands I've noted. Maybe the person would call herself a high priestess, but she would nae be respected or treated as one."

"Are Lucinda and Robert Ellsworth-Kent registered as a high priest and priestess?"

"I've been looking at our list while we've talked, and the answer is no. They are nowhere mentioned."

Before the women knew it, they realized they had talked with Rosamund for more than an hour.

"We've kept you too long, Rosamund. You've helped immensely."

"I ken you have troubles," she said. "I pray they will be solved by the gods."

Elsbeth and Sue were exhausted and hungry. They stopped on their walk to the hotel at a restaurant for dinner.

"We're starved," said Sue to their kilt dressed waiter.

"What do you suggest?" Elsbeth added.

"Let me bring you a five-course meal, and I will explain each dish," he offered.

"That's good for me," said Sue, with Elsbeth nodding.

He returned fifteen minutes later with self-explanatory prawns in whiskey, then soon thereafter with two cups of Cock-a-Leekie, a traditional chicken soup that included prunes. That was followed by salmon Balmoral, a fish coated with oatmeal, and then the main dish—clapshot, consisting of turnips and potatoes with a little infamous Scottish haggis. Finally, dessert was Strathbogie mist, a mix of pears and ginger wine.

"Did you like your meal?' Sue asked as they walked out and headed quickly toward their hotel.

"It was *so* different, but made up of food common in the U.S., except for the haggis."

"What *is* haggis? I ate it, but I didn't know what it was."

"Sheep intestines," Elsbeth exclaimed. "I didn't eat mine. I'll say no more."

"Nae another word, or I'll have to run for a loo!"

It was very dark and getting bitterly cold. At the hotel they went to their room and quickly dressed for bed, each wearing two sweaters.

"Beth, what do you think of our day?" Sue called out in the darkness after she turned out the light.

"I want to sleep on it. But I'm not sure Lucinda and Ellsworth-Kent were married, nor was Lucinda made a high priestess that would be accepted. Paganism takes time and education and experience and commitment. None of that was present with Lucinda and I'm not sure Ellsworth-Kent was a legitimate high priest."

"What does that mean to us?"

"That's what I need to sleep on. Pleasant dreams. We can talk in the morning."

The following day they visited some sights they had heard Macduff mention, in the morning to St. Magnus, the Earl's Palace, and the Bishop's Palace, and a guided tour in the afternoon to Maes Howe, the Ring of Brodgar, and Skara Brae. At their last stop, the Standing Stones, they met a young man by the name of Scott Sinclair, who taught courses on Pagan traditions to those aspiring to be high priests and priestesses.

"Do many who are unqualified try to become high priests or priestesses?" Sue asked Sinclair.

"Aye," he replied. "In the last year several dozen were turned away."

"Do you know of a High Priest Einar of Kirkwall?"

"Nae. I think I'd know anyone by that na. . . . Wait a minute. A few years ago a man with a double name tried to be accepted as a high priest, but he was rejected. Word was out that he'd served time in a prison on the Isle of Wight in England. He was strange and scary. He disappeared.

"His name was Robert something . . . Ellsworth something . . . Lent! Ellsworth-Lent. A year or so later the Scotland Yard people were poking around here, looking for someone by that name. Claimed he was wanted in the U.S. for killing four or five people."

"I believe you mean Ellsworth-*Kent*. Any sign of him since?"

"Nae. . . . Well, maybe. A friend of mine—he's nae a priest, nae even a Pagan—who works for the Pagan Federation as an accountant, was talking last month about Kent. He said the man was back a few months ago, claiming to be a high priest. My friend didn't like the man and told him he shouldn't hold himself out to be a Pagan priest. They had a big argument and my friend threatened to call the police. The man left."

"Was anyone with this man?"

"I dinnae think so. But I dinnae really know."

"Is your friend around?"

"Dead! Got himself killed."

"How?"

"Found his body washed up on a beach about seventy miles southeast of here near Scapa Flow. Called it a drowning while diving on some scuttled WWI German warships. Some have doubts about the drowning. Me, too. He was a careful man and an accomplished diver. Always went with someone. You know, the buddy system. Someone was with him, but it wasn't one of his friends. The person hasn't come forth. I'm suspicious."

"And you're certain Ellsworth-Kent didn't have a lady companion when your friend talked to him?"

"I'm nae sure. All I know is my friend didn't mention anything about a companion."

"So he *might* have had someone with him?"

"Aye. That's possible."

Elsbeth and Sue had to return to Florida for the start of classes. They had made extensive notes of their conversations and were pleased with their findings.

Both hoped Macduff and Dan would agree.

46

ST. AUGUSTINE BEFORE THE MOVE TO MONTANA

ELSBETH AND SUE VISITED WITH ME ON THEIR return to Gainesville. Their notes embarrassed me because I hadn't been thorough in Kirkwall on my way home from Italy. I had checked only the National Registry government records, not those of the Pagan Federation.

With my help the two drafted a report of their trip and attached the original notes they had made every evening in Scotland. We sent Dan Wilson and Grace Justice copies. Both suggested that we three talk. Dan's office arranged a conference call.

"Beth and Sue did exceptional work in Kirkwall," Dan exclaimed on his phone. "I've sent a copy of their report to our mission in London and asked them to follow-up and send someone to Kirkwall to learn if any more about Lucinda can be discovered."

"What do you two think about whether Lucinda has remained with Ellsworth-Kent?" asked Grace.

"There isn't any evidence that establishes that Lucinda was or for that matter wasn't with Ellsworth-Kent in Kirkwall," I observed.

"I suspect she wasn't there," Dan said. "She wasn't seen by anyone Elsbeth and Sue talked to in Kirkwall. That included the people at the National Registry and the Pagan Federation and Sinclair, who teaches Pagan traditions. His friend who died at Scapa Flow didn't mention that Ellsworth-Kent—who Sinclair and his friend were referring to when they said Ellsworth-*Lent*—had anyone with him, male or female."

"Are we agreed that Ellsworth-Kent and Lucinda didn't marry in Kirkwall?" I asked. "They may have tried, but they didn't have a ceremony before a recognized celebrant. And Lucinda never divorced me. . . . Even assuming you agree, that doesn't answer whether she wrote a new will leaving everything to Ellsworth-Kent. But he doesn't get anything based on an alleged marriage."

"At least not a marriage celebrated in Kirkwall, but Lucinda's letter didn't say that Kirkwall was where the ceremony took place," said Dan.

"It did say they were married while they were staying *near* Kirkwall at Skye Brae," I replied. "For that ceremony to be legal, it would have to be registered with the Pagan Federation in Kirkwall or with the National Registry."

"I suspect no marriage took place in Kirkwall, on the Orkney Islands, or anywhere else," asserted Dan.

"Then why did Lucinda say it did?" asked Grace.

"Duress. Drugs. She may believe she's married to Ellsworth-Kent. But that doesn't deal with *our* marriage never being officially ended. I've never received anything relating to a divorce," I commented.

"If she were alive, why wasn't she seen in Kirkwall?" Grace inquired.

"Ellsworth-Kent wants us to believe they're married. I think we agree they're not, at least without better evidence then we have," answered Dan. "Lucinda sent us a letter and more recently the tattoo photo. I want to believe she sent those because she's been drugged or remains under his control all this time."

"If she's been drugged, why wasn't her handwriting shaky?" asked Grace.

"I don't know. Could he take her off drugs, force her to write the letters, and then put her back on drugs?" I asked.

"If she went off the drugs, why didn't she try to escape?" wondered Grace.

"It's not easy to keep a person on drugs for so long. And, if the dose is varied, to get her to where she can write and then put her back under their influence. Why? What were his intentions?"

"One goal. Ellsworth-Kent hates Macduff Brooks. He wants you to suffer," said Dan.

"By playing games at Lucinda's expense?" asked Grace.

"Yes," responded Dan. . . . "Let's go on to other questions. Ellsworth-Kent has pretty much failed in becoming a celebrant, and he's not a high priest. Where's he headed? Assuming Lucinda is with him and drugged, what will he do with her?"

"I think we've answered those questions," said Grace. "We don't know. But we've ignored the possibility that Lucinda is content with staying with him, whether they're married or not."

"I can't accept that," I stated, discouraged by my own reasoning. "If you both disagree, then we shouldn't do anything. I assume she either is forcibly living with him, or she's dead."

"You're right, Mac, and as regretful as it appears to be, she may be dead," concluded Grace.

"Case closed?" I asked.

"No!" clarified Grace. "It remains an ongoing investigation. But we live our lives."

"Dan, we need your view. Grace and I have personal feelings for each other that affect our thinking."

"I can't make the decision," said Dan. "Grace is right about the probability of Lucinda being dead. But *you're* the one who has to act, Mac. You have legal standing to ask a Florida court to rule that Lucinda is deceased. But Florida law states that seven years must pass before a missing person is legally presumed dead. And you're not emotionally ready for such a procedure."

"Could we get a ruling in Montana in less time?"

"No, seven is common across the country."

"What if Lucinda is ruled officially dead and five years later she walks in very much alive? After all, my daughter walked in *seventeen* years after my believing she was dead."

Unable to speak any more, I wanted the matter settled. But what Elsbeth and Sue had discovered in Kirkwall gave me increased hope.

I'm not ready to have Lucinda declared dead. But I won't give up Grace. . . . I've got a few days to think about it. I'm leaving tomorrow for Montana.

47

FIVE DAYS LATER IN MONTANA

THERE WERE FIVE MESSAGES WHEN WUFF AND I arrived at the Montana cabin after tiresome hours on the road. As more interstates were built to make travel time shorter, many more cars were built making each trip longer.

All five of the calls were from Ken Rangley, Chief Deputy of Park County Sheriff's Office in Livingston, my long-time friend and occasional fishing companion.

"Ken, five calls in four days. Are you that anxious to talk?"

"Yes. Deputy Jackson, who was reinstated to the Gallatin County Sheriff's office force, is gunning for you."

"It has to be connected to the two deaths on the Gallatin."

"*Murders*, not deaths," Ken replied. "Do you want to debate the proper adjective?"

"Murder assumes *intent* on the part of the killer," I said. "If one of the adjacent property-owning ranchers was only trying to keep his livestock from wandering off his property, is that intentional homicide?"

"Probably not," Ken said. "It depends on whether one of your clan—lawyers—is believed or disbelieved by a jury. . . . Will it help if we talk about questions you may be asked by Jackson?"

"It will help if you give me the best answers," I said.

"First question. Who was or were the intended targets?"

"Are you assuming the two who were killed were not?"

"I'm almost sure of that," Ken answered. "But even if the person who put up the barbed wire only wanted to make a statement and didn't think *anyone* would be killed, he or she has committed a crime—at the very least manslaughter."

"OK," I said. "Assume the wire was strung intending to hurt *specific* people and not anyone who might come along. It could be their targets were actually Martin and Glendon. There was no motive we know about to kill Martin or Glendon rather than one or more of us, meaning Sue, Liz, or John Kirby in addition to Elsbeth or me."

"Who wanted to kill either Martin or Glendon? Rudolfo Martin worked as the Assistant Librarian at the public library in Bozeman. He had a master's degree in library science. Born and raised in Bozeman, no criminal record, and a member of the Central Baptist Church. Married for thirty-eight years, he had three children, all apparently good kids. He's easy, Macduff—not a likely target."

"He sounds as good a citizen as some of those seemingly nice, well-adjusted, promising, church-going folk who go into a theater and shoot fifteen people," I said. "But I agree about Martin. We can go on to the next, Ruth Glendon."

"She was thirty-three and taught at Three Forks High School. On weekends she worked as a volunteer at the Sacajawea Inn, giving tours of the historic building to guests and town visitors. Last year she won the county teacher of the year award."

"Family?" I asked.

"Divorced twice. No children. Currently dating both another teacher at the high school and a Three Forks police officer. Nothing in her record suggests anyone wanted her dead."

"Former husbands?"

"One serving in Afghanistan. Been there for two years. The other died at thirty-eight of an unexpected heart attack."

"I think *you* were the target, Macduff," said Ken.

"But I wasn't near the area at the time of the first death."

"Elsbeth was. *And* she was present at the second. She could have been the target."

"Damn! Between worrying about Lucinda and Ellsworth-Kent, I have to worry about someone being after *Elsbeth*."

"I'm only saying that Elsbeth or you, as well as John Kirby and both Sue and my daughter, Liz, *could* have been a target. But *you* were the most likely."

"Don't include Liz," I said. "And probably not Sue. Also eliminate John Kirby; he joined us at the last moment. Elsbeth as the target bothers me. But I thought it was more likely to have been me, as you believe. I was only on the river for the second float. That takes us back to Elsbeth, and that worries the hell out me. Losing Lucinda followed by losing Elsbeth would have ended it for me. I would have walked into Herzog's office and turned myself in."

"So you think it might be *Herzog's* work? And not Ellsworth-Kent's?"

"No, I'm being melodramatic. Herzog's busy as president, not searching for some fictitious person in Alaska. . . . Damn, I shouldn't have raised that. I'll explain when I see you in person."

"Alaska? You're a strange one, Macduff."

"You're not the only one who's said that. Next question?"

"Are we agreed the two killed were *not* the targets?"

"Yes."

"And you may have been the target, Mac. Or Beth."

"Yes," I said, hardly a whisper.

"I think we've covered the *who*," said Ken. "What about the *why*?"

"Because he disliked some specific people, most likely you," I answered. "Or he disliked anyone who fished. Or who fished on that particular part of the river. Maybe he was after Sue because she's Elsbeth's friend."

"Or Liz because she's the daughter of a sheriff's office head—me—with the usual array of enemies. There are too many 'whys' if we don't know the who."

"Does it matter who owned the land next to where the two died?" I asked.

"There are some landowners known to string up barbed wire to keep any boats off the river. If the landowner where the barbed wire was strung was one of those, he should be investigated."

"In the Gallatin case the land was owned by Ted Turner."

"Forget it. He's one of the most responsible land owners in Montana. Cross him off," said Ken.

"But his land could have been used by the killer without his knowing," I added. "I suppose someone who disliked Turner could be trying to frame him, or at least bring him into the public limelight to embarrass him."

"Macduff, there are too many possibilities about why the two were killed, who might have done it, and why. Maybe Martin was sleeping with the killer's wife. Or Glendon had been threatened by a student she flunked at her high school. They could have been specific targets."

"Maybe they were the wrong specific targets, Ken. We're thinking only of *our* families as possible targets. It could have been *anyone* who was scheduled to float with a local guide and had an enemy who knew that. . . . I need a break to think about what we've said. Can I call you back in an hour?"

"Where are you?" Ken asked.

"At the cabin."

"I'll come by. I have an appointment on Tom Minor Road at three. I can stop at your place at one."

"Fine. Stop at Albertson's and bring me a turkey on rye?"

"Sure. I'll buy two and join you."

An hour later after we finished lunch sitting on folding chairs we took down to the edge of Mill Creek, which was flowing with springtime vigor, Ken turned and asked, "Where did we leave off? Let's start with why there's inactivity investigating these two deaths by the Gallatin County Sheriff's Office. If the two deaths were in my county and the question was why we are not doing more to find the killers, our answer wouldn't be what you'd like to hear."

"What would your answer be?" I asked.

"First, consider any county's experience in dealing with murders. Not many murders occur in Montana. Between the shuttle gals murders and the wicker man and mistletoe murders, we exhausted our resources in Park County. We survive because of taxes. If we had asked for increased property taxes because of those killings, our citizens would have asked why. When we told them why, they would have run you out of town, Mac. It's partly why Deputy Jackson in Gallatin County was so nasty to Elsbeth."

"That means the level of justice depends on what the citizens are willing to pay?"

"Always. The theory of justice is overruled by the theory of don't spend more than you have."

"If you do have the money, how is it allocated?"

"By decisions of the county sheriff."

"Do you think Deputy Jackson, whatever his influence is in Gallatin County, could be pushing to allocate funds to other issues more to his liking?"

"No doubt. That's common practice anyplace."

"Meaning that a case that might be solved could be sitting on the back burner and never be seen again?"

"Exactly."

"Why would Jackson choose to put the two Gallatin cases on the back burner?" I asked.

"Elsbeth was testy. She challenged him. But more importantly, she embarrassed him in front of his peers. That's enough to make someone seek revenge. Jackson sought revenge."

"I'm not sure we're getting anywhere. What will it take to jump start the investigation?"

"More than seems to be forthcoming."

"Leave it for now," I concluded, more confused and disappointed than when we began to talk.

48

A FEW DAYS LATER IN BOZEMAN

KEN RANGLEY AND I AGREED ON THE KNOWN facts surrounding the two Gallatin River murders. Would Deputy Jackson agree? We would soon find out. He called late one afternoon and said Elsbeth and I had a choice of arriving at his Bozeman office the next morning at 9:00 a.m. sharp, or be visited at the cabin within an hour by a couple of deputies who would invite us to go with them and wouldn't take "no" for an answer. We agreed to meet Jackson in Bozeman and prepared for an unpleasant day.

Elsbeth and I went alone and arrived promptly at nine. Jackson was waiting. He was at his desk with coffee and a box of donuts. He didn't offer us either.

"Where are the other three?" he demanded, speaking so anyone in the next room would hear him exercise his authority.

"Elsbeth and I don't control what Sue and Liz do. We didn't talk to them. That's your job. I assume they're not coming," I said. "Sue is at her family home in Jackson, Wyoming. You could call Liz in Livingston. Best to call her dad. He's the Chief Deputy in Park County. Elsbeth and I can answer anything you want to *again* discuss about the first death that you can't remember. If you decide you need to talk to Sue or Liz, I suggest you call them. You specifically talked to Elsbeth and me about coming. You never mentioned the others."

"Where's Kirby?"

"Probably fishing right now with some client on the Snake River in Wyoming. That's the way he earns his living."

"You didn't tell him to come?"

"That's right. That's your job. And I think he's outside your jurisdiction."

"You trying to obstruct my investigation?"

"Deputy, you talked to all these people at the scene, and you haven't asked to meet them again until now. Why?"

"I make my schedule, Brooks. Don't tell me my job!"

"Have it your way; time distorts people's observations."

"Let's get to business, Macduff. You too li'l lady," he said acknowledging Elsbeth's presence for the first time.

Elsbeth went to the door, closed it, turned, and spoke.

"Some rules of the game, Deputy Jackson," Elsbeth asserted firmly. "If you don't tell me you accept them, I'm gone. You can send someone after me if you wish, but I won't say a word when you've brought me in because Wanda Groves will be with me. I want an apology for the way you treated me and my friends at the first death. . . . Agreed?"

Jackson stammered as he reached into the box, took a donut, and stuffed it into his mouth.

"Take your time. Enjoy your breakfast. Tell me when you're ready whether you agree or not," Elsbeth said.

Donut crumbs were tumbling down Jackson's uniform shirt front; one large sugar-coated crumb hung from his gold badge.

"What makes you think a bratty college kid is going to tell me what to do?"

"O.K. Let's talk about Alice Evans, Deputy," Elsbeth said, a reference that caused an instant reaction from Jackson.

"Well," he said, his brow beginning to sweat. "That won't be necessary. I don't know any Alice Evans. . . . I'm sorry about our first meeting, Miss Brooks."

"Let's get started," Elsbeth replied, making me wonder even more who this Alice Evans was. "What can we help you with, Deputy Jackson?"

That exchange deflated Jackson. A touch of sweat darkened his shirt front. He lost concentration and asked benign questions while fumbling through his notes. After thirty minutes, he looked at Elsbeth.

"I think we've done enough for today. Thank you for your help, Miss Brooks," he said as he got up from his chair and walked around the desk and held her chair. "You may go."

"*Who* is Alice Evans?" I asked Elsbeth as we left the building. "Jackson certainly changed his manner when you said her name."

"I don't know her, but Liz Rangley does and told me about her. Alice is a beautiful young lady from Livingston who grew up with Liz. She's a sophomore at Montana State and pays for her education by working for an escort service in West Yellowstone. Liz told me after the first death on the Gallatin that when Deputy Jackson questioned us she recognized him.

"Some months ago Alice had told Liz about her evenings with Jackson in West Yellowstone. When I talked to Liz last night, I told her I expected a bad day today because we were ordered to appear before Jackson and answer some questions. She passed on to me all Alice had told her about Jackson. I thought I'd see how Jackson would react if I mentioned Alice. He certainly reacted; I never expected that much instant apology."

"What do you think this means about the Gallatin deaths?" I asked Elsbeth.

"We've heard the last from him about the Gallatin deaths. We're now *former* suspects. Same for Liz, Sue, and John."

"So it's over."

"As far as suspecting us, yes. . . . But I'm not happy with the idea that two apparently good people were killed and the matter may have been closed prematurely—a cold case for the county. I'm not through with this."

"I'm not sure I want to ask, but what do you mean *you're* not through?" I asked.

"I have a few ideas I want to pursue. Nothing big. At least not yet."

"I wouldn't dare to try to stop you. You're as stubborn as your mo . . . as Lucinda. . . . But, be careful."

"OK."

49

ANOTHER MORNING ON INSPIRATION POINT

PALMER BROWN WAS ONCE AGAIN SITTING ON the top of Inspiration Point above Jenny Lake in Grand Teton National Park. Over the past year he had made seven trips to the same place for the same purpose. He had not been to the point for months, not because he had changed his mind about murdering his wife, but because he needed time to have her assets ready for a quick transfer to him after her "accidental" death.

He had come from his Jackson house where he'd had an unpleasant conversation with Brenda Lacy about his failure to contribute to their considerable assets that had made them one of the wealthiest couples in Jackson Hole.

"Before we married," she had stated, "my net worth was *growing*. Then you took over managing my investments."

"That's right, my dear."

"Between the poor performances of the new investments you recommended and what you've spent on your 'lifestyle,' we're down to about $39 million."

"All investments fluctuate. We needed more long-term investments, which have value at the *end* of the term. Be patient."

"I use 'we,'" Brenda Lacy explained, "because I love you, and I put your name along with mine on the investments, and we are each the sole heir of the other."

"That's as it should be for two who love each other."

"We have to change the way we live," she said. "We spent $3 million last year."

"Let me hear your views; you're usually correct," he said.

"First, I'm taking your credit cards, Palmer, and I'll approve or disapprove all expenses over $500. We'll trade in your Mercedes and buy you a Ford Explorer SUV. It may be a Ford, but it will be the fancy Platinum model. And you may keep the King Ranch pickup truck we use mostly around our property."

Palmer did not say a word, but thought, "Thank God we have charge accounts that don't need a card. I simply sign and the bank directly pays the balance each month. . . . I never liked the Mercedes. It's too ostentatious. The Ford will prove how modest my expenditures have been, if the issue is raised after she's gone."

"The Palm Beach winter house goes," Brenda Lacy added. "We can do with a condo penthouse in Hobe Sound. Anyway, I'd like to get away from the 'new money' social climbers in Palm Beach."

Palmer's unspoken thoughts continued. "Social climbers in Palm Beach! What about the same here in Jackson Hole? Next thing you know she'll want us to move over the mountain to Driggs in Idaho and live among the potato farmers."

"Do I make myself clear, Palmer?"

"Yes, dear" was all that Palmer would say.

"You do have to dress well, my love," she added. "We have an image to maintain. But $3,000 for a pair of shoes was too much."

"You're right," Palmer said, but at the same time thinking, "I love those shoes. I bought them at Harrod's in London. Harrod's had some for $34,000 a pair, so comparatively I really didn't spend too much. Besides, they're so *very* comfortable."

Sitting on the granite near the edge of the point, Brown realized he had to proceed with haste. At any time Brenda Lacy might come to understand his true intentions, throw him out of the house, and file for a divorce. And likely place their assets exclusively in her name. Worse, she might discover they had not lost money investing as he had told her, but because monthly he was transferring funds to an account in Bermuda in his own name.

Brown knew he must keep up appearances of a happily married man until the very end, which he now decided must come soon. Any suspicions about her death could go hard on him. Enough to mean life in prison or even execution. He would never own the dozen acres along the Snake River with the luxury log home that he had visited with a relator only three days ago. Nor the modest jet he coveted to fly him back and forth between Florida and Wyoming.

He stepped to the edge of the point, looked around to assure no one was watching, and dropped a large stone, watching it smash and break apart on boulders below, thinking how the same would happen to Brenda Lacy.

Sitting again, he placed a final "X" on the paper where he'd dropped the stone. There were eight such marks, and he decided that the best location to push Brenda Lacy off was the last. She would bounce on the way down, and there was no chance of her surviving when her battered body reached the bottom.

When Brown was finally rid of Brenda Lacy, he intended to turn his attentions to a person he had hated for several years, who had ridiculed him and walked away unscathed. For a long time he had imagined various ways he might kill that person.

50

THE SAME WEEK

I WAS DREADING GOING FOR THE MAIL AFTER receiving the earlier two postings from Lucinda. The handwriting on each had been hers.

The positive side to opening the letters was not the content, but the possibility that they told me Lucinda was alive when they were written. They didn't tell me how alive she was, however. She could have been drugged and sent the mailings against her will. Or she could have sent them on her own while living contentedly as the wife Ellsworth-Kent.

Considering how he treated her in the past, leading to the attempt to kill her—and me—on the final summer solstice of the wicker man and mistletoe murders, I think the latter is untenable. Drugs raise important questions about what she's been given and how much and how often. How long could her body consume them without permanent damage and ultimately death?

I have terrible nightmares contemplating Lucinda's life. There isn't a day I don't envision her return. I think about that even when I'm with Grace Justice and have illusions that I'm with Lucinda. But if she is dead and Grace becomes reluctant to wait month after month for some kind of commitment, I may end up a three-time loser with desirable women, including my wife El's death on the Snake River two decades ago. The third is my daughter. If Juan Pablo Herzog successfully turned his vengeance on her, there would be nothing worth living for, and he would have achieved his original intent: to take my life after I suffer the loss of those closest to me.

I was thinking about that walking to the mailbox at the beginning of the gravel road. There were a few letters. The first, from John Kirby, was four pages again explaining why his Georgia Bulldogs were going to win the National Championship in football. Over a decade of football seasons I have accumulated from John thirty pages of repetitious, unsupported testimony on that subject. It never proves true and each year Georgia is more distant from the glory days of 1980.

A second letter was from our New York City investment advisor with the good news that we had a seventeen percent increase in our portfolio value last year.

The third letter was from a Bermuda law firm I was not familiar with. I opened the envelope and began to read:

Dear Mr. Brooks,

We represent Robert Ellsworth-Kent although he does not reside in Bermuda. He has retained us to assist in arranging and carrying out the transfer to his name of all the assets belonging to his wife, Lucinda. We have a power of attorney from his wife granting him legal authority to make such transfer.

We understand those assets to be principally located in an account in the name of Macduff and Lucinda Brooks, located at an investment firm in New York City and totaling an amount exceeding ten million U.S. dollars. We also claim title to real property in New York City; Paradise Valley, Montana; and St. Augustine, Florida.

By this correspondence we are instructing you to provide a full record of all assets held jointly by you and your former wife, Lucinda. Please submit to us by return mail the name of the investment firm, the account numbers for the investments, and a list of all other properties you jointly owned.

Most respectfully,
George Hamilton

To say I was astounded by the letter is using mild language. But its flaws were so apparent to me I had to assume Attorney Hamilton was either very poorly trained in law or is engaged with Ellsworth-Kent in a fraudulent attempt to take Lucinda's and my assets and place them solely in his name.

However much I disagreed with the letter, it compelled me to attend immediately to what I had briefly thought previously: If Lucinda is dead, what will happen to the assets she and I have jointly shared? Attorney Hamilton has affirmed what I feared Ellsworth-Kent might propose: move the assets from the joint ownership of Lucinda and me to the sole ownership of Ellsworth-Kent.

It's time to call Wanda Groves, our Bozeman attorney and good friend. I wonder if she will consider herself still to be Lucinda's attorney as well as mine. That's fine. It's Ellsworth-Kent who is the problem and who we have to keep from getting his hands on our assets.

51

A FEW DAYS LATER IN BOZEMAN

I HAD NOT TALKED WITH WANDA GROVES SINCE shortly after she helped me with the shuttle gal murders and dealt with then Park County Chief Deputy James W. (Jimbo) Shaw. Wanda recently passed the twenty-year mark of practice in Bozeman, and I look forward to her being available when I need her during the next twenty.

"Macduff Brooks!" she exclaimed when I called her. "Back in trouble again?"

"It's been over a decade since you helped me with Shaw," I answered. "That's a name I expected never to say again."

"If you ever see Shaw again, I hope you're carrying a gun," she said. "But it's unlikely because he's passing the years in a cell in solitary reserved for him for the rest of his life in our state prison at Deer Lodge. He should have been executed but the Governor commuted his sentence."

"And you, Wanda? I haven't read anything about you being disbarred and in prison."

"Disbarred! Prison! You're as bad as ever. I was 'attorney-of-the-year' in Montana last year."

"And this year you're the president of the Montana Bar. I know all about you. . . . Well deserved."

"Thanks. I can't say I've heard much about you. When I think of your name, I have visions of shoot-outs on your drift boat. You call it *Osprey*, don't you? I also heard something about you getting in trouble in Cuba, and in Florida involving gill nets and more recently airboats."

"All in a day's work for a fly fishing guide."

"Is Lucinda why you called me? Or have you been mistreating Wuff?"

"Yes and no, in that order."

"Macduff, I know this is a sensitive subject. Is there anything new about Lucinda's abduction?"

"Nothing good. It's been more than a year. No ransom demand, no body found. I'm told that means she's almost certainly dead. But there's some hope."

"Why? Some contact?"

"In a way." I explained the first letter from Lucinda and the more recent image of a Celtic tattoo allegedly somewhere on Lucinda.

"What can I do to help?" she asked.

"Another letter came yesterday."

"From Lucinda?"

"No, from an attorney in Bermuda named George Hamilton. I scanned it and sent it to you a few minutes ago."

"I have it. Let me download it, read it, pull your file, and call you back."

Thirty minutes later my cell phone rang. It was Wanda again.

"Macduff, we need to act immediately."

"Why am I not surprised? What should I do?"

"First, revoke the power of attorney you granted Lucinda. I'm sending a form as we speak. Sign it and send it back, and I'll forward it with an email to your Manhattan investment broker. It doesn't have to be notarized but, nevertheless, I want you to have that done immediately. Notarization is not mandatory under Montana law but New York may give it more attention if it is notarized.

"We keep the power of attorney *you* have over Lucinda, recognizing she may have already or intends to revoke that power. I'm assuming she hasn't tried yet. And I'm going to send an email immediately, instructing your investment advisor to reject all communications from Hamilton that refer to any assets in the name of Lucinda or you. Hamilton should be warned he may be an accomplice in a fraudulent attempt by Ellsworth-Kent to obtain assets to which he has no right.

"Macduff, a quick note on your marital status. Is there anything on record that ends your marriage to Lucinda?"

"No," I answered.

"What about Lucinda's alleged marriage to Ellsworth-Kent in Kirkwall? You said Elsbeth and her friend discovered no marriage is on record in either the public National Registry or at what they call the Pagan Federation. I can't imagine a Montana court giving any recognition to whatever the Pagan Federation did, even though under Scottish law—if properly celebrated and reported—the marriage could have been lawful. But the Pagan Federation would have to acknowledge the proper celebration of that marriage, and it hasn't. I'll contact the Federation and get a letter affirming that. And, I want you to do something else today! Where do you have bank accounts?"

"One account is here in Montana at the Emigrant branch of the Bank of the Rocky Mountains. The other account is in Florida at the main office of the Ancient City Bank in St. Augustine."

"Joint accounts?"

"Yes, with right of survivorship."

"Go to Emigrant when we finish talking. Open an account in your name alone. Move all of what is in the joint account to your new account and then cancel the account you have drained of assets. Then call the Ancient City Bank and do the same. Don't let either bank give you any trouble. You have a clear legal right to those assets; that's the purpose of a joint account. You don't need to use your powers of attorney for making those changes. If you have multiple accounts in either or both banks, such as checking, savings, money market, on-line, or others, do the same with each account.

"Next are your investment assets. Where are they?" she asked.

"All in a joint account in the Mellon Private Bank in Manhattan. It's where Lucinda worked. Our contact there is Henry Mellon."

I gave Wanda the account number.

"Roughly, what's it worth?" she inquired.

"Last month the total was slightly over twelve million. It's our most valuable asset."

"I want you to call Henry Mellon right after we finish. Tell him about Lucinda and your concerns that Ellsworth-Kent is trying to obtain all her assets. Tell Mellon I have been your and Lucinda's attorney for over a decade. I believe he'll put a stop to any attempt by Ellsworth-Kent or Hamilton to access the assets.

"After you've talked to Mellon, I will call him and see what he recommends and needs from us. I'm hopeful he will create a new account solely in your name and transfer all the investment assets into that account. I can explain and fax to him the powers of attorney you both gave me. Tell him I will provide whatever he wishes verifying my use of the powers to close the joint account and open a new one.

"I'll ask Mellon if he knows the tax implications of the transfer, but I expect you're willing to pay whatever tax might be due rather than lose the entire amount to Ellsworth-Kent and have it end up hidden in some account in Bermuda, where Hamilton might shift it to God knows where—a numbered account in the Cayman Islands, Liechtenstein, or Panama."

"I'll pay any taxes," I said, without hesitation.

"Lastly, your real property, which includes two Montana properties, the log cabin you're sitting in as we talk and the ranch further up Mill Creek. Also, we need to deal with the cottage in St. Augustine and Lucinda's Manhattan apartment. Tell me about them," she asked.

"The Montana log cabin and Florida cottage were originally in my name alone. The large ranch near the log cabin was in Lucinda's name alone. When we married, we transferred all three into our joint names, with right of survivorship. But we left the Manhattan apartment in her name alone."

"Why?"

"Lucinda insisted we do the same as with the three other properties and have it jointly owned. If she predeceased me, I would receive the apartment; each of our wills leaves all property to the survivor, with Elsbeth next in line. . . . But I wanted her to keep the apartment so she'd have one property exclusively in her name. Maybe that wasn't wise financially, but I felt better. She resisted but finally agreed. . . . What do we do? Can we use the power she gave to you or the one to me to transfer the apartment title?"

"I'll take care of your cabin here in Montana using the general power Lucinda gave me. There's no question Montana will recognize it and transfer both the cabin and the ranch either directly to you or to a trust for the benefit of you and Lucinda, with me being the trustee. I'll try the same for the Manhattan property. They *should* recognize the powers. I want to get the real estate transfer recorded as soon as possible. Let me go and get started."

I called the Emigrant bank and asked the branch manager to close our joint account, open a new one for me, and deposit the balance in the new account and close the current one. She said she would call back.

All kinds of visions passed through my head over the next few hours. If Ellsworth-Kent already had transferred to himself any assets held under Lucinda's name, jointly with me or otherwise, even if she did return to me we would face a very different future if we couldn't have the assets returned. As much as I love to guide, it isn't a pathway to wealth or at my age even survival. I don't guide as much as the years pass. I would do as many float trips as I'm able to do physically, and Lucinda might find a job with an investment firm in Bozeman, but that's too far to commute. We might have to move from Mill Creek and even sell the Florida cottage. I hated to think of the impact on Elsbeth.

When the Emigrant bank branch head called back and said to drop by and sign some papers I felt better. I went to the bank, signed the papers, and walked away knowing at least I had $21,462.89 solely in my name.

Wanda called again as I was thinking about which leftovers I would have for dinner.

"Have you done what I asked?" Wanda began.

"Yes. I've talked with people at both banks. My dealing with the Ancient City Bank differed a little from the Emigrant bank. Ancient City said they would put a hold on the account while they investigated the validity of the power executed here in Montana. I told them if they didn't comply by tomorrow noon you would file a civil suit immediately. I have every expectation that their attorney will tell them they *must* comply, close the account, and transfer all the funds to a new account in my name alone. I also suggested that if they delayed I would transfer all my accounts—I have a money market account as well as the checking—to another bank by the day after tomorrow. The amount is considerable. I said also that Elsbeth would transfer her new account from the bank. . . . There should be about seventy-five thousand in our Florida joint account. We were planning a major purchase and some needed repairs to the cabin; also we used that account for Elsbeth's college expenses."

"It's my opinion that Ellsworth-Kent *himself* has no right to any of Lucinda's assets," Wanda noted, "unless she has given them to him as a gift. But a gift could be voided if ruled fraudulent. Of course, Lucinda could *bequeath* them to him, married or not. But in such case we could challenge probate. I've never dealt with this kind of conflict, you may want to go big time and retain a Manhattan law firm."

"Not a chance, Wanda. The most financially ambitious lawyers may be in Manhattan, but that's not the same as the best and the brightest. Keep at it. The most I'll approve using a New York lawyer for is transferring the apartment title."

"Thanks for the encouragement. This is a difficult case to discuss on the phone. I've done the immediately needed work. Can we have lunch or dinner and talk about the investment assets issue, plus some other matters that deal with Lucinda."

"Soon, please. I'm not sleeping much."

"Tomorrow? I know you like Ted's Montana Grill. Outside if it's warm enough; inside if it isn't. About 7:00 p.m.?"

"I'll be there."

"Bring Wuff. I'd love to see her."

"More than me?"

"That's between me and Wuff."

I'm certain Wanda believes she represents Lucinda, Wuff, and me in that order.

My aging sheltie Wuff was handed over to me by Judge Amy Becker a dozen years ago. Judge Becker and Wanda are close friends in Bozeman. If Wanda represented Wuff against me before Judge Becker, I'd end up in solitary confinement.

As a puppy, Wuff was abused by previous owners—a couple that was splitting. Wuff came to live with me and traded that abuse for a life of being served foods almost on time and sleeping in every room on soft Orvis beds with her name on the side. She enjoys summers in Montana and winters in Florida and never complains about the five days of travel twice a year. She spends those days sound asleep on comfortable cushions in the back of the SUV. I wish *I* could sleep crossing the Great Plains.

Dinner with Wanda was a good idea. The rest of today and tomorrow making notes about issues I think Wanda may help to resolve will consume my attention.

52

TED'S MONTANA GRILL THE NEXT EVENING

TED'S IS A FAVORITE, NOT BECAUSE I KNOW THE owner, but because I like what he does raising bison.

Wanda and I arrived at Ted's at the same time, and all the outside tables by the front entrance were empty. We sat and watched as Montana State University students walked by, a lilt to their stride promoted by the ending of exams.

"Macduff," Wanda observed, "you look older, no wiser, haggard, tired, and frustrated. Wuff looks much better."

"Guiding and raising a sheltie are demanding work."

"I know you don't guide that much, and when you do, if your clients cause you the least bit of trouble, you shoot them."

"That's exaggerated. I've shot only *one* person on *Osprey*, a dozen years ago on the Snake in Jackson Hole."

"Shooting a dead body doesn't count. You shot Park Salisbury *after* Lucinda had already killed him with several shots from her Glock, while *you* fumbled through your guide box looking for your own Glock. By the time you found it Salisbury was dead."

"What would you like to drink?" I asked to change the direction of the conversation.

"Wine."

"Color?"

"White. What do you suggest?" she asked.

"*Chardonnay, pino grigio, white Burgundy, sauvignon blanc, riesling, or gewürztraminer?*"

"I'd prefer *pouilly fume or fuisse!* What are you having? I remember you consume Gentleman Jack?"

"Consume? I call it sipping. I'll sip two or three tonight."

"Are we going to get too cold sitting here?"

"No. And I want to hide from your disparaging remarks. Plus, I doubt Wuff is welcome inside."

"I don't plan to disparage you any further tonight. We have serious matters to discuss."

"Where do we start?" I asked. "Maybe I should ask who are you representing?"

"You. I'm protecting your interests."

"Aren't you also Lucinda's attorney?"

"Yes. As long as you and Lucinda are alive and married, I try to represent you together as a family. You two requested that. If Lucinda died, the will I prepared for her would be probated with you as the executor. If you died, the will I prepared for you would be probated with Lucinda the executor. I would assist either executor as needed, more so if Lucinda were executor. I know you were a lawyer, which I never talk about."

"This is a different situation," I observed.

"It's not something we planned for," Wanda said.

"We don't know if Lucinda is dead and her will should be probated," I said. "One week I'm sure she's alive. The next week I'm sure she's dead. If she's dead, the will governs. If she's alive, it's more complex. She could be living voluntarily with Ellsworth-Kent. Or she could be in some kind of bondage, and he forced her to write me the letter and later send me the image of the tattoo with a single written sentence."

"If she's captive," Wanda said, "we should be able to stop any attempt by her to transfer your jointly held assets to Ellsworth-Kent or even put them in her name alone and exclude you," suggested Wanda.

"But not knowing if she's alive, how do we do that?"

"We've already done that with the checking accounts. They are now both solely in your name."

"And the four properties?"

"Deeds of transfer to you have been filed, along with copies of the power of attorney Lucinda gave you. No immediate opposition, but I'm a bit uncertain whether the City Register office in New York will accept those documents. That's not our major concern."

"Which is the Mellon held investment portfolio."

"Yes. Let's talk about that."

"Before we do, why do you think Ellsworth-Kent has concentrated only on this account?"

"Remember," she interrupted, "it wasn't Lucinda who contacted Mellon, but Ellsworth-Kent purportedly acting on her behalf and using a general power of attorney he claimed she gave him.

"I think he's dropped any thought of obtaining the real property or checking accounts. He wants the investment portfolio put in his name. Unless Lucinda is living with him voluntarily—which I don't believe is conceivable—he will have no further use for her when he gets the account funds. She'll be gone." I suggested.

"Refer to her as gone if you wish. I read 'gone' as 'dead.'"

"Assume she's alive; how do we proceed?"

"I talked to Henry Mellon today," said Wanda, "after sending him instructions to close the joint account and transfer all the assets to a new account in your name."

"Won't he do it?"

"He said he received a similar instruction from Lucinda the day before," exclaimed Wanda, "and adding that after the account was closed, Mellon was to transfer the assets to a new account solely in the name of Robert Ellsworth-Kent. Mellon was more than a little suspicious."

"What's Mellon going to do?" I asked.

"He didn't want to commit himself," Wanda replied. "I told him that if Lucinda was dead, her purported request had to be denied, and it was up to probate to deal with assets she owned at her death. I also said that, assuming Lucinda was alive, he should demand something more than an unsigned request that I was convinced was a fraudulent attempt by Ellsworth-Kent to abscond with her assets. Mellon then asked, 'What if Lucinda was acting according to her own free will?' I told him that required a court to determine. Fortunately, he agreed to put a lock on the accounts, pending further information."

"What if I need to cash in some of the stocks or bonds in the account, for something like tuition for Elsbeth?"

"You can't do it until we've straightened this out and a court rules," said Wanda. "I'll get something filed immediately in a New York court. You have enough in your two checking accounts to pay Elsbeth's tuition."

"Yes. Wanda, you may not know that Henry Mellon was devoted to Lucinda when they worked together. I suspect he wanted to marry her."

"That probably doesn't help us," she said.

"But Mellon agrees that Lucinda's abduction, the letters, and Hamilton's request all point to suspicious activity," I said. "Mellon wants to protect Lucinda."

"Macduff, I want you to inform both the Kirkwall based National Registry and the Pagan Federation about Lucinda's and Ellsworth-Kent's alleged marriage. Tell them that Ellsworth-Kent is holding himself out as a high priest who was married in Kirkland, apparently at a Pagan ceremony, and that due to the information Elsbeth and Sue discovered, whatever alleged ceremony he believes they participated in appears nowhere on the Pagan Federation or National Registry records. Ask for a written statement to affirm that."

"I've done that. Without response," I said.

"Follow up. Do it again. Call them," she suggested.

"Wanda, how does the request from Hamilton in Bermuda fit into this? He expects some response."

"Ignore him," she instructed.

"Ignore him! Why?" I asked.

"Hamilton wants Lucinda's assets. He's started by demanding from you a complete list of all assets to which Lucinda had *any* claim. What he needed were the account numbers for those assets."

"What do we give him?" I asked.

"Nothing," she asserted. "I suspect he's somehow going to receive a contingent fee, regardless of the Bermuda attitude towards that form of compensation. I was very suspicious of his motives."

"Wanda, do you think Lucinda is dead?"

"Don't assume that Ellsworth-Kent killed her trying to get the financial information and she wouldn't tell him. She probably doesn't know the numbers of the checking or investment accounts."

"But Ellsworth-Kent did learn about the Mellon account."

"Patience, Macduff. We have the checking accounts. We'll soon have the real property. And Henry Mellon is not going to transfer anything to Ellsworth-Kent, or Lucinda, without a court order. Ellsworth-Kent can't go to court in New York. He's wanted for the five wicker man and mistletoe murders."

"Using your knowledge about Lucinda, with your best feminine intuition, *is* she alive?" I asked.

"Yes. She's tough. She hates Ellsworth-Kent. She told me a half-dozen times about how he treated her and how awful the five murders in the West were. I am surprised she hasn't killed him."

"He was in the British elite Special Air Service, known better as the SAS. They are the best England has," I said.

"Lucinda's better. We have to keep thinking that, Macduff."

"I will. Time for some food?"

"I hoped you'd ask," she said. "I'm famished."

53

INSPIRATION POINT THE NEXT DAY

PALMER BROWN AND HIS WIFE BRENDA LACY were the only two people on the trail leading up to Inspiration Point as the sun rose behind them and began to absorb the night's chill. He was excited about what soon was to occur.

"Palmer, I don't like heights. Can we turn around?"

"My dear, it's not much further. I'll hold your hand. I promise you will never see a better view."

"Well, all right. But you know I'm afraid of heights."

At the top they stood together and looked out across Jenny Lake. The first tour boat was leaving the dock. It would be at the landing below Inspiration Point in fifteen minutes, and the tourists would reach the point twenty minutes later.

She linked their arms and leaned against Palmer.

"I have something very exciting to tell you, Palmer. You know I've wanted to set up a foundation to help preserve this magnificent national park. The legislators in D.C. don't provide nearly enough money for expenses, much less improvements."

"How will your foundation work?"

"It will have a board to determine how the income should be spent and initially will have about $1 million to work with."

"That's a nice gift. A million will be very helpful."

"No, silly. The income should be a million or two *each year*. I'm giving nearly *all* of my money to the foundation."

Palmer couldn't believe what he was hearing.

"You'll be quite comfortable, dear. You have your own funds, and I'm leaving you $1 million," she said.

Palmer's own funds were down to about $200,000, but that did not include the $2 million he had secretly shifted to his personal account from their joint accounts. That $2 million grew nearly $120,000 annually. He would have to put aside some of his earnings to cover inflation and would have at best about $200,000 a year to live on, far less than what he expected if he inherited her entire estate. Her proposal was a disaster. He was shaking and pulled away from Brenda Lacy's hold.

"When did you do all this," he asked.

"Last week. This afternoon I'll meet with my lawyer and sign all the papers."

Palmer had to act fast. His mind raced. Normally he carefully calculated what he did. But now he couldn't think beyond the amount of money that was at stake.

"Brenda Lacy, look at me. I'm so proud of you for your plan about the foundation. I want a big kiss."

She turned toward Palmer, her back to the drop off, and kissed Palmer as hard and long as she could. Her eyes were closed when she realized she was losing her balance.

"Palmer! Grab me!" she cried out as she tipped back.

She reached out to Palmer, but he didn't reach back. The last thing she saw was Palmer standing there smiling. He leaned out and watched her tumble down, bouncing off the granite wall. She seemed to fall in slow motion. He watched her land among the trees at the foot of the point. No one could survive such a fall. He turned around to see if anyone had seen them. Sounds of voices coming up the trail were increasing, but he was certain no one had yet arrived.

As the first climbers reached the top, Palmer was running toward them, screaming unintelligibly. He feigned loss of consciousness and fell. Several climbers knelt over him, one with a neckerchief soaked in water.

"She fell over!" he gasped, 'regaining' consciousness he had never lost.

"How?" asked one climber.

"She was next to me and so happy she turned and kissed me. And then she stepped back. The last thing I remember was reaching for her. Our fingertips touched, but she was gone."

Palmer sat down, put his face in his hands, and sobbed, praying he wasn't too late to inherit her fortune.

One of the climbers pulled out her cell phone and called 911. She was patched through to the park's emergency services and forty minutes later a boat arrived with park wardens and medics. When they began to question Brown, he told the wardens his prepared story. One called up from below that they had found the body and would transport it to the medical examiner's facility in Jackson.

"I need to see her one last time," pleaded Palmer.

"You don't want to," said a warden. "Her body was badly damaged from the fall into the trees. We'll take you to town."

Brown played the role of the grieved husband to perfection. After meeting with Operations Lieutenant Huntly Byng of the Teton County Sheriff's Office, and assuring Byng that he would not leave the county, Brown went home to their big house on the bank of the Snake River. The maid was off, and he had the house to himself.

He filled a flute with Moët & Chandon *Champagne* to the very top and took it to the terrace.

"This is mine!" he exclaimed, looking around at the property and spilling his drink. "All of it is mine! A few more hours and her wealth would have gone to her damn foundation. I can't wait to get rid of her things. Tomorrow I'll pack all her clothes and shoes and everything else that reminds me of her and take them to Goodwill. Then sell her tacky Caddie. One thing I *must* do to look good is give a substantial donation to the Grand Teton National Park in her name."

In the morning a sheriff's vehicle drove up to Palmer's residence. Two men got out and walked to the front door.

"Mr. Brown," said the one in uniform, "I'm Lieutenant Byng. We met yesterday. With me is Sergeant Roscoe, in charge of investigations, including homicides. Roscoe wore charcoal trousers and a dark blue blazer but held his badge out in front of him."

"Homicides?" Brown said, choking on the last of his morning coffee.

"Yes."

"Come in," he said reluctantly, surprised at their presence. "What can I do for you?"

"Come with us to town to our office, please," said Byng.

"But I talked with your people yesterday at some length right after my wife's tragic accident."

"We know that. But we have some new questions. We understand your wife had an appointment yesterday afternoon with her local attorney, Charles Claudel. She was setting up an extensive well-funded foundation. Her attorney called us late yesterday when she didn't show up to sign critical papers. He said her death prevented the creation of the foundation."

"Give me a minute to call my attorney and ask her to meet us at your office," requested Brown.

"You go ahead."

54

THAT AFTERNOON IN JACKSON

PALMER BROWN WAS NERVOUS AS HE DROVE TO town closely behind the deputy's car. He hoped his attorney, Jennifer Longstreet, would be waiting to meet them.

He was ready to play the role of the grieving widower. But he worried that Brenda Lacy's attorney, Charles Claudel, may have given Roscoe enough information to establish a motive. Brown understood that the substantial wealth of Brenda Lacy raised red flags about her death.

The interrogation room at the sheriff's office was what Brown expected from having watched so many police mystery TV programs. It was stark and furnished only with a plain table and two uncomfortable, straight-backed metal chairs. He was asked to sit in one of them, aware he would be facing a large, dark, glass wall, which he correctly assumed hid more sheriff's investigators or deputies.

Roscoe sat in the chair facing Brown. Byng left the room for a minute, returned with a chair, and placed it next to Roscoe's.

"Let's get started," said Roscoe, smiling.

"Let's wait," responded Brown. "My lawyer will be here any minute. She instructed me on the phone not to answer any questions until she arrived."

"But we're investigating an occurrence that may prove to have been an accident. You hardly need a lawyer for that."

"You accepted it yesterday for what it was: a tragic accident. There is no reason for me to be here," said Brown. "Let's wait for Ms. Longstreet."

Sergeant Roscoe was visibly disturbed and began to tap his pencil on the yellow legal pad on the table in front of him.

Brown finally recognized Roscoe. He had graduated from an obscure for-profit law school in California, passed the bar exam on his third try, came to Jackson, and opened a practice. He attracted few clients and after two years ran for an opening on the local court, but lost by a large margin and took a position with the county sheriff's office. It wasn't that he was incompetent; his personality simply wasn't conducive to attracting people as clients or voters. He proved to be a good crime investigator.

"Mr. Brown, were you and your wife having marital problems?" Roscoe asked, smiling.

"We can talk about that when Attorney Longstreet arrives. But the answer is no."

"Had she raised the question of seeking a divorce?"

Brown looked at Byng, ignoring Roscoe's question.

"Mr. Brown, had you discussed a divorce?" asked Roscoe.

Brown looked at Roscoe and smiled and didn't say a word.

"Now Mr. Brown, if you're not going to cooperate and talk about your wife's death, we can. . . ."

"No, you can't, Sergeant," said Brown, glaring. "Whatever you're thinking, if Longstreet is delayed, we're delayed. No more questions. Don't even ask me what time it is."

Roscoe began tapping his pencil again. He wasn't smiling.

Another fifteen minutes passed before Attorney Longstreet arrived, strolled into the room as though she hadn't given a thought to being late, gave a cordial hello to Byng, set down her briefcase on the table, pulled out a legal pad and two ball point pens, and only then acknowledged Roscoe with a nod.

"Roscoe, get me a chair," she demanded. "I don't think I should have to stand to do this."

Flustered, he left the room and quickly returned with a chair. Longstreet sat without a word of thanks.

"I think we're ready, Sergeant," Longstreet said, having won round one.

Roscoe turned to Brown.

"Mr. Brown, tell me why you and your wife were on Inspiration Point yesterday morning."

"For the view and the exercise," Brown answered.

"But you were there very early. No other climbers were near the top?"

"I don't know about other climbers. Brenda Lacy and I were looking out over the lake to see the sunrise."

"When your wife was pushed off the edge, were any other climbers in view?"

"Roscoe," interrupted Longstreet, "you know better. Mrs. Brown's death was an accident. Don't refer to her being pushed off. Palmer, don't answer any questions that refer to your wife's death as anything other than a terrible accident."

"All right. I could hear other voices when Brenda Lacy fell, so I assumed others were on top of the point. But I was looking at Brenda's beautiful hazel eyes when she lost her balance and accidentally fell."

"Could you have bumped her and caused her to fall?" Roscoe asked.

"No. I was holding her and kissing her. It was her birthday and special to be sharing it from the top of Inspiration Point."

"Did you push her?"

"That's ridiculous," exclaimed Brown.

"Sergeant," interjected Longstreet, "you've asked how she fell, and my client has told you. She fell backwards. It was an accident. What evidence leads you to believe otherwise?"

"Are you aware, Ms. Longstreet," responded Roscoe, "that Brenda Lacy Brown was going to sign some documents yesterday afternoon when they returned from Inspiration Point? Do you know signing the documents would effectively cut off Palmer Brown from being bequeathed all but a token amount of her millions?"

"I'm not the one being questioned here," responded Longstreet. "Please direct your questions to Mr. Brown."

"Are you aware, Mr. Brown, that yesterday afternoon you were going to be cut off from your wife's considerable wealth?"

"No."

"Are you certain?"

"*Certain*. If I had thought that, would I have taken her to Inspiration Point as part of her birthday gift from me? Would I have had lipstick smeared on my mouth? Sergeant, *please*."

"Were you and your wife having marital problems?"

"No."

"None at all? No arguments? No physical abuse?"

"We had the usual differences of opinion. Nothing serious. I resent the suggestion of spousal abuse."

"So you were what you'd call a happy couple?"

"Very happy. Yes."

"Had your wife told you of her plans for the foundation?"

"Many times," Brown lied.

"So you knew you were going to be cut off from the wealth you'd been enjoying?"

"My wife had substantial assets. She could set up the foundation and remain wealthy. She didn't need to cut me off."

"Did you know she was changing her will to substantially keep you from inheriting her wealth?"

"Sergeant, I have my own wealth. I don't need my wife's money to live comfortably."

"What is the source of your own wealth?"

"Inheritance."

"How much did you inherit?"

"About $4 million," he answered, hoping Roscoe would not ask from whom he received it or how much was left.

Roscoe was flustered; he hadn't researched Brown's background and how he came to such wealth. Roscoe knew Brown could live comfortably if he had inherited $4 million.

"So your position is, Mr. Brown, that when you took your wife to the top of Inspiration Point you knew nothing about what your wife was going to do that afternoon, and you did not push her off the edge so you would not be cut off?"

"That is exactly my position. I'm glad we had the opportunity to make that clear. My wife's death was a tragic accident and an immeasurable loss to me. Money was not an issue in her accidentally falling."

"Lieutenant, any questions?"

"None," Byng said, disturbed by Roscoe's failure to ask about Brown's background, more about the source of his wealth, and any history of violent outbursts other than a year ago when the Sheriff's office was called to remove Brown from a local bar, an incident Roscoe didn't ask about.

There were also some scratches on the back of Palmer Brown's neck, Byng noticed. Could they have been from Brenda Lacy trying to save herself from Palmer's pushing her off the edge? There would have to be more investigation before Byng was satisfied they were dealing with an accident.

55

THREE DAYS LATER

THREE DAYS LATER ROSCOE WENT TO PALMER Brown's house once again.

"Hello," Brown said, opening the door and concerned that Roscoe was staring at him with a grin. Behind Roscoe were two uniformed policemen. Neither one looked very cordial.

"Can we come in?" Roscoe asked.

"Do I have a choice?" asked Brown, not moving aside.

"I have an arrest warrant," said Roscoe, waving a paper at Brown, "for the premeditated murder of your wife."

He felt the steel handcuffs being placed onto his wrists behind his back. The deputies walked him to the car and assisted him getting in the back. On the ride to the sheriff's offices, Brown tried to remember what he had said to Roscoe after Brenda Lacy's death. He was glad Lieutenant Byng had been there; he at least appeared not to have drawn any premature conclusions. Brown, worried that Byng wasn't present this time, may have had reason to worry. Roscoe clearly rejected the idea that Brenda Lacy had accidentally fallen.

Roscoe allowed Brown to call Attorney Longstreet from the car, and she was at the sheriff's office when Brown arrived.

"Palmer," Longstreet said quietly as they walked into the building, "this time I mean it. Look at me when you're asked a question. If I nod, go ahead. If I shake my head, don't answer.

Answer any question as briefly as you can. Don't open up other avenues. Roscoe is good at his work."

Roscoe was the only other person in the interrogation room when he began his questioning. He sat opposite Brown and Longstreet. Brown knew others were behind the glass-paneled wall and hoped Byng was among them.

This time there was no water on the table. Longstreet took a bottle from her bag and set it in front of Brown.

"Mr. Brown," began Roscoe. "This won't take long. I won't repeat questions I asked you three days ago. Let me start with a different matter. . . . Did you ever strike your wife?"

"Never."

Roscoe picked up a sheet of questions and moved his finger part-way down, apparently trying to find something.

"Three years ago you were seen by a Jackson police officer arguing with your wife outside Albertson's. The policeman came over and asked if anything was wrong. His report stated that you pushed your wife into your car. Is that accurate?"

"Partly, she wanted me to go back and get some fruit she had on her grocery shopping list, but forgot to put in her cart. I told her I wanted to get home because the second half of a pro football game I'd been watching had started. She said something like, 'you watch too goddamn much of that stupid sport. Go get me the fruit.' I helped her into the car, shut her door, got in, and drove home."

"Did you take her to the emergency care facility?"

"No. She was not injured. She told me to take her home."

"A neighbor reported that your wife was wearing a sling the day after that incident."

"She slipped on the ice on our driveway carrying the grocery bags, and fell on her shoulder."

"Did you take her to an emergency clinic?"

"No. She refused to go. I offered to take her," Brown said, not having remembered any such conversation.

"But she had to wear a sling?"

"That's right. She found the sling in a drawer in closet. She had worn it several years before when she had a similar fall. Mr. Roscoe, my wife had poor coordination from taking heart medicine," responded Brown, again bending the truth.

"Mr. Brown, we have a witness to your pushing your wife off Inspiration Point."

"I don't understand," said Brown. "After she fell, I ran to where several people were arriving at the top of the point. They couldn't have seen Brenda Lacy fall."

"Maybe they didn't. But a hiker was already at the top, having camped out in Cascade Canyon. She walked back from the canyon toward the point and was in the woods. She claims she saw you push your wife off the cliff."

"That's impossible!" Brown exclaimed. "I looked around for help and no one was there."

"We're going to hold you tonight. Tomorrow you'll appear in court for a bail hearing."

"Can they do this, Ms. Longstreet?" Brown asked.

"They can. We'll go before the judge in the morning and ask that you be released on bond. I'm sure he'll agree."

"What about this alleged witness?" Brown asked Longstreet.

"I wasn't aware of that. She apparently came forth this morning; her comments were the reason you were arrested."

"What can you do?"

"First, we want to get you out on bail."

56

THE FOLLOWING DAY

THE BAIL HEARING LASTED ONLY FIFTEEN minutes. Attorney Longstreet asked the judge to release Brown *without* bail, but the judge rejected that request because of the seriousness of the allegations that Brown intentionally took his wife to Inspiration Point to push her off, there was a body, and an eyewitness had come forward. He noted that Brown had no prior arrests and agreed that his possible inheritance of nearly $40 million was a significant reason that Brown would remain in the area and not become a fugitive.

The judge granted bail in the amount of $2 million and after posting bond Brown walked out into the crisp air of Jackson a free man, at least for the time being.

Attorney Longstreet insisted Brown go with her to her office where they spent two hours discussing the case. She said they had to concentrate on the alleged eyewitness and unless she could discredit the new witness they would face a trial with an uncertain outcome.

57

THE FOLLOWING WEEK

A TTORNEY LONGSTREET FOCUSED ON PALMER Brown's case intensely the next few days. She interviewed the prosecution's alleged eyewitness, Gail Garcia, who at first seemed to be a stable, intelligent young woman who would impress any jury. Longstreet learned that Garcia went camping with her boyfriend, Robert Casis, for two nights four miles west of Inspiration Point, and decided that an interview with the woman's boyfriend was necessary after interviewing Ms. Garcia.

"Ms. Garcia, where was your boyfriend when you watched the accused push his wife off the cliff?" asked Longstreet.

"He was coming along behind me."

"Meaning he walked a little slower but was close to you?"

"Not really. He left the campsite later than me."

"How much later?" Longstreet asked.

"I don't know."

"When did he arrive at Inspiration Point?"

"After I did."

"By how much time? How many minutes?"

"I'm not sure. After I saw the woman pushed off the cliff, I went down the trail to the boat dock. I asked two people waiting for the boat if either had seen the woman go over the cliff."

"And?"

"No one had."

"Apparently, you didn't wait for the police."

"I was confused and not myself. Seeing what had happened, I didn't want to be involved. I went to the boat dock."

"And took the boat back to the Jenny Lake parking lot?"

"No, I walked back."

"How far?"

"Two miles."

"When you got to the parking lot, what did you do?"

"I was scared. I drove home."

"Was your boyfriend with you at that time?"

"No."

Longstreet was disturbed by something about the relationship between the two campers.

"When was the last time you talked to your boyfriend?"

"I'm not sure."

"Have you seen him since the death?"

"We're not dating anymore."

"I'll ask you again. When was the last time you saw him?"

"At the campsite."

"The night before the accident?"

"No, when I left him that morning. I didn't wake him."

"Were you trying to get away from him?"

"I guess so. I don't remember much."

"Had you been drinking the night before?"

"Yes."

"And smoking pot?"

"A little."

"Were you high?"

"I guess."

"What happened that night with your boyfriend?"

Garcia paused, and her face began to show anger. "We had an argument."

"Serious?"

"Yes. The son-of-a-bitch had promised to marry me. He was to give me a ring that night. He didn't. He said he was breaking off our relationship."

"What was your reaction?"

"I smoked some more pot. And then some more. And then drank some booze, and then had more pot."

"Ms. Garcia, what was your condition when you were on the trail out of Cascade Canyon and reached Inspiration Point."

"I was damned pissed off. Men! They're all alike."

"When you allegedly saw Brenda Lacy Brown go over the cliff, what was your physical and mental condition?"

"I guess not too good."

"Do you remember your hike back to Inspiration Point?"

"Not really. I had too much weed."

The following day Longstreet interviewed Robert Casis, who was with Gail Garcia on the camping trip.

"Mr. Casis, how long have you known Gail Garcia?"

"About four months."

"Where did you meet?"

"At the Silver Dollar in Jackson."

"Were you both drinking?"

"Of course. That's what you do at the Silver Dollar."

"Did you ask her out?"

"The next week I decided to ask her out and called her."

"She accepted?"

"Yes."

"What did you do together?"

"I asked her to do a day hike around Jenny Lake."

"Did she agree?"

"Yes. We hiked some days later and met a couple of gals who had camped up Cascade Canyon. They said it was great. Gail asked me to take her to the same place."

"You agreed?"

"Yes."

"That was the camping trip that led Ms. Garcia to say she saw Palmer Brown push his wife off Inspiration Point?"

"Yes."

"Had you promised to marry her?"

"Not a chance. She was just a date."

"Did you and Ms. Garcia drink the night before?"

"Yes. Too much."

"Explain that."

"I brought a full bottle of Jim Beam bourbon. She had a bottle of some cheap vodka."

"How much did you drink?"

"On the first night we each had a couple of drinks."

"You camped two nights?"

"Yes. On the second night after we'd each had about five drinks—and were both smashed—Gail pulled out some pot."

"Which you began to smoke?"

"Yes. It was too much on top of the liquor."

"How much did you drink and smoke?"

"I don't remember. I remember Gail was pretty wild."

"What do you mean?"

"She thought we should climb Grand Teton."

"The next day?"

"No, that night. She was crazy. I fell asleep."

"And she was still smoking?"

"And chanting."

"When you woke in the morning, was she awake?"

"Yes, sitting on her bedroll smoking the last of the pot."

"What was her condition?"

"Scary. She was over the top. We had an argument, and she got up, grabbed some of her things, and started off down the canyon in the direction of Jenny Lake."

"Did you follow her?"

"Yes, I was worried about her."

"Why?"

"She wasn't walking straight. She was still yelling at me when she disappeared."

"And you were behind her?"

"Yes, a hundred yards more or less."

"Was she walking normally?"

"No. She stumbled several times and fell once. She looked drunk or stoned. Probably both."

"Ms. Garcia claims she arrived at Inspiration Point in time to see Palmer Brown push his wife over the cliff."

"That's not possible. I arrived close behind her. There were already a dozen people at the top, all in a frenzy. She didn't get to the top in time to see the Brown woman go over. She's imagining it."

"Why would she lie?"

"I think Gail has problems. From our conversations at the campsites she said all men were liars and cheats and only interested in sex. She was scary. I'll be more careful who I hike with. If she had the opportunity she would push *me* off a cliff."

"Thank you, Mr. Casis."

Longstreet was ready for a hearing on her motion to dismiss the charges against her client. At that hearing the court took little time to make a decision.

"Mr. Brown has no prior criminal record," said the judge. "Furthermore, he is a prominent member of the community. We both coach little league football. The report of the authorities places too much weight on Ms. Garcia's comments. Mr. Casis had no reason to lie to this court, and I place considerable weight on his testimony. The charges are dismissed. Mr. Brown, you may go."

That afternoon Brown bought a bouquet of red roses and took them to the boat dock on Jenny Lake and then to the top of Inspiration Point. He stood near the edge and quietly said his goodbyes to Brenda Lacy, throwing the roses off the cliff.

"Thank you, my love, for leaving me all of your property. I will spend it carefully and think of you always. Be content wherever you are. I hope you enjoyed the trip down."

Brown returned to Jenny Lake, drove to the Silver Dollar bar in Jackson, ordered a bottle of the most expensive *Champagne* they served, *vueve clicquot*, poured a flute, and toasted Brenda Lacy. He also toasted the judge for his decision and Robert Casis for his testimony.

By now, Casis was almost to the Wyoming-Colorado border, wondering how he would spend the $50,000 in cash in a backpack in his car's trunk.

"I'm through with Wyoming," Casis thought out loud, as he passed the Welcome to Colorado sign. "That Brown was a pretty nice dude. I don't know why he killed his wife."

Back at the Silver Dollar, Brown sipped the last of the *Champagne,* left a hundred dollar bill on the bar as a tip, and mumbled, "I have more money than I'll ever be able to use. . . . I can buy *everything.* I can even buy someone's life."

58

THE SAME EVENING IN GUATEMALA CITY

AT THE VERY MOMENT PALMER BROWN WAS sipping the last of his drink in Jackson, Juan Pablo Herzog was settled deeply in an arm chair in his residence in Guatemala City, reading several reports in his lap and sipping the same brand of *Champagne—vueve clicquot*—Brown was drinking that same evening in Wyoming.

The reports referred to the suicide note Ralph Johnson had left in Barberino Val d'Elsa, Italy. Herzog had read them over and over. Having them was worth the loss of Alarcon and Olviedo. Now, General Hector Ramirez would deal with Walter Windsor. Herzog thought that someday not too distant he might soon join General Ramirez in Alaska to end finally the life of Maxwell Hunt. Herzog would accomplish that fatal act slowly, imposing on Windsor before he died a measure of physical pain equal to the mental anguish Herzog had suffered.

Herzog stood and walked out into the resplendent garden. He thought of his niece María-Martina Herzog, his nephew Martín Paz, and a second niece Luisa Solares. Herzog was convinced that María-Martina and Martín had been killed by Windsor, who earlier had lived as Professor Maxwell Hunt. Luisa had not been killed, but he had lost her loyalty to him by her succumbing to the fruits of university life in the U.S.

Luisa no longer mattered because Herzog now knew about Windsor. She could stay at UF and add a JD to her Masters. He hoped she would return to Guatemala at about the time his term as President ended. She would become *his* lawyer when he returned to private life, and he would pay her generously from what he was accumulating as President.

While he considered that future, the guard at the front entrance called and said General Ramirez had arrived.

"Escort him to me immediately," Herzog responded.

A few moments later Ramirez joined Herzog in the garden.

"General, it is good to see you. I assume you have read all I have sent to you about former Professor Maxwell Hunt."

"I have, Excellency."

"I want you to go to Anchorage. I have appointed you as a consular officer stationed in Alaska. You will have diplomatic immunity."

"That is impressive, Presidente. I will begin the search for Windsor immediately. I can leave for Anchorage in two days."

"I want you to work carefully and not let it be known you are searching for Windsor. Remember that Windsor is hiding and watchful that his true identity does not become known. The CIA helps him do that.

"The method of your search I leave to you. My hope is that by the time I leave the presidency in a little less than three years, you will have sent me more exact information, specifically Windsor's home address."

"I will do that," said Ramirez, although he thought that if he found and killed Windsor, he would be praised and bestowed with honors by Herzog when he returned to Guatemala. Herzog rose, quickly followed by Ramirez. And then Herzog did what few had ever seen him do. He gave Ramirez the traditional Latin abrazo—a hug of affection used in greeting and saying goodbye to special people.

General Ramirez left thrilled with the meeting and especially the parting abrazo. As the driver opened the door on the general's official car and Ramirez settled in the back seat, he began to think aloud what was ahead.

"It should not be difficult to identify all the persons named Windsor in Alaska." But he began to realize there were obstacles. He opened his cell phone and pulled up Alaska, discovering it to be the largest state by area but only the 47th by population, which was yet to reach three-quarters of a million. The search might lead him to some of the more than 300 islands that make up the Aleutians. Commercial fishing was an important industry throughout the state.

Then Ramirez thought, "What if Windsor has adopted a different name? Many Alaskans have migrated from the lower 48 states to escape something. Also, I have been assuming Windsor would have adopted a man's name and I would only have to limit my search to about half the Alaskan population. But what if Windsor adopted a name used by males and females, such as Morgan or Jordan or Jamie?" Ramirez began to realize his search might be more difficult than he imagined.

Herzog returned to his quarters a contented man. Now he could focus on executive matters, knowing he would receive reports from Ramirez, and by the end of his presidency, he would know exactly where Windsor lived.

And maybe have proof that Windsor was dead.

59

SAME TIME IN BERMUDA

ATTORNEY GEORGE HAMILTON CALLED ME AT 6:00 a.m. I thought he was playing tricks until I realized the time in Bermuda—four hours later than in Montana. It was 10:00 a.m. at Hamilton's office.

Hamilton had to be British; he sounded like an educated product of Oxford or Cambridge.

"Mr. Brooks, I sent you a letter two weeks ago and haven't had a response from you. Perhaps your postal system was not working in your vast undeveloped wild West with the same efficiency it operates here on our tiny but highly civilized island."

"You may be right," I said. "We are much less anal retentive than you island folks. . . . I did receive your letter."

"And?"

"I read it," I answered.

"And?"

"Where does your client reside?"

"I'm not at liberty to disclose that."

"Would you tell your local police where he lives, if they ask?"

"What does that have to do with my letter?" he asked.

"Ellsworth-Kent is a fugitive. You must not know that or you wouldn't be helping him. You're harboring a multiple murderer and you are committing a crime under Bermuda law."

"I'm only protecting my client."

"From what?"

"You."

"I've committed no crime, and you obviously know *exactly* where I live," I said.

"Might we talk about the substance of this matter and not trivial details?"

"Fine. You claim your client Ellsworth-Kent has a power of attorney."

"That is correct."

"You stated that the power is from his wife, Lucinda. Would it interest you to know he does not have a lawful wife?"

"That's ridiculous. I have a copy of the power in front of me: 'I, Lucinda Ellsworth-Kent,' it begins, 'being the lawful wife of Robert Ellsworth-Kent. . . .' It goes on to grant full power from Lucinda to her husband."

"She's granting the power as the lawful wife of Ellsworth-Kent?"

"Yes."

"Do you have a copy of their marriage certificate?"

"No, the ceremony of marriage took place near a town called Kirkwall on the Orkney Islands of Scotland."

"Did you ask Ellsworth-Kent for a copy of the marriage papers?"

"Time was of the essence. I took his word."

"Now you might take *my* word. There are only two ways under Scottish law that they could have married properly at Kirkwall. One would have been a civil ceremony. None has been recorded at the National Registry."

"But it was a religious ceremony, not a civil ceremony," replied Hamilton. "My client is a high priest. He and Lucinda, who is a high priestess, were married in a *Pagan* ceremony."

"Do you have a copy of their marriage celebration that must have been filed with the Scottish Pagan Foundation?"

"No," he said more quietly than before.

"Assuming that they were not and are not now married, how can your client Ellsworth-Kent be representing Lucinda in doing something only she can do?"

"Because of the power of attorney."

"Which in this case was a power granted specifically by a *wife* to her alleged *husband?*"

"Yes."

"Attorney Hamilton, assume you have given your wife a power of attorney to act on your behalf."

"If you wish to play games, all right."

"Can she have you married to someone you don't know by appearing herself on *your* behalf at the wedding ceremony?"

"I would think not."

"And then come home and inform you that on your behalf she has had *you* married?"

"That would be strange."

"So there may be limitations to the power given?"

"Well, yes," Hamilton admitted.

"Could that not include the inability of one allegedly given a power to act for the person who granted the power?"

"Yes," he mumbled nearly inaudibly.

"May I suggest *you* consider what power you have? Assuming you conclude, as I have, that Lucinda and Ellsworth-Kent were *not* married, would you still insist that I must do what you demand in your letter?"

"I'll have to think about that."

"Please do, and get back to me. While you're thinking, please consider that a Pagan high priest or priestess must be listed in the Pagan Foundation's records. In this case Lucinda and Ellsworth-Kent are not," I said and hung up.

I immediately called Wanda Groves in Bozeman and told her about the letter and my conversation with Hamilton.

"Macduff, I wish you'd talk to me before you get involved in a conversation like the one you had with him. You waiver between being a good lawyer and a pain in the ass."

"Did I mess things up?"

"You could have, but to the contrary, I suspect you confused him."

"Sorry. You sound busy," I said. "I'll let you go. Call me as soon as you hear anything."

"One other thing," Wanda said. "I'm going to call the police in Bermuda and talk about Hamilton committing a crime by aiding and abetting or even harboring a fugitive."

"Let me know about that as well," I said, and hung up.

I called Henry Mellon in Manhattan and explained the whole matter.

"Fortunately, Mr. Brooks, there have been no further attempts by Lucinda or Ellsworth-Kent to take over the investment account," Mellon said. "As you know, I've blocked that account."

"I don't like to do this, Henry. It makes me feel there's been another stage after the abduction where I'm losing my hold on Lucinda. When she's back with me—if that happens—we'll restore the account as jointly held assets."

"Thanks, I thought you would."

60

EARLY SEPTEMBER

THAT EVENING ELSBETH AND I ENTERED THE Chico Hot Springs main dining room and were seated in a quiet corner.

"The dinner is on me," said Elsbeth. "It's time I paid you back for all my freeloading. Besides, I get a great discount."

"Do I wait another three years for the next invitation?"

"At least. . . . What's up with you?"

I told her about my phone conversations with George Hamilton in Bermuda and Wanda Groves in Bozeman.

"It looks as though Ellsworth-Kent is not going to get Lucinda's assets, those she solely holds and those she shares with me jointly. Your inheritance seems safe."

"Dad! I want *Lucinda* back. I'm not worried about any inheritance. . . . I'll have my law degree."

"I want to leave you financially comfortable. So you can keep the cottage and, if you wish, also the cabin here."

The window was open, allowing a chilled breeze to surround us. Elsbeth got up, shut the window, and sat again.

"Dad, before we finish, I want to talk to you about Palmer Brown. He made six or seven trips alone to the top of Inspiration Point, allegedly plotting where he'd push his wife off."

"Why does he interest you? Are you planning to take *me* to Inspiration Point?"

"It's a thought. . . . I read everything I could find in the lo-cal papers and on-line about him and Brenda Lacy Brown. I even called and talked to Lieutenant Byng in Jackson."

"Where are you headed with this? You mentioned both the Gallatin murders and Palmer Brown's incident with his wife on Inspiration Point. Those were *unconnected* deaths."

"OK, I know that's what *you* think. . . . When I researched Palmer Brown, I found he was much like you. There is no rec-ord of his existence as Palmer Brown before he moved here."

"So?"

"So I went to Jenny Lake with a photograph of Brown and talked to several employees at the boat dock. One of the boat drivers said he thought that once or twice Brown was on his boat returning from the boat landing below Inspiration Point.

"A woman who works on the dock said she saw Brown maybe a half-dozen times. She remembered he always wore a University of Minnesota Alumnus sweatshirt and a Minnesota Vikings cap on backwards. I did a name search in Minnesota and found nothing. Byng got access to the University of Min-nesota records. A Palmer Brown never attended.

"Why did Brown make so many trips to Inspiration Point?" she asked rhetorically. "I believe he made at least a half-dozen. I believe he was *planning* Brenda Lacy's death."

"Do you have anything more?" I asked, intrigued with her search. "Remember that Brown was acquitted. He can't be tried again for her death. You know what double jeopardy means."

"I do have more," she said. "I'm certain that Palmer Brown was formerly Heinz Kunstler, like you were formerly Professor Maxwell Hunt."

"*Kunstler?* Sounds German."

"It is. He lived in Frankfurt where he owned a few apart-ments that he rented, giving him a modest income."

"What are you trying to prove?" I asked.

"Be patient," she said, exasperated.

"Kunstler married a wealthy woman named Greta. Her family owned vineyards and produced a high quality Rhine wine. After only three years of marriage, Greta died."

"Germans die, just like us."

"*Dad!* Listen to me. . . . On a holiday trip Heinz took Greta to a high cliff in the valley at Lauterbrunnen in Switzerland. She 'fell off' the cliff and died. Kunstler and Brown are similar in height and weight. They were about the same age. I've compared photos; there were some in the Swiss newspapers."

"And you see a link between the deaths?"

"Wait 'til you hear the rest. . . . Swiss newspapers thought Kunstler pushed his wife Greta off the cliff. A Swiss prosecutor pursued the matter but concluded it was an accident."

"That's all interesting. You're as curious as Lucinda."

"And another fact in the Swiss death matches Palmer Brown's actions at Inspiration Point. Heinz Kunstler had been on top of the cliff five or six times before Greta fell and died."

"What are you going to do about this?" I asked.

"I've typed it out and sent a copy to Byng in Jackson and Rangley in Livingston. I thought they would like to know about Brown's German background. Byng can pursue it more if he wants to."

"Are you going to search more?"

"You bet. It's fun and better than crossword puzzles."

"Don't get in trouble. And don't get me in trouble."

"I'll try," she said. "It's time to send *you* home and let *me* get some sleep. I'm on duty early at the front desk."

"So what if Palmer Brown was jailed, tried, convicted, and executed for pushing his wife off a cliff?" I said aloud to myself, walking up the stairs to my cabin. "Do I care? Not a high priority considering my own problems. I'd prefer to read Lucinda pushed Ellsworth-Kent off a cliff and was coming home.

"Other than Lucinda, my main interest is Juan Pablo Herzog," I continued. "Sometime he is going to realize he's been had by Ralph Johnson's lies in his suicide note stating that Professor Hunt had become Walter Windsor and worked in Alaska at something to do with fishing. Most everyone in Alaska seems to have something to do with oil or fishing! I suspect that sometime in the future Herzog will be back on a more focused track to find me—maybe by 'purchasing' the memory of one of the remaining CIA agents who was involved with my change to become fishing guide Macduff Brooks."

Despite the problems with Jackson, it would be good for the citizens of Gallatin County if the sheriff's office solved the Gallatin River murders. Whether it was only a coincidence that our boat was the first to encounter the bodies hanging from the barbed wire is perplexing. Were we really *involved* in those two murders? Were we the intended *victims?*

Mainly, however, I'm a wreck from worrying and wondering about Lucinda. Even if she is found and wants to come back, she won't be the same person as the one who was abducted. I've slowly moved on with my life, and Grace Justice has been an important part of that. She has not pushed for some kind of long-term commitment, but she is not getting any younger and is much in demand by many who would like to step in and replace me. Should I encourage that?

I think I'll ask Grace. In fact, I'll call her and ask if she would like to fly out here to Montana and fish.

61

TWO DAYS LATER

WHEN I CALLED GRACE, SHE WAS THRILLED with my invitation to fly out and fish during the Montana September "hopper" season, tossing a grasshopper imitation onto an opposite bank and pulling it off into the water, enticing brown trout hidden under the bank. An FFF Master Casting Instructor, Grace had never been trout fishing west of Arkansas.

Two days later when Grace got off the flight to Bozeman from Salt Lake City, following a long leg from Atlanta after a short hop from Jacksonville, she looked spectacular, wearing mutely embroidered jeans and a light turtleneck sweater that left no doubt about her eye-catching figure.

"I'm so excited to finally be in Montana," Grace said, wrapping her arms around me and pressing her lips hard against mine.

"That felt *so* good," she said when she let go. "I've missed you. It's been a long, lonely summer. I haven't been fishing once, but I did go to your cottage one afternoon and walked down and sat on your dock for an hour or two. The cottage looked so empty without you."

"I need to give you a key," I offered. "You might like to take a break and stay over there when I'm in Montana."

"I'd rather stay over when you're *not* gone. . . . I'm freezing, Macduff. This is a very thin sweater."

"It is, but I'm not complaining. You look ravishing."

"Are you a ravisher?"

"Not until I've finished a Gentleman Jack—or two."

We walked toward the crowded baggage area where several flights were arriving at nearly the same time. Grace tucked her arm tightly around mine and laid her head against my shoulder.

"Mcduff? Is that you?" came a voice from behind us.

I turned and there were my attorney, Wanda Groves, and Livingston Deputy Sheriff Erin Giffin. Both were close friends of Lucinda and appeared in shock to see me embraced by another woman.

"Say hello to Grace Justice," I said, looking far more guilty than the cat that swallowed the canary.

"Hi, Grace. I'm Erin. I think Macduff has mentioned you. You're county police back in St. Augustine?"

"Close. I'm with the Florida State Attorney's Office. And you're a deputy here?"

"A little east on the other side of the Bozeman Pass."

"I'm Wanda Groves," said the second person. "I'm the Brookses attorney. Are you here on business? I've done some work for Macduff recently on the man who abducted Lucinda."

"I know about both Ellsworth-Kent and his Bermuda attorney," replied Grace.

"We're meeting some people coming off the Denver flight," Erin said. "I see them coming in. We need to help with their bags. Good to see you both. Enjoy your stay, Grace. Bye, Macduff. Make sure Grace keeps warm."

I was glad that neither Grace nor I said she was here solely for pleasure. I hoped they assumed we were working on a Florida case together. But that wouldn't have involved the kind of kiss Grace induced.

Quickly the two were gone. My enthusiasm about Grace's arrival deflated like a pierced balloon. I hadn't given a moment's thought how I would react if we ran into any of Lucinda's close friends. The expressions on the faces of Erin and Wanda were the needle that pierced the balloon.

"Hungry?" I asked as we loaded Grace's bags into my SUV.

"Yes. I had a sumptuous free lunch of peanuts and tepid water on the plane. Delta's infamous cuisine. That proved to be my lunch. I'll bet the CEO of Delta had a very different lunch that same day. . . . Where are you taking me?"

"To Ted's Montana Grill in the old Baxter Hotel. As you might expect, being associated with Ted Turner, they serve bison chili, bison meatloaf, bison pot roast, bison nachos, bison steak, or burgers. *Bison* burgers that is."

"Do we sit outside?"

"It's too chilly. Snow's expected tomorrow."

"Snow?" Grace said, shocked. "It's *September!*"

"We had quarter-sized hail in a storm in July, which covered the ground with a couple of inches," I explained. "And yesterday we had the first snow of the fall, about four inches that melted by nightfall."

"Eating inside will be fine. I'm already shivering."

I parked, and we walked into what was once the two-story hotel lobby. "Ted's takes up about half the main floor," I said.

"It's beautiful, Macduff."

"It was once the town's social center. Now it's residential and commercial space and generates a lot of pride being on the

National Register of Historic Places, which seems to fit with Ted Turner's preservation of that historic animal—the bison."

"I can't believe I'm here. When did you invite me?"

"Forty-eight hours ago sounds about right. It took you so long to accept."

"As I remember, it took about ten seconds."

After dinner the drive over the modest but seasonally demanding Bozeman Pass to Livingston took only thirty minutes. No trace of snow was left from the day before. Before heading south into Paradise Valley, I drove Grace through the center of the old downtown of Livingston. Another half-hour, and we entered the gravel road to my log cabin.

When I'd invited Grace to Montana, I hadn't given a moment's thought to Lucinda's presence in the cabin in photos on every wall of every room.

"You miss her terribly Macduff, don't you?" Grace said as she entered the living room.

"Yes. I don't know what she suffered. She can't be alive. I've set next New Year's as time to come to grips with her being gone. I'll remove these photos and put them into albums to give to Elsbeth, who thinks of Lucinda as her mom and best friend. This room is too painful to look at forever. The same is true for the Florida cottage."

"It's unfair, Macduff," she said, taking my hands in hers. "You went through something similar to this two decades ago with El. But then you knew right away that she was gone. There's still a chance with Lucinda. . . . Don't give up. But you're right; closure has to come, and you're the only one who can make it work. . . . Should I have come here?"

"Yes," I said, and nothing more.

I was up early the following morning, sitting on the porch with coffee and wrapped in two blankets. Grace was inside pouring another coffee and looking around the cabin.

About the time the morning sun rose above the surrounding Absaroka Mountains, Elsbeth's car pulled in. She and Sue got out, opened the rear deck, and lifted out several bags, which they carried carefully past me and into the cabin without saying a word. I followed them inside where they opened the bags and produced a steaming breakfast for four that their colleagues at Chico Hot Springs had prepared.

"How's this?" Elsbeth asked, hugging me and then doing the same with Grace.

"What's going on?" I asked.

"Grace called me and said she was coming out to fish with you. I told her that Sue and I'd be here for breakfast, and we'd bring the food. Let's eat while it's hot."

"Grace is staying four days," I explained. "Then she has to get back for a trial beginning Monday. Will you bring us breakfast every day?"

"Not a chance. I expect you'll both come to Chico a couple of times. We serve great meals. . . . When are you two going fishing?"

"Every day, starting in an hour upstream on Mill Creek. Tomorrow we'll float a section of the Yellowstone River. The day after that we head for Yellowstone Park to see the sights before the park closes for the intemperate seasons. Grace first and last visited there when she was a teen. On her last day here, we'll float the Gallatin. I talked to Jason in Bozeman, and he said the recent rains have made that possible."

"Come to dinner with us your last evening?" Sue pleaded.

"A deal!" Grace answered.

62

THE NEXT THREE DAYS

M ILL CREEK WAS ON ITS BEST BEHAVIOR. THE
upper section near the campsites was covered by burnt
trees rising above a forest floor thick with brilliant wildflowers
beneath the charred trees. The day produced a dozen eight- to
ten-inch cutthroats at their most colorful. I won't say which of
us did better, but Grace allowed me credit for two!

We floated the Yellowstone the second day, starting near
the Tom Miner Bridge at Carbella and drifting a full sixteen
miles to Emigrant.

"That looks like a very long way and a lot of hours for you
to row," said Grace, looking at a map of the river while finishing a dawn breakfast.

"It is a long way, and it demands more than I like to row.
So I won't."

I was serious, and a few miles downriver from Carbella,
near Point of Rocks, I leaned forward from the guide seat,
tapped Grace's shoulder, and when she turned around said,
"*Your* turn."

"What do you mean 'my turn,'" she replied, netting a fat
twenty-incher.

"You've never rowed one of these drift boats. If you're
coming to Montana more often, you need to learn. How about
a trade? You give me good advice on casting and not make

your usual snide remarks about my dropping the tip of my rod or making another wind knot, and I'll teach you to row a drift boat from this middle guide's seat."

"I'm content with where I am at the bow."

I moved from the guide seat to the rear, picked up my rod, and cast.

"What are you doing, Macduff? No one's rowing!"

"Not my turn. I didn't promise to guide you every minute we're on the water. Get in the guide's seat. Earn your keep!"

"Men!" she grumbled, adding, "I've rowed a dingy. When I did, I always sat with my back toward the bow and faced the transom. Now you have me *facing* the bow. That's not right. What do I do?"

"Row! The same way you did in the dinghy. But here you aren't rowing toward something like an anchored boat or a dock. You're rowing backwards *against* the current and keeping a good distance from obstacles ahead."

"It would be easier to go *with* the current."

"You are, but you row to stay *off* the current and have some control where we go. Merely drifting wouldn't provide that control."

"I think I'm getting it," she said. And she was correct. I didn't say a word until thirty yards ahead we saw a pile of tree limbs in the middle of the river.

"I don't want to hit that scary pile of trees we're heading to. What do I do?" she asked.

"Point *toward* it."

"Oh, thanks. That's sounds like a death threat."

"I mean it. Angle the boat so we're facing the tree. We're off to one side now and want to stay there. By keeping us at an angle, the current is going to sweep us safely past the tree."

"Wow," she said as we passed twenty feet to the side of a dangerous mass of trunks and branches. "You were right!"

"That happens sometimes. You owe me a casting lesson."

"I wouldn't know where to begin."

Our third day wasn't an all-day fishing event. I planned an hour spent dropping a few flies on the Firehole River near Old Faithful. But mainly, the day was to be a trip through the park.

"Why aren't there many cars here," she said as we drove through Gardiner, passed under the Roosevelt Arch, and approached the park entrance behind only two vehicles.

"Most of the park has begun to close. When kids go back to school, the number of visitors drops dramatically. In July we might wait here for forty minutes to enter the park."

"Only a few people sounds good. Also true of park lodging?"

"Yes. We're having lunch at the Old Faithful Inn. No reservations needed. No lines. I usually book lodging for the last few days before the summer season is over and most of the park has closed. Yellowstone can't be described. Or even attempted to be shown by *National Geographic* on TV. It has to be experienced."

"You've been coming here long?" she asked.

"Since I was four. My grandparents brought me out, and I whined until they did it again the following year. I kept whining, so we came back every year. It became an annual family event until I went off to college."

We stopped alongside the Firehole River at Fountain Flats, surrounded by geysers and steam. The oncoming fall was cooling down the river from the combination of the water that drains into the river from geysers and the warm air temperatures of summer. Now the fall water was cooler every day, and the trout were coming back into the main Firehole. We fished a bit, and each caught a single brown trout by throwing grasshoppers onto and under the far banks.

After a leisurely lunch at the inn, we continued our drive to Yellowstone Lake, north to the upper and lower falls, Canyon Village, Mount Washington, the Lamar Valley, Gardiner at dusk, and soon were home at the cabin.

The evening was warm enough to sit on the cabin porch overlooking Mill Creek, but fleece vests were followed by sweaters that, in turn, were followed by blankets.

"An incredible day, Macduff. Only one more. I hate to leave."

"Tomorrow will be different. The Gallatin's much narrower than the Yellowstone. There's not much water this time of year, but it's worth trying to float."

"Isn't the Gallatin where you've told me a couple of murders took place not long ago? Barbed wire hung across the river that caught a couple of fishermen by their necks and jerked them out of their boats so they hung on the wire and bled? They must have suffered agonizing deaths."

"We're going to fish that same section tomorrow. But there've been no similar barbed wire incidents for months. It was some crank who's gone on to other activities. Most of the guides, including me, think it was a nasty, paranoid riverfront landowner who occasionally strung barbed wire across the river. He was harassed so much by the county sheriff's deputies after the two deaths that last month he sold out and moved to Utah."

"Is Elsbeth going with us?"

"She wants to, but she's working. It's just the two of us."

63

THE NEXT MORNING

THE DAY DAWNED CRISPLY AND CLEARLY, AND the air was deafeningly still. The rising sun disclosed the sharp, dark edges of the mountains against the blue sky.

I made breakfast—eggs Benedict, Canadian bacon, and Hollandaise sauce on split English muffins. All carefully arranged on a carved, well-worn wooden Mexican tray, I carried it to Grace who was beginning to stir to the enticing fragrances from the kitchen. She rolled over and modestly pulled up the covers. I left her to enjoy the meal and went out to rig my inflatable boat for our day on the Gallatin.

"Where do we put in Macduff," she asked a half-hour later as we drove through Livingston and west over the pass. Bozeman was quietly opening to what portended to be a day of calm and clarity, the temperature expected to hover around seventy.

"We keep going through the middle of Bozeman a half-dozen miles to what is called Four Corners, hang a left, and go south another ten miles watching the Gallatin Mountains close in on us." I think Grace heard me, but she still looked sleepy.

Forty minutes later a couple of miles beyond the road to the Williams Bridge, we bumped down off U.S. 191 and backed the trailer to the river's edge. The launching site is not clearly marked on most maps, likely because it's not used often since you can't fish from a vessel. That wouldn't prevent us from floating the river and stopping and wade fishing as often as we wished.

We loaded the inflatable and shoved it into the water.

"Am I rowing you or are you rowing me?" Grace asked. "You tried to teach me to row two days ago. It can't be much different in an inflatable."

"It isn't, but it's different on this *river*. We may have to get out to pull and push where it's too shallow to float. The bottom's made of round stones that for centuries have tumbled here from upstream. They are slippery. Be careful. . . . Sit up front to begin," I suggested. "I'll point out places you might enjoy knowing about."

"Like waterfalls and dams?"

"No waterfalls, but there are occasional diversion dams. We'll finish near one close to the old boarded-up Gallatin Gateway Inn."

"I'm rigged except for a fly. What do you suggest?" asked Grace when we first stopped to try our skills, which she defined for me as *luck*.

"Try a fairly small black rubberlegs and trail a tiny midge pupa. I'll hand them to you. I'm going to do the same with a greenish rubberlegs and a Prince Nymph. If they don't work quickly, we'll try something different.

"We just went under the Williams Bridge," I said a half-hour later. "I'm pulling us in ahead on the right, a hundred feet before a favorite spot."

We set the anchor, hopped out, and scanned the river.

"Throw right along here, at the bank downstream, and if you can make a good cast without losing your rig in the trees behind us, the far bank may be productive."

"I've got something," Grace called out ten minutes later as a brown trout broke the surface giving us a hint of its unique color. "It's hooked on the midge!"

"It *was* on the midge. . . . But it's gone—easy to lose one on a barbless hook. We'll find anoth . . . You've *got* another! Maybe the brown's back for another try."

"But this is on the rubberlegs."

"Keep your rod tip *up*."

"I'm supposed to be giving *you* lessons," said Grace. "You should focus on *rowing* lessons."

"You're a Master *Casting* Instructor," I noted, "not a master on playing and landing fish."

"Get the net and be quiet," she ordered, as she brought the brown close enough for me to reach out with the net.

"Pure brilliance," she said.

"It is beautiful," I agreed.

"I meant a brilliant *landing* of my first Gallatin River trout."

"There'll be more," I added as I lifted my own rod to set the hook in another trout, this time a rainbow."

"Was yours hooked on the rubberlegs or Prince?"

"The Prince. Old and reliable. Like Gentleman Jack."

"You would make that comparison," she added.

An hour later and a mile further we stopped again and, standing in the water, I commented, "We're doing OK, but I want you to try something different. Replace the rubberlegs with a different stonefly and change your midge pupa for an egg dropper."

"Why an *egg* dropper?"

"Trout like eggs, just like you. Eggs Benedict for you at seven; egg droppers for trout at eleven. I'm the perfect host."

"So you choose what fly to use based on what you had for breakfast!"

"Why not?"

"Macduff," she called out five minutes later, lifting her rod tip, "I've hooked one on the egg dropper."

It was her fourth fish, each on a different fly.

"Your turn to row," I said as we pushed the inflatable boat back into the river.

"I guess that's OK. I'm not allowed to fish from the boat so I might as well be rowing."

"How do you like the Gallatin?" I asked an hour later.

"It's a dream! Different from the Yellowstone, as you said. I have to pay attention because the water changes so rapidly."

"It'll be that way the rest of the float. We're about half-way, almost time for lunch. I'll look for a good place."

Watching along the bank for a place to pull off, I assumed Grace was looking ahead. But she was distracted momentarily, searching for a fly on the floor of the boat. When she sat up and looked ahead, she screamed, *"Duck Macduff! Quick!"*

Dropping to the floor, without looking I felt something scrape across the top of my head. Instinctively reaching up, my hand came away bleeding profusely.

I looked back to see Grace yanked out of the boat. There was barbed wire stretched across the water from one cotton-wood tree to another on the opposite side. Blood spurted from Graces neck, and she was not moving.

Slipping into the guide's seat, I rowed to the shore. Glances toward Grace brought not the slightest movement as she dangled from the wire, the barbs embedded in her throat.

It was faster to run along the shore than to row back against the strong current. When I got back and waded out to Grace, I caught my already bleeding hands in the wire and struggled to remain standing, jerking free only at the cost of further deep cuts. When I reached Grace, I touched her neck and felt no pulse. I couldn't possibly free her from the barbs without wire cutters.

Calling 911 meant reaching for my phone and letting go of one hand. I might have been able to cut the wire on the far side of her and pull her body back to the shore. But my wire cutters were on my inflatable, and I had no choice but to leave her and work my way back to the shore; I was tiring and chilled and shivering from the cold water.

On the bank I stood by the tree where one end of the barbed wire remained securely nailed and made the 911 call. I was uncertain what to do next. No movement from Grace and the amount of blood on her head and jacket made me realize she was dead. The suddenness of striking the wire may have broken her neck.

A few minutes later a siren wailed in the distance, and I stepped onto the bank to wave the emergency van toward us. Standing and watching the van, I felt something strike my lower side, heard a shot, and fell back down the bank into the shallows along the edge of the river. I reached down and brought up my hand, soaked with fresh blood seeping through my shirt and combining with the drying blood from my head. Another shot came, but I felt nothing; the bank apparently blocked the shooter's view. A flurry of different sounding shots followed a few seconds later.

Then silence as I lost consciousness, lying motionless in the cold shallows and the current that absorbed the continuing flow of blood from my side.

64

AT THE BOZEMAN HOSPITAL

"DAD!" CAME A DISTANT SOUNDING VOICE. IT was Elsbeth. She wasn't distant at all but standing next to my bed, patiently waiting for me to open my eyes and reassure her there was a bit of life left in me.

"Hi, daughter," I mumbled, slurring the few words I could get out. "What . . . you doing here? You have . . . work today."

"That was yesterday. You've missed a day. The police are outside, less patient than me. They want to ask you questions. I want a hug," she said, carefully setting her head against my cheek and trying to hold back tears.

"Mr. Brooks?" said a voice on the other side of the bed. I looked and saw a tag that said "Dr. Carter."

"I'm *he*," I murmured.

"You are fortunate to be 'he' and not the 'late he.' You took a high caliber bullet into your back that nicked a kidney and went back out, passing through your belt. It destroyed what was an impressive, intricate silver buckle. I've patched up the kidney. You buy your own new belt and buckle."

"Who . . . shot me?"

"One of your former fishing clients from Jackson. I assume he gave you a bad evaluation as a guide."

"Was he caught?"

"In a manner of speaking. He's resting on a slab at the morgue."

"Then I . . . go home now?"

"When you're free of infection, at best in two days."

"And," added Elsbeth, showing a faint smile, "if you answer all the deputies' questions and aren't taken directly to jail."

"Young lady," interrupted Dr. Carter, looking at Elsbeth, "you and your friend killed the man who shot Mr. Brooks. You both fired your guns several times. The police are more interested in talking to you than your dad."

"They already have talked to Sue and me. And we shot the guy a bunch! I had my dad's .357 magnum Ruger revolver that carries five soft-nosed cartridges. I emptied it and hit him four times. Sue used Lucinda's Glock that holds fifteen rounds. She fired twelve and got him seven times. She needs more practice."

"You mean he was hit *eleven* times?" the amazed Dr. Carter asked.

"That sounds right. We felt like Butch and Sundance. We were running side-by-side directly at him and firing. We each fired our last shot from about seven feet. Whether he knew it or not, he was dead by that time, on his knees staring at us, his rifle on the ground."

"Elsbeth. Is Grace . . . OK?" I asked. "She didn't look like she was alive . . . I couldn't take . . . off the barbed wire."

"She's dead, Dad. Grace broke her neck and cut an artery on the wire. We don't think she suffered long."

"Did I hear her say that Grace was gone?" I thought but couldn't ask. "First El, then Lucinda, and now Grace?"

I turned on my good side listening to Elsbeth and was amazed at what she related about what had happened.

"Who's the person . . . you shot?" I asked her. "*Who?*"

"His name was Palmer Brown," explained Elsbeth. "A name you know. His first shot dropped you, and he got off a second that missed when Sue and I surprised him. He turned and fired at us, but by then he had one of my bullets in his chest and two of Sue's in his lower groin. I'm not certain what Sue was aiming at, but I have an idea. Her shots destroyed his sex life and mine took everything else."

"Palmer Brown?" I said to no one in particular. Elsbeth was close beside me. Dr. Carter was by the door, looking incredulous. "A client of mine a year or . . . ago," I went on. "Not a good person . . . in my boat. When he got out . . . said he'd kill me. . . . Is he same person . . . got charged . . . pushing . . . wife off . . . cliff in Grand Teton Park, but no jail? Acquitted?"

"He *was* acquitted and released," Elsbeth said. "Not this time. I'll tell you more about him when you're better. But yes, I'm convinced he *pushed* his wife off Inspiration Point last month. And I'm sure he did the same to his first wife in Germany."

"Elsbeth, why were you . . . and Sue . . . near the Gallatin?" I asked a half-hour later, feeling a little better. "You were at work . . . said you couldn't float with Grace and me."

"Sue and I started tracking Brown two weeks ago, after reading the old German and Swiss news articles and hearing from you that a client named Palmer Brown had once threatened you. He got away with killing two wives, and we thought he might next go after you. We were right."

"You were on the . . . two floats on the Gallatin when the two fisher . . . were killed. Was Brown involved with . . . incidents?" I asked, relapsing into a black hole.

I woke an hour later. Elsbeth was still sitting beside me and said, "I don't want to fill your head with ideas *before* you talk to the county police. Two Gallatin County Sheriff's Office people are outside. Why don't you do the best you can and talk to them. Then you and I and Sue will get together, and I'll tell you more about Palmer Brown and his wives."

"OK," I stuttered.

"You should be warned that one of the two deputies outside is the guy who arrived at the first Gallatin murder—his name is Jackson. He wasn't nice to me. Be careful. Ask him if he still visits Alice Evans."

"I will. I'm ready . . . for him."

"I know how tired you must be, Dad."

"Go home and get . . . a rest," I pleaded. "I'll want . . . sleep after Jackson and . . . colleague left. Come back . . . evening."

Sue walked out with Dr. Carter who went to see other patients. She stopped where the two deputies were sitting. Ignoring Deputy Jackson, she said to the other—Deputy Rose Stein— "You can go in but for a brief time. He's sedated and in some pain."

Turning to Jackson, Sue said, "Remember me? I'm one of the little ladies from the first barbed wire murder. The murder you've never solved. Like you've done with the second murder. My friend and I saved you from being a three-time loser by taking care of Palmer Brown ourselves. If you treat Mr. Brooks the way you did Elsbeth and me, I'll ask the county commission for your badge, and I'll call Alice Evans."

Sue and Elsbeth turned away and left, passing Dr. Carter who had stopped in the hall and listened. Carter whispered as they went by, "Good for you. He needs to be put in his place.

He's been in here before throwing his weight around. A badge can be a terrible thing to give a person."

Jackson and Stein entered my room and stood at the foot of the bed. Before Jackson could say a word, Stein began.

"I'm sorry what happened to your friend, Ms. Justice, and to you. We won't keep you long. Reporters would like to talk to you; several are waiting outside the hospital's front entrance for your daughter and her friend. They're both local heroes. . . . Fishing should pick up again on the Gallatin. A lot of people stayed away after the first two deaths, and we weren't able to solve either one."

"Deputy Stein, what can I tell you that . . . haven't already learned?" I murmured, quickly tiring.

"Let's start with Brown's motive," Stein suggested.

"I guided him . . . couple of years ago. It wasn't . . . successful trip. He said he would get . . . even." I was struggling to speak.

"What did Brown have against Grace Justice?" Stein asked.

"Nothing. . . . Brown . . . after me, not Grace, hoping I'd be . . . one to get hung . . . barbed wire."

"Do you think Brown was connected to the first two murders on the Gallatin?"

"I'm not . . . thinking . . . seriously about anything. When I'm no longer . . . medication . . . will think about that." I couldn't say more, beginning to drift off. But I could tell they were arguing.

"I think we ought to go and let him rest," said Stein to Jackson.

"Hell, shake him."

"Back off, Jackson." Stein ordered, adding, "Do you have anything to ask that's so important it can't wait? Look at him; he's exhausted."

"I have some questions. I want them answered *now*," Jackson said loudly to me. "You have a history of being a trouble-maker."

It maddened me. I wanted him gone.

I whispered, "Jackson, I've heard . . . litany about . . . past dozen years, from deputies, guides, and . . . owners, stories that sound . . . like fiction. . . . We've gone over . . . deputy Jack . . . you never understood what I told . . . about some previous incidents. You call . . . Rangley in Livingston or . . . Byng in Jackson Hole. They . . . about . . . my earlier involvements."

"This is *my* turf, Brooks. I don't give a damn about Livingston or Jackson Hole."

"Deputy," I said, turning to Stein, "can talk . . . few days. And . . . Wanda Groves . . . be with me."

"Damn you, Brooks," interrupted Jackson. "I keep telling you that you don't need no goddamn lawyer when I ask you questions."

"Maybe not . . . you need a lot more . . . Jackson . . . a *lot* more. Go see . . . girlfriend, Alice Evans."

"I'll see you behind bars, Brooks," said Jackson, turning toward the door."

"Mr. Brooks, we're going," Deputy Stein said, interrupting and pushing Jackson out of the room.

"Tell me about Alice Evans," Stein asked Jackson as they walked down the hall.

I passed out again before they reached the elevator.

65

THREE DAYS LATER

"I'M TAKING YOU HOME, DAD," SAID ELSBETH. "Dr. Carter thinks you'll recover faster in your own bed."

"No argument from me. The nurses like me so much here they wake me every half-hour to make me take a bunch of pills, scribble something on my chart, check the maze of attached tubes, ask 'How you doin', or for a dozen other reasons I can't remember. A full night's sleep at home sounds like the best medicine. Let's go."

The landscape on the drive home looked especially bright and dynamic, from the layer of new snow on the mountains to the last of the fall wildflowers on the valley floor. It felt good to be alive a little longer than Palmer Brown had intended. Surviving being shot makes one appreciate having a life not cut short by some insane fanatic. . . . I looked over at Elsbeth who was looking over at me."

"You're driving. Shouldn't you be looking ahead at the road?" I said.

"I do occasionally. But I'm your caregiver and have to look at you. You look crummy—like you usually do after being shot fishing. It was so peaceful living in Maine. Why did I ever search for you?"

"How would Sherlock Holmes ever have solved so many London murders if he'd lived peacefully in Maine? . . . Can't you find the killer before he shoots me, rather than thirty seconds after? You know, Elsbeth, I haven't yet heard from you about what happened after I was shot and collapsed."

"You know Sue and I arrived and shot Palmer Brown. That's it!"

"That's *not* it; start with why you were on the Gallatin when Brown shot me. You were heading for work when Grace and I left the cabin that morning."

"Sue and I left right after you. But not for work. It's complicated. You know from our recent dinner conversation what I learned about Brown and his first wife in Switzerland, where he was charged and then acquitted because the authorities accepted his statement that she died of an accident—falling off a cliff near Interlaken. Once Sue and I gathered that information and set it alongside the facts of the Inspiration Point death of his second wife—wealthier by far than his German wife—we thought we had identified a murderer. We wrote down all the details and sent a report to Dan in D.C."

"You told me that over dinner at Chico's. Before I was shot. Is there more?" I asked.

"Yes," she said. "You had told me about the float you did with Palmer Brown and how you dealt with him when he got out of control."

"Go on," I said.

"The first two Gallatin murders hadn't been solved. Sue and I thought that maybe Palmer was involved in those murders. I was on both those trips. Were they practice runs for Brown? You were on the second float but had been scheduled to be on the first. Remember? Liz Rangley took your place."

"What made you think Palmer Brown was involved with those floats?" I asked.

"Something I never raised at our dinner," Elsbeth said. "It was very trivial at the time. When we launched that first day on the Gallatin, a man wearing Montana Fish, Wildlife & Parks shirt and hat was walking the shoreline a little upstream from where we put in. He walked down and talked to us for a couple of minutes and agreed to take some group photos of Sue, Liz, and me. He was very nice. After you left for the third float, while Sue and I were on our way to work, I suddenly guessed that that FWP Warden had been Palmer Brown in disguise. Apparently, I was wrong, but it did make me turn the car around and head for the Gallatin. I was using your vehicle that day and it had one of your rifles and a pistol on the rear seat. Sue and I flipped a coin to see which of us would carry which gun."

"So I was saved because you won a coin toss! You know Sue isn't too good with guns. . . . Did you think on your drive to the Gallatin that you would find me? Grace and I could have been anywhere on several miles of river."

"I knew where you planned to put in and take out. I guessed about where you'd be at the time we'd get to the river. And I assumed the killer would string the barbed wire about where it was on the first two floats."

"So it was a coin toss and a guess that saved me?"

"You might say that. But it wasn't that. You don't understand women's intuition."

"Now you're telling me it was a coin toss, a guess, and women's intuition that saved me."

"Something like that. But there was more. The third float with you and Grace came after Palmer Brown had been acquitted of killing his second wife on Inspiration Point. He was ready to concentrate fully on a new challenge. You were that challenge."

"He would make sure my neck snapped?"

"Correct. He hated seeing you alive and was determined to kill you and thought his new fortune allowed him to get away with anything. He didn't plan for what happened and he lost his focus when he saw it was Grace who was killed. He used his rifle and after hitting you with his first shot he figured one more would have you join Grace. If Sue and I hadn't shot him, you'd be dead."

"That doesn't explain how you were there with guns blazing. You were supposed to be at work?"

"I need to add a few more facts. Some I learned from Deputy Stein while you were in the hospital. After Sue and I were certain Brown killed his two wives, and I remembered you telling us about how he hated you after the float a year ago, we were worried he was planning something. With Dan Wilson's reluctant help, we bugged Brown's phone, trying to learn what he was planning."

"But he acted alone, which meant he wouldn't be talking on his phone with some accomplice," I commented.

"That's right, but he did use his phone. He called several outfitters and explained he was talking photos of Macduff Brooks to be in a new pictorial piece in the *Bozeman Magazine*, a follow-up to the interview article Celeste Ransome wrote.

"Brown asked the outfitters to let him know when you would be floating the Gallatin so he could take some photos of you floating by. One called Brown in Jackson two days before you and Grace floated, right after you had told one of the Bozeman outfitters and arranged for a shuttle service. The outfitter told Brown about your plans.

"He drove north that evening, stayed at Big Sky, and got up early the next morning to be at the Gallatin River before you started your float. He stretched the barbed wire at daybreak and waited near the riverbank to watch you arrive and be caught on the barbed wire. He didn't plan on Grace rowing from the guide's seat. Grace saved you at the cost of her own life."

"Elsbeth, I loved Grace in a desperate way that she struggled to accept. She knew what you and Lucinda meant to me. And she knew the two of us would never marry. But she hung on, and I didn't discourage her."

"And now you feel you betrayed Lucinda?"

"I avoided making the choice I should have made."

"Admitting that Lucinda was dead?"

"Or not. Logic told me Lucinda was dead. It still does. My heart, when it was working, told me she was alive. But not whether she was a mistreated prisoner or living voluntarily and happily with her ex."

"Grace is gone, Dad. Can you accept *that*?"

"In time, I suppose so. Right now, no."

66

ON THE EVE OF LEAVING MONTANA FOR FLORIDA

GRACE'S DEATH WEIGHED HEAVILY ON EVERY thought that entered my mind. The State of Florida had lost a fine Assistant State Attorney who was mentioned frequently as the future head of the statewide office.

The fly fishing community lost a Master Casting Instructor who donated her instructional skills exclusively to fund-raising events.

Sue, Elsbeth, and I, and Lucinda when she was with us, lost a person we had befriended for different reasons.

Grace entered my life a month after Lucinda left me to return to live and work in Manhattan. Lucinda thought I would never make a commitment to her, especially when she discovered she had breast cancer and wrongfully assumed—in her words—that I wouldn't "retain damaged goods." I knew nothing about her cancer and thought she was bored with our life and needed the cultural and professional attractions of Manhattan.

Grace stepped in and filled a sudden void in my life, in addition to giving me advice when a local deputy in St. Augustine named Turk Jensen gave me trouble when one of the gill net murders occurred on my flats boat. By the time Lucinda returned, I had become close to Grace in more than a professional way. When Lucinda came to know and admire Grace, they joined forces to play important roles in solving the gill net murders.

As years passed after Lucinda returned from Manhattan and we married, she and Grace became close. They were good days, even better when Elsbeth came into our lives. She grew to consider Lucinda her mom and Grace a close adult friend.

Lucinda's abduction brought Grace closer to me as both a social and a professional friend. It became close enough to cause Elsbeth and others to doubt my loyalty to Lucinda, who—were she alive—remained my wife. A month ago Elsbeth and I had the first harsh words over my relationship with Grace.

I accepted that seventeen months was long enough to presume that Lucinda's absence had led to her death. I could face that and ask a court to rule her dead. But what would I do living with Grace if Lucinda miraculously showed up? That was where I stood when Grace was murdered.

The next day I left to drive to St. Augustine. One task when I arrived would be to administer Grace's estate. I would do as I promised when a year ago she asked me to be her executor. The days ahead without my three around—Lucinda, Elsbeth, and Grace—will not pass easily.

There is a bright contrast to my losses occurring since the time of Lucinda's abduction. Guatemalan Juan Pablo Herzog is expectedly now chasing me in Alaska, where he deceptively learned that I moved to live as Walter Windsor, engaged in something to do with commercial fishing. This respite from his pursuit will not last forever. When Herzog finishes his term as President of Guatemala, he will have time to focus his search, and he is likely to be furious when inevitably he learns the truth about the wild goose chase Ralph Johnson sent him on.

That appears to leave all my problems resolved or, in the case of Herzog, at least deferred. Could that really be true?

But where is Lucinda?

67

DELAYED DEPARTURE TO ST. AUGUSTINE

WERE IT NOT FOR ELSBETH ATTENDING THE University of Florida at Gainesville, only a two-hour drive from our St. Augustine cottage, I would have no reason to drive east to Florida. I could stay in Montana and fish alone, walking along the banks on Mill Creek, wading the Gallatin, or drifting on the Yellowstone.

Juan Pablo Herzog keeps an eye on and occasionally visits Gainesville, which is not the best place for me to be. He has sent two nieces and a nephew to Gainesville to help him. Two were killed, and one has refused to return to Guatemala. I doubt Herzog has ever been to Montana or Wyoming. It's obvious that they are safer places for me than Florida.

I have more friends in Montana than in Florida, a reflection of that concern for my safety. Gainesville is where I taught for twenty years and worked when my conflict with Herzog began. I'm careful when I visit Elsbeth and Sue at their rented house in Gainesville, and have not gone anywhere I might meet old colleagues or friends. I wear some form of disguise when I have the urge to see a UF soccer game. Grace had fortunately kept me away from Gainesville by persistently asking me to fish with her on the salt flats near my cottage. Losing Grace troubles me every day.

In Montana I know a dozen fly fishing guides in Emigrant, Livingston, and Bozeman, and I can drive a few hours to Jackson Hole in Wyoming to visit and fish with John Kirby. Plus there's Huntly Byng who heads the Teton County Sheriff's Office investigation staff in Jackson. I also have friends in Montana: Ken Rangley and Erin Giffin on the Park County Sheriff's office staff, and both my Bozeman attorney, Wanda Groves, and local Judge Amy Becker. Erin, Wanda, and Amy are exceptional women.

My loyal canine companion Wuff is past the mid-point of a sheltie's expected life and will increasingly need me as her best friend. She'll happily live anywhere I do, Florida or Montana.

Florida is where I lost Lucinda nearly two years ago. By now there is little hope she's alive. Emotionally, I can't go near the old Castillo in St. Augustine, where I watched Ellsworth-Kent physically abduct her and take her who knows where.

Once Elsbeth finishes her studies in another year or two, she may be off to law or graduate school or a new job anywhere from Florida to California. I'm not getting any younger, and this time I may sell the cottage and follow her.

Only because of Elsbeth's insistence, I've been packing for the trip east. I have a few boxes ready but have delayed putting them into the SUV because a torrential downpour arrived from Idaho, has thus far left six inches of water, and shows no sign of stopping. It's not the warm and within reason welcome rain from tropical depressions we receive in Florida, but a rain that chills you to the bone if you give it a chance.

I've spent much time recently inside my cabin, moping about and looking out at Mill Creek. That's where I was when the phone rang one morning. I thought it was from Elsbeth engaged in one of her promised frequent checks on me, but it was from Budapest, a location I haven't thought about for years, since I visited Hungary for the State Department three years after El's death, was declared *persona non grata,* and was escorted out of the country by the communist government for actions not in the best interests of Hungary. At least there I didn't face anyone like Herzog.

I took a final bite of a blackened English Muffin and opened the cell phone.

"This is Macduff."

"Macduff Brooks, the fishing person?" It was a lilting feminine voice with an accent.

"The very same. Who do I know in Budapest?"

"You don't know me. My name is Mira Cerna. Please call me Mira. I'm Hungarian and live on the side of the Danube we call 'Pest' and pronounce 'Pesth.'"

"That's very interesting. You bring back good memories of a mostly pleasant two-month visit in your country before the Berlin wall fell and Eastern European countries were out from under the thumb of the USSR."

"It was a large and hurtfully pressed thumb," she noted.

I liked her soothing voice the more she spoke. It was one of those unusual voices where the tone, rhythm, and accent were so charming that it was easy to be distracted listening to the voice rather than the content.

"Mr. Brooks, do you have a half-hour to hear a story?"

I didn't want to take the time for a half-hour story, but I was enjoying hearing her speak Her voice made me realize how much I missed the same voice qualities shared by El and Elsbeth.

"Why would you want to tell me a story?" I asked. "Is it your hobby to call strangers and tell stories? No one other than my parents has told me a story for decades."

"I could tell you a story about a bear who said that 'if you live to be 100, I hope I live to be 100 minus one day, so I never have to live without you.'"

"My wife El used to say that often," I noted. "Every American kid knows about Winnie the Pooh. Was it translated into Hungarian?"

"Probably, but it was read to me in East Sussex, England, where A. A. Milne lived."

"Is A. A. Milne your pen name?"

"If so, I'm long dead," she said, laughing.

"If we're going to go on quizzing each other on children's books, you'd best call me Macduff or just Mac."

"It has to be Macduff; Mac sounds like you change tires in some gas station."

"I agree, but these days some people don't want to waste two syllables where one will get your attention. I never know when someone looks at me and says, 'Hey, Mac' whether they know it's my name or they call all males 'Mac.'"

"We've certainly gotten off the subject of my call," she said. "Sorry."

"Yes, we have."

"You OK?" she asked.

"Almost. You remind me of someone," I said softly.

"Lucinda?"

This wasn't what I needed. After a long pause, I said, "Ms. Cerna, I don't know what you want but I don't care to hear it."

This time I set the phone down and turned it off, walked to the kitchen, poured a cup of coffee and took it out onto the porch and down the few steps to Mill Creek. It was still raining. but I didn't care. After ten minutes I was drenched and shivering and finally realized the caller had not given me any reason to act so precipitously.

I headed back to the cabin, refilled my cup and sat in a rocker facing Emigrant peak. I was about to make my bed and do some household chores that had to be done before I set out for Florida, when the phone rang again and again was from Budapest. It had to be Ms.Cerna.

Staring at the phone and listening at the third and final ring before it cut off automatically I quickly picked it up but didn't say anything. After nearly a minute of neither party speaking, I said, "I should not have acted so impolitely, Ms.Cerna."

"Mira," she whispered.

"Mira."

"Tell me what you'd like me to say," she asked.

"Everything you know about Lucinda."

"I will. Promise to let me finish?"

"I'll try."

"I'm an academic at Eötvös Loránd University. It's across the river in Buda."

"Years ago I knew a wonderful member of your law faculty. I once asked him why he didn't defect to the West. He was well known and would have been welcome at many universities. He turned to me and said, 'I will never leave Hungary. If you don't have a horse you should cherish your donkey.' . . . You're at a fine university. Do you teach?"

"Yes. At the Faculty of Education and Psychology. More specifically I teach and research issues of hypnotherapy."

"Is hypnosis a legitimate academic study in Hungary?"

"Hypnotherapy is legitimate. How do you view it?"

"Something used by devious male cranks to seduce women or by magicians to get applause."

"Maybe also by someone named Robert Ellsworth-Kent to seduce someone named Lucinda Brooks?"

I was trembling and unable to respond but after a long pause, pleaded, "Don't do this to me."

"Sorry. I didn't know how to tell you. I hesitated because I knew it would be upsetting."

"It's more than upsetting. I can envision Ellsworth-Kent forcing Lucinda to have sex with him."

"He didn't have to force her," she said.

"I don't believe you."

"A skilled hypnotherapist knows how to convince the subject that a spouse never loved her or him and the person who most devotedly loved the subject was someone else."

"By someone else you mean the hypnotist?" I asked.

"Exactly, or, as I prefer—the hypnotherapist."

"Meaning Lucinda is *willingly* living with, and having sex with, Ellsworth-Kent?"

"Yes. She has been convinced by hypnosis that she loves him."

"Was this partly drug induced?"

"Not at all. She is doing this freely. She *believes* she loves him."

"How could this have happened?"

"That's complex."

"Are you convinced Lucinda was hypnotized more than a year ago and remains so?"

"I am. Hypnosis doesn't go away. Once she was under hypnosis, if the hypnotherapist didn't bring her out or if she didn't come out by some other event, it remained in place."

"For years?"

"Forever," she said.

"Won't it kill the person?"

"No. It's natural and safe. There are no dangers to the person hypnotized."

"How did Lucinda ever succumb to hypnosis?" I asked.

"It's not because she was weak and unhappy. Her hypnotherapist took over control of her."

"How?"

"He convinced her that she loved him without any interruption from the time they were first married in London."

"But we know he had abused her."

"He never reminded her of that," she explained. "Remember that hypnosis can alter one's recollections. He told her she still loved him and wanted to spend the rest of her life serving him."

"And she believed him?"

"Thoroughly."

"You say 'he.' Was Ellsworth-Kent a hypotist?"

"He was. And he's very good."

"How did he achieve that?"

"That's where I come in; I'm sorry to admit I helped train him."

"Tell me. And don't leave out anything, no matter how disturbing you think it will be to me."

"About a year ago Ellsworth-Kent called me and offered me a very substantial sum—$500,000 and all expenses—to fly and meet him and bring him up to date on hypnotherapy methods."

"Did he say why?" I asked.

"Not at the time."

"Where did he want you to meet him?"

"A small island in the Bahamas."

"Named?"

"I was told it was Man-O-War Cay, which I learned is pronounced and means 'key.' Have you been there?"

"Yes, but I went to another island, Elbow Cay—to the south of Man-O-War—and visited the small community called Hope Town with the picturesque candy-striped lighthouse. I was also at Hope Town more recently."

"For something related to airboats?"

"How do you know that?"

"I think if I start at the beginning you won't keep asking how I knew something."

"Go ahead," I said, no less concerned and anxious.

68

MIRA'S PHONE CALL CONTINUES

"BEFORE I ACCEPT ANY ENGAGEMENT, I HAVE my research associates investigate the person who wishes to retain me," said Ms. Cerna.

"You did that in this case?"

"Please don't interrupt. We'll play 'questions and answers' when I'm through. . . . The report they prepared began with your arrival in Montana over a decade ago. Strangely, my associates did not discover anything about you before that time. I assumed you moved to Montana after changing your name, but since it was a year or so before you met Lucinda, I didn't have to know your early history.

"Let me tell you who we talked to over the past year with different degrees of willingness to talk about *any* part of your life before Montana. Not one would say anything about that time and little about you since. The persons in the West included Ken Rangley, Erin Giffin, Wanda Groves, Amy Becker, Mavis Benton, a few fishing guides in Montana and Wyoming, and a few store owners in Emigrant. In Jackson Hole we talked to Huntly Byng and John Kirby.

"Our attempts in Florida were different, but no more productive. We talked only to Grace Justice and Jen Jennings. I thought it strange that you had considerably more friends in Montana than Florida.

"We accumulated numerous newspaper articles that mentioned you. They covered your conflict with Park Salisbury, the so called 'shuttle gal murders,' and a year or two later the 'wicker man and mistletoe murders.' Those articles were mostly from newspapers in several cities in Wyoming, Montana, and Idaho.

"Florida newspapers showed a similar pattern. First were reports about the 'gill net murders,' then some episodes in Cuba, and lastly the matter of airboats.

"The report we prepared focused on your relationship with Lucinda, from your first meeting her at the ranch she owned on Mill Creek, her being shot on your boat by Salisbury and the consequent amnesia she suffered for several months, then leaving you to resume her work in Manhattan, and your initiating the friendship—or more—with Grace Justice that ended when you and Lucinda rejoined.

"One difference in investigating you and Lucinda was that—as I mentioned—*your* life seems to have begun when you arrived in Montana. Contrastingly, Lucinda's history was traceable to grammar school.

"I mention all this so you know I began the hypnotherapy only after learning a great deal about both of you.

"We also investigated Robert Ellsworth-Kent's early years in England and his brief marriage to Lucinda. He believed you stole Lucinda from him by deceptive actions that prevented her from returning to England from New York and resuming their life together. We learned that he was purportedly behind the wicker man murders, although that was never proven and was denied vehemently by him.

"Ellsworth-Kent had studied hypnotherapy in Scotland years before he met Lucinda and used that knowledge on Lucinda in the brief time between their fleeing St. Augustine and my arrival from Hungary.

"I'm getting ahead of myself. I had accepted Ellsworth-Kent's offer and flown to the Bahamas from here in Budapest. I was met at Nassau and flew by private plane to a small private landing strip on Man-O-War Cay. At least I thought I was on Man-O-War Cay.

"A man who didn't give me his name was waiting for the plane and drove me to a large home surrounded by high walls where Ellsworth-Kent was waiting for me. Lucinda was sitting next to him in the living room. She did not get up to greet me and appeared tired and complacent.

"Although Ellsworth-Kent denied it, I was essentially a captive. There were guards at the house, both at the outer gate and doors. The house belonged to a friend of Ellsworth-Kent who I never met while I was there.

"I was told in no uncertain terms that I could not go out because it was unsafe. Ellsworth-Kent said he had an obligation to protect me from street crime and especially rape, which he claimed were out of control on the island.

"A superb cook prepared whatever we asked for, the weather was far milder and sunnier than in Budapest, and I had an exquisite guest suite on the top floor from which I could see the emerald bay. It was beautiful, I was kept busy, and I had no need to leave the house. I was told there was no town to visit, that the island was solely residential with food and other supplies brought by ferry from another island.

"I met with Ellsworth-Kent the first night after Lucinda went to bed. She had been quiet at dinner but smiled often. She sat next to Ellsworth-Kent, and they often kissed. She showed no signs of distress.

"Ellsworth-Kent told me he had begun hypnotherapy with Lucinda the day they arrived in the Bahamas. His goal was to convince her that she had been in an abusive relationship with you, Macduff. He first focused on gaining her trust so that she believed he was a good man who would never suggest she do anything that was immoral or illegal. He used a few good experiences that she remembered, and he built around them untruths she did not previously think were untrue.

"I hope you accept hypnosis as a fact of life. We sometimes say we are under the spell of another. Everyone becomes involved with hypnosis to some degree, although many reject its use and even deny it's existence, probably because it is depicted in fiction as being unsafe and dangerous. Of course, so is smoking and drinking and using guns. No one dies from hypnosis.

"Ellsworth-Kent was careful in his use of words while I was with him. He wanted to learn as much as he could from me about improving his hypnotherapy skills and stressed that he would never use hypnotherapy to harm Lucinda. He loved her enough to carefully use hypnosis so he could be with her and hoped that someday she would be rid of all positive thoughts about you and want nothing more than to spend her life serving him. I believed him. That shouldn't seem too complex, Mr. Brooks. What more can I tell you?"

"Did he try to convince her I was bad?"

"No, and he never tried to get her to commit an immoral act, such as to kill you. He did convince her that you loved others such as Grace and Erin, and could never be exclusively devoted to Lucinda. He would not tell her that you were intentionally bad, but that it was simply the way you were. And then he worked on convincing her that he was the one she truly loved."

"And she began to love him and reject me?"

"She did not reject you as an evil person. Ellsworth-Kent convinced her that you were not her true love."

"How did he avoid becoming another Rasputin of Russia?"

"Rasputin used hypnosis to seduce women. He loved them and *left* them. Ellsworth-Kent was not a seducer; he wanted to live with Lucinda forever."

"Or perhaps he wanted to hurt me."

"That's part of it, but he never said that to Lucinda. You were another person not good enough for her."

"I will probably have much to ask you in the coming weeks," I noted. "But I have questions now. How has Ellsworth-Kent managed to keep her under hypnosis since you left and returned to Budapest? That's a long time. Also, can hypnotherapy be used by Ellsworth-Kent to access and acquire Lucinda's financial assets? We have considerable jointly owned property? Lastly, why have you told me all this?"

"I should have mentioned that since returning to Hungary I continued to address her case by phone discussions with Ellsworth-Kent. He's very smart and quite clever. There were times when he was uncertain how to keep her under hypnosis, and I recommended directions he could consider depending on her actions. For example, on one day more than a year ago, she began to ask about you. He called me, and we talked. He supported her interest but always in the context of you being good but he being better.

"One day for the first time in months Lucinda again referred to you. It worried Ellsworth-Kent until I discovered it was your birthday. With Ellsworth-Kent's help, she put aside her interest for that day.

"Your question about access to records, Macduff, is something I haven't thought about or ever experienced. Which of you maintained your joint financial records when you were together?"

"I did more often. She, of course, wrote checks for household expenses, but I received our monthly bank and investment statements, and told her how we were doing. She asked questions on occasion."

"Has she tried to access those assets since her abduction?" asked Cerna.

"Not the Montana or Florida bank checking accounts. Nor did she make any attempt to change the real property ownership. Maybe she told Ellsworth-Kent that all the bank and property interests were solely in my name. Recently, I have transferred both to my name exclusively, with the intention of transferring them back to joint ownership if she survived and returned to me.

"There is one account," I noted, "our investments, which Ellsworth-Kent and a lawyer in Bermuda tried to shift from my name. The joint investment account was our most valuable asset by far. The investment house in New York at my request has frozen that account until a court rules on the ownership. My lawyer and I are trying to keep it from being transferred to an account owned exclusively by Ellsworth-Kent."

"I was never informed about any of those financial matters," said Cerna.

"I don't know how the court will react to my disclosure that Lucinda has been under hypnosis for so long. I suspect it will rule in my favor, perhaps requiring the investment to be placed in a trust for our joint benefits with a trustee's consent required for any change by either of us. That is quite acceptable to me. I'll call my Bozeman lawyer and New York broker after we talk and inform them about our conversation. . . . Now what about my question asking why you decided to tell me all this?"

"Macduff, without trying to praise my own work, I generally am considered to be one of the half-dozen most respected hypnotherapists in the world. I do not want my reputation tarnished, and I do not want Lucinda hurt. Or you. I'm not inclined to further assist Ellsworth-Kent because while I understand his professed love for Lucinda, access to her wealth seems to be an equal motive. I was not told about that."

"Can Lucinda be brought out of the hypnosis?"

"Yes. Hypnosis goes on only until it is stopped. But I would prefer to see that happen slowly. And I would like to help."

"If Ellsworth-Kent learned that you talked to me, how do you think he would react?"

"He wouldn't sit idly by with so much money at stake. He might have her die from an 'accident.' He might go after you."

"Or you," I added.

"That's true."

"I'll let you go," she said. "Call me as soon as you know more. I'm going home and have a large glass of Swack."

"Swack? Is that cyanide in Hungarian?"

"It's an herbal liqueur made here. You should try some."

"Ever hear of Gentleman Jack?"

"No."

"*You* should try some."

69

MONTANA THE DAY BEFORE DEPARTURE FOR FLORIDA

ELSBETH CHALLENGED MY UNACCOMPANIED return from Montana to Florida by car. She was leaving to drive across country with Sue and wanted me either in her car or driving right behind her. I declined again, planning to have only Wuff with me for the five-day event. It would give me time to think about the call from Budapest, which I hadn't shared with Elsbeth. But I had talked to Wanda, Dan Wilson, and Henry Mellon, and we intended to talk again after I reached Florida. I also wanted to think about how to deal with Attorney Hamilton in Bermuda when he next contacted us.

"Dad, when will you learn to let me help you when you need help?" Elsbeth asked on the phone from her room at Chico Hot Springs.

"When I'm past eighty I may listen to your pleas. At least *some* of them."

"I'm not talking about your aging. I mean recovering from another of your misadventures. You were shot! It wasn't the first time. And remember that the real target was *you*. I won't even try to rehash the other murders in or around your boats. Now, little more than a week after being shot in the side, you're packing to drive all by yourself to Florida! Who do you think you are? Clark Kent?"

"You need to head to Florida and attend to your classes," I said, trying to change the subject. "You've missed enough at UF since Lucinda was abducted. Don't worry so much. I'll have Wuff for company. She's a little slower and has some gray hairs. But she has the same protective loyalty, and she won't sit next to me telling me what to do every fifteen minutes."

"I'm texting you every fifteen minutes until you reach the Florida cottage."

"That's OK. *If* I can find my cellphone when you text."

"I'll be waiting for you at the cottage, even if that means missing classes."

"I plan the drive so I don't arrive at the cottage until the evening, well after your last class of the day, or even better, I'll arrive on a Saturday or Sunday."

"Don't be thinking about Grace and Lucinda while you're driving with dozens of tractor-trailers," she said.

"I'm more likely to worry about what you and Sue are up to. Leave your guns at home; you can't take them on campus."

Elsbeth and Sue packed their belongings after their last shift at Chico's, and joined me at the Montana cabin to help me finish some leftovers in the refrigerator that would otherwise be tossed out.

"Dad," said Elsbeth, as she ran up the steps, "Wait 'till you hear what I've discovered."

"What is it?"

"I just talked to Wanda in Bozeman. She said something about Hamilton; she said she wondered whether he really was a lawyer. That troubled me so I called the Bermuda Bar Association and asked about him. More specifically I asked if he were in good standing. They looked up his name and found nothing. They double checked and said there was no George Hamilton admitted to practice, nor even one lawyer with the surname Hamilton."

"That's incredible! Who's writing and acting as Hamilton?"

"I believe I know. Or at least have a hunch. . . . It's Ellsworth-Kent trying to find out information and get the investment portfolio for himself. Think about that on your way across country! . . . We have to run."

They said goodbyes and disappeared down my driveway, intending to drive through the night and make only one stop—in Vicksburg—to stay with a friend. As soon as I saw them off, I started my own packing. There was less to take without Lucinda present.

Now there was more for me to think about other than Mira Cerna's call.

70

TWO WEEKS LATER IN FLORIDA

W ANDA, HENRY MELLON, AND DAN WILSON were stunned by Mira Cerna's disclosures and the discovery that there was no attorney named Hamilton in Bermuda. We agreed that I would call Wanda, Henry, and Dan when I reached St. Augustine, or immediately if I learned anything new.

"Lucinda is alive!" I called out, starting my cross-country trek in my SUV the next morning, first driving toward Livingston. "Mira Cerna is coming to Florida to go with me to find the house on Man-O-War where she stayed with Ellsworth-Kent," I said to a car empty except for Wuff and me. "Dan Wilson promised to send an agent to the Bahamas to search for him. Hamilton is out of our lives! Hooray!"

Wuff looked at me strangely, hearing sentences that didn't contain any of her vocabulary such as sit, stay, or bad dog.

Herzog is starting a wild goose chase in Alaska. For the first time in more than a year, I felt there was a chance for closure to the worst days of my life.

No more than five minutes after I rose the morning after arriving at the Florida cottage, my phone beeped that a message from Dan was waiting for my attention. I needed to call him, and also Wanda, Henry, and Elsbeth.

Sitting down on my favorite porch rocker, I looked at the list of recent phone messages and opened the one from Dan. The subject was marked only "IMMEDIATE ATTENTION."

When I opened and read it, the direction of my life was once again altered:

Macduff. Call me. Last night the partial remains of the body of Robert Ellsworth-Kent were discovered washed up on a beach at Abaco in the Bahamas. A few parts of a second but unidentified body of a woman were nearby. Dan.

EPILOGUE

Elsbeth's Diary

These had been difficult months, ending with two bodies washed up on a Bahama beach. The good news was that one was identified as Ellsworth-Kent. The bad news was that the other was assumed to have been Lucinda.

The autopsy of Ellsworth-Kent didn't disclose any traces of drugs or alcohol. The autopsy of what was left of the woman didn't disclose anything. The coroner couldn't conclude that any foul means had been used and wrote down as the cause: accidental death by drowning.

I have tried to remember what happened so I might include it in this diary, but Dad wouldn't talk about Lucinda being the unidentified body. He did tell me about Mira Cerna, who confirmed that Lucinda had been with Ellsworth-Kent in the Bahamas.

Why Ellsworth-Kent was in the Bahamas wasn't clear. His photograph was shown throughout the islands, but no one identified him, except for the owner, Rusty, of a local popular Hope Town bar and grill named Casa Colada. Rusty said he was absolutely certain the person in the photograph had an English accent and manners and had been at the bar several times with an attractive but extraordinarily quiet woman with whom he sat each time at the same table in a corner. They were always alone.

At the time I didn't know what to do. I hugged Dad a lot and tried to convince him there is a plan for everyone, and it can't be as bad as he envisioned.

M.W. GORDON – The author of more than sixty law books that won awards and were translated into a dozen languages, he wrote one book on sovereign immunity in the U.S. and U.K. as a Scholar-in-Residence at the Bellagio Institute at Lake Como, Italy. He has also written for *Yachting Magazine* and *Yachting World* (U.K.) and won the Bruce Morang Award for Writing from the Friendship Sloop Society in Maine. Gordon holds a B.S. and J.D. from the University of Connecticut, an M.A. from Trinity College, a Diplôme de Droit Comparé from Strasbourg, and a Maestria en Derecho from Iberoamericana in Mexico City. He is a pretty competent fly caster, an average small plane pilot, and a terrible oboist. He lives in St. Augustine with his author wife Buff and their sheltie, Macduff.

AUTHOR'S NOTE

I enjoy hearing from readers. You may reach me at:
macbrooks.mwgordon@gmail.com
Please visit my website: www.mwgordonnovels.com

I answer email within the week received, unless I am on a book signing tour or towing *Osprey* somewhere to fish. Because of viruses, I do not download attachments received with emails. And please do not add my email address to any lists suggesting for whom I should vote, to whom I should give money, what I should buy, what I should read, or especially what I should write next about Macduff Brooks.

My website lists appearances for readings, talk programs, and signings.